Myths Within

by
David Creighton

gage EDUCATIONAL PUBLISHING COMPANY
A DIVISION OF CANADA PUBLISHING CORPORATION
TORONTO ONTARIO CANADA

Canadian Cataloguing in Publication Data
Creighton, David
    Myths within
Includes bibliographical references and index.
ISBN 0-7715-1784-X
1. Mythology — Juvenile literature. I. Title.
BL311.C74 1992   j398.2   C91-095702-9

Text design: Michael Gray/*First Image*
Cover design: Susan Weiss
Illustrations: Michael Gray/*First Image*, Jean Galt
Developmental Editor: Jeff Siamon
Gage Editorial Team: Ann Downar, Tim Johnston, Carolyn Leaver, Darleen Rotozinski, Carol Waldock

ISBN: 0-7715-1784-X

1 2 3 4 5   FP   96 95 94 93 92
Written, printed, and bound in Canada.

Gage Educational Publishing Company wishes to thank the following educators for their evaluation and helpful advice:

Betty King
Integrated School Board, NF

Glen Kirkland
Edmonton Catholic Schools, AB

David Kneeshaw
East York Board of Education, ON

Anne Payne
Fr. Lacombe High School, AB

Donald Porter
School District 26 & 27, NB

Bill Prentice
Swift Current School Division No. 94, SK

Tom Rossiter
St. John's Roman Catholic School Board, NF

─────────────

John Barnes
Eastwood Collegiate, ON

Catherine Feniak
David Thompson Secondary School, BC

Gordon Francis
Ascension Collegiate, NF

Lucille D. Hawkings
Camille J. Laronge Collegiate, AB

Robert Hughes
Aurora High School, ON

Peter Kingston
McMaster University, ON

ACKNOWLEDGMENTS

My first debt is owed to the people who shaped the myths in the first place. These include North American Native people, whose tales I have retold as authentically as possible.

The book also owes much to scholars who have explored the myths' meanings, and Joseph Campbell's name would appear first if I were merely to list the most persuasive. But *Myths Within* is based on the work of many others, for there is simply no end to the complexities of myth.

I explored these ancient stories with my students in several Ontario high schools, asking them in their journals to focus on the myths within. Moved by the honesty and depth of these journals, I asked them if I could keep photocopies of passages. Later I thought of including several in this book — one for each of its 25 themes—and the authors graciously gave permission to have them used in this way.

I would like to thank my editor, Jeff Siamon, for assisting in the effort (as he put it) "to cross over the lines of literature and thought." I am also grateful to Jim Henderson for bringing me into the Macmillan fold (with *Deeds of Gods and Heroes*) in the first place.

Above all I thank my wife, Judy, for unfailing encouragement and her own editorial assistance.

PHOTO CREDITS

Contents

What the Myths Mean

To Cross Our Bridges

The cover of this book shows a bridge, reflected in canal waters at sunrise. Bridges are symbolic, and we speak of a "bridge over troubled waters," "bridging the gap," "crossing that bridge when we come to it."

From the hour of birth until that of dying, we pass over many bridges. En route from one experience to another we feel love and loss, pleasure and pain, triumph and defeat.

And for humanity since its beginning, guidance in these journeys has appeared in stories known as *myths*. They explain how those bridges have been crossed before. They help us to see the larger picture.

Myths tell how things came to be, and what is likely to lie ahead. They tell about how we relate to the world, how heroes and gods battle against evil, how life keeps getting snuffed out and then born anew.

These are stories that we share, and every people has them. Myths are infinitely precious, giving a shape to the past as well as a direction into the future. They are often retold, and thus may be defined as "traditional sacred stories."

In some cultures, story-tellers still keep the old myths alive. But most of us are unlikely to learn the traditional myths except through the occasional film version and books such as this one. So we fashion "modern myths" from TV shows, popular songs, news reports, opinions of parents and friends, formal education, and trial-and-error experience.

Myths absorb our attention. With their help we struggle to settle our problems, to cross our many bridges. And sometimes those problems are magnified by a confusion of myths.

We worry about the health of nature, wondering if our myth of progress has been wrong. We elect leaders for promoting attractive myths, which collide with those of other countries and are upheld by weapons of inconceivable deadliness. We pile impossible hopes upon our heroes, and brood over rumours of evil conspiracy.

Such stories flow in our bloodstream, run riot in our souls. These are the *myths within*.

Myths are often dismissed as falsehood, made obsolete by enlightened science. This is unjust criticism, because always they convey truths. The following story, a famous myth from ancient Greece, provides a focus on the most fundamental things in life.

Ariadne's Thread *Greek*

In the city of Troezen, young Theseus often went to sit on a big mossy rock. His mother, Aethra, told him that some day he must gain the strength to push it from the ground.

Theseus met with no success until he reached young manhood. Struggling with all his might one day, the hero managed to shift the stone. And there before him, in a cavity, were sandals and a gold-hilted sword.

"These belonged to your father," said Aethra. "He is Aegeus, king of Athens, and you must go to him now."

"I have been given sandals, so I must walk," Theseus replied. Aethra urged him to travel by boat, as the journey by land held many dangers. But he was determined to take the coastal road and, kissing her goodbye, set out at once.

Perils faced Theseus indeed, but he overcame them all. One was Procrustes, the surly innkeeper who insisted that the guests must fit his bed—by being stretched to the right length, or by having their extremities cut off. Theseus simply seized this villain and lopped off his head.

When Theseus entered Athens, he went to the palace and approached the king, now aged and care-ridden. Father and son recognized each other, and they embraced at last.

But an atmosphere of gloom ruled the land, for the next payment of human flesh was due. Fourteen young people would be fed to a monster—a man with the head of a bull, called the Minotaur. It lived on the island of Crete, within the twists and turns of a great labyrinth.

"Let me be one of the fourteen," Theseus cried, "and I will kill the Minotaur!"

Aegeus agreed, though he was filled with sadness. "Your ship has a black sail," he told his son, "and if you manage to return, a white one must be raised as a signal of your good fortune. I'll be watching for it."

Theseus promised to remember. Then he joined the doomed youths who, amid terrible cries of grief, went down to their ship and sailed to Crete.

The king of that land, Minos, had a lovely daughter named Ariadne. She was the half-sister of the Minotaur.

Ariadne, at the very first glimpse of Theseus, fell passionately in love, and that night, she secretly sent for him.

Her heart ablaze, Ariadne whispered, "The labyrinth is very large, with many corridors that will confuse you." Then she handed him a ball of thread. "As you enter it, begin to unroll this," she said. "If you kill the Minotaur, find the way back to the entrance by following the thread."

Theseus, encouraged by this advice, gazed into Ariadne's eyes. "You're a gift from the gods," he said.

Without hesitation she asked, "If you can escape, will you take me to Athens as your wife?" And captivated by her beauty, he readily agreed.

"Now quickly," said Ariadne, "hide these in your cloak." She gave him the thread and also a sword for the killing.

That same night the Athenians, led by Theseus, were thrust into the labyrinth. Its dim passageways immediately began to curve jaggedly, but he remembered to unroll the thread.

Soon they smelled the rank odour of the Minotaur and heard the shuffling of its brutish feet. Then it stumbled into view and charged at them, bellowing.

Theseus drew the sword and swiftly plunged it into the Minotaur's throat. Spouting a stream of blood, it collapsed and died.

The Athenians embraced one another in a frenzy of relief. Then Theseus, following Ariadne's thread, brought them safely out of the labyrinth.

Theseus and the Minotaur

The princess stood at the entrance, overjoyed at the hero's triumph. Cautiously the young people returned to their ship, hauled anchor, and slipped out of the harbour. They were safe at last.

Soon their boat was in the waters of another island, Naxos, where everyone disembarked to rest. Here Ariadne, dazed by love, walked with Theseus before both fell asleep.

Toward evening Ariadne awoke to find that Theseus was no longer beside her. She looked out to sea and saw, far out on its grey waters, the Athenian vessel.

Theseus had left her, and as the bitter tears flowed, she cried out to Zeus for vengeance. And her prayer was answered—for Theseus, his mind in a turmoil of emotions, forgot to raise the white sail.

Near Athens on a plateau, King Aegeus kept vigil. He scanned every approaching ship, seeking the one that had taken his son away. When it appeared bearing the black sail, he flung himself to death on the rocks below.

As the ship came ashore and loved ones were reunited, Theseus looked in vain for the father he had known such a short while. Then he heard the cry, "Aegeus is dead!" and was overcome with remorse for his grievous error.

The people acclaimed Theseus to be the new king of Athens. During his reign, for the first time, the Athenians drove out foreign invaders, the female warriors known as Amazons. He married their leader, Hippolyta, and they had a son who met a tragic end—being banished by Theseus and then dying when his chariot crashed.

Theseus won high renown among his people by making Athens the centre of government for the outlying villages. He became the Athenians's greatest hero.

Myth, Ritual, Symbol

In tribal societies a distinction is made between **folktales**, called "false stories," and the myths or "sacred stories" of gods and heroes. Also there is **legend**, which gives an exaggerated account of real events— whereby celebrities become "legends in our time" with life-stories embroidered by colourful additions.

Myth and legend often blend together. The hero of "Ariadne's Thread" may well have existed, and the story does refer to something that really happened: villages being unified under the rule of Athens. Even the Minotaur has had a basis in fact since 1900, when a large structure near Cnossos on Crete was found to contain many images of the bull.

A myth often connects with **ritual**, a sacred ceremony marking key moments in peoples' lives. The Minotaur story may relate to rites involving animal masks and an actual labyrinth—with youths going toward apparent death, then experiencing rebirth as a way out is discovered.

Always presiding over the labyrinth is a woman. And indeed, Ariadne in ancient times was a goddess known as the "Mistress of the Labyrinth." On the Greek island of Delos, dancers once held a rope symbolizing Ariadne's thread while miming a path into the labyrinth's centre and out again—a representation of life's continuity.

Rituals belong to myth, and so do those meaningful images known as **symbols**. T-shirts, for instance, often serve as billboards to express personal mythology. And while reading the myths, we must always keep a focus on what is symbolized. So now, the labyrinth—what does it mean?

Here the prospects of youth are blighted by a cruel custom, we might say. Or, the Minotaur's brutality is defeated by the power of love. Or, the problems of life fail to trap us because someone shows a way out. Or, a woman's guidance is offered. Or, a hazardous bridge is traversed into new realms of experience.

The labyrinth means many things, for it is an especially rich symbol. Its basic seven-corridor shape is known around the world.*

Anyone visiting the great French cathedral of Chartres will see a huge labyrinth traced on its floor. Worshippers once followed its path on their knees to imitate the soul's wanderings. It was a form of baptism, subjecting the devout to discomfort so that on emerging, they knew what it meant to be saved from death.

Heroic Lives: Seven Stages

Front and centre in the Minotaur myth is that dazzling figure, the **hero**. Adventures of the hero, female and male alike, recur throughout the stories of this book. It is divided into seven parts, according to the pattern of the hero's life.

Here is how the experiences of Theseus and Ariadne follow this pattern.

The first phase is that of the **JOURNEY**, as when Theseus makes his dangerous trip by land. Ariadne undertakes no such ventures, but shows spirit by plotting elopement with him. And for all of us, life becomes a journey as its strange events unfold.

Meeting the **GODDESS**, the second stage, happens when Theseus is visited by Ariadne—the Mistress of the Labyrinth who holds its key. The goddess must be discovered by every hero, male and female, for her special wisdom is all-important.

*See pages 141-142.

Heroes must learn how to use their **POWERS**. Ariadne offers special devices—the sword with which to kill the Minotaur, the thread that will permit escape—and Theseus uses them well. In the same way, we all must find and nurture our powers, whatever these might be.

On life's journey, all must expect to suffer **PAIN**, often symbolized by monsters lurking in the dark. To meet the Minotaur is a horrifying experience for Theseus, but he manages to do the deed. For Ariadne, pain lies in her betrayal by Theseus.

To the victor belong the spoils. And mythology tells of **TRIUMPH**, as when Theseus is crowned as king and defeats the Amazons. Ariadne, meanwhile, goes on to marry one of the greatest gods, Dionysus.

The greatest delight, that of **LOVE**, might also be the greatest challenge. Although Theseus wins a bride, his actions suggest certain shortcomings in the romance department. It is quite the opposite with Ariadne.

The heroic journey's ultimate end is to enter **PARADISE**, a land of peace and happiness. For both Theseus and Ariadne, this means the rewards of marriage and the honour of prestige—goals shared by many of us.

Myths are both old and new. So in each chapter, you will find a long-established myth followed by a parallel one from our own time. Among the biggest of these modern myths is that of Superman, created by two teenagers in the 1930s.

Lois, Clark, and Superman *American*

One night in 1934, 17-year-old Jerry Siegel had trouble sleeping. "I'm lying in bed counting sheep when all of a sudden it hits me," he recalled. "I conceive a character like Samson, Hercules, and all the strong men rolled into one. Only more so."

Thus in the mind of a scrawny Cleveland youth, Superman was born. Next morning Siegel ran to the home of his friend Joe Shuster, who immediately did the drawings for a dozen strips.

Superman was given a second identity, that of a "mild-mannered" reporter named Clark Kent. Shuster came from Toronto, with fresh memories of the Daily Star's comic section. Thus Clark Kent was put to work on the "Daily Planet," which also employed a feisty woman named Lois Lane.

In the boys' class at Glenville High School was a girl named Lois Amster, who hoped to become a reporter. Shuster had a crush on Lois, but only older boys attracted her attention. Interestingly, Shuster once said of himself in high school: "I was mild-mannered, wore glasses, and was very shy with women."

Superman took shape as the first comic-book super-hero. But the newspaper syndicates rejected the concept as "crude" and "immature." Not until 1938 was the story accepted by an editor—who, as was the custom, put his own copyright on it. When the story hit the stands, in *Action Comics #1*, every copy was sold.

Superman is born on the planet Krypton, the only son of the great scientist Kal-El and his wife Lara. When his father realizes that the planet will explode, he sends the infant hero to earth in a rocket.

Raised by two small-town Americans, Superman from an early age shows amazing powers. But these must be hidden from people, he is told, "or they'll be scared of you!"

Disguised as Clark Kent, Superman begins his newspaper career. But whenever evil erupts, he enters the nearest telephone booth to shed his meek identity and vault into the sky.

When Superman's adventures were told in a radio serial, the lead-in brilliantly set the scene: "Faster than a speeding bullet! More powerful than a locomotive! Able to leap tall buildings in a single bound! Look! Up in the sky! It's a bird! It's a plane! It's *SUPERMAN!*"

This is the "Man of Steel," who aims "to strike terror into the hearts of evil-doers." He uses X-ray vision to hunt down criminals. Superman wages an ongoing battle with arch-enemy Lex Luthor, a mad scientist intent on ruling the world from his underground hide-out.

But Superman must be wary of Kryptonite, a green metal from his native planet, for it alone is able to rob him of his powers. Again and again he defeats evil and rescues Lois Lane, who yearns to be his wife.

Many superheroes followed Superman's example. All wore costumes that made them look somewhat like angels: cape, boots, underpants worn on top of longjohns, bearing a stylized insignia. All had stupendous powers, all led charmed lives, and all vowed to visit mayhem upon the wicked.

Superman

But in the 1960s, *Marvel Comics* brought out a new concept. "Heroes," Stan Lee of the rival company explained, "should be like normal people who happen to have a superpower or two." And *DC Comics*, publisher of Superman, eventually reshaped the myth in these terms. Clark Kent gained more self-assertiveness, Lois Lane showed greater maturity, and Superman became more "open" about his feelings.

Back in 1938, when Siegel and Shuster witnessed the success of their comic, they sued for their rights—but lost in the courts. So they suffered poverty as Superman grew into one of the greatest modern mythic figures. Not until 1974 did his creators, aged and in poor health, receive any share in the royalties.

Hero-Cycle

Turning from the Theseus myth to that of Superman, we find many parallels. Someone of lofty birth, but raised in humble circumstances, goes on a journey. While no goddess appears, the girl-on-a-pedestal of Joe Shuster's youth lives on in the person of Lois Lane.

Superman, appearing whenever Clark Kent's mild-mannered exterior is shed, displays very considerable powers. He penetrates an underworld, that of the devilish Lex Luthor. Superman in every venture triumphs, thus winning Lois Lane's love. And gratitude from every decent citizen represents a kind of paradise.

This is the **Hero-cycle** of mythology, as mapped out in the book's seven main sections. Here is a chart showing how the hero-cycle is followed by Theseus and by Superman.

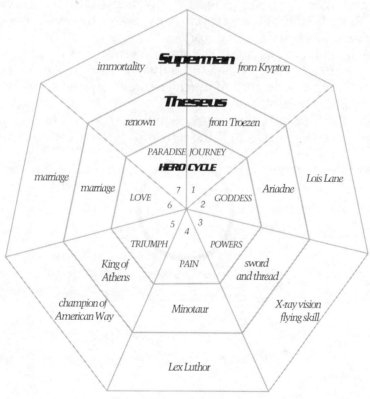

The hero-cycle,
for Theseus and for Superman

This book presents 25 themes of mythology. Two large hero-cycle charts on pages 312-313 give an overview of the myths and stories in these chapters. A great myth will express many themes, of course, but here each is classified according to whichever theme it best reveals.

Me Myself in the Exact Middle of a Living Story

Our lives may not seem especially heroic. Yet big stories do happen—stories of quest and rebellion, sacrifice and rescue, betrayal and love. These amount to a personal mythology, which may be more dramatic than we give it credit for.

Our personal myths are stored away in our memory—some for ready recall, and others far back (being hard to deal with). They dramatize our lives. A phrase used by the Welsh poet Dylan Thomas, in a story about his childhood fantasies, expresses this well: *Me myself in the exact middle of a living story.*

Huge dreams are inspired by comic books, thrillers, rock videos, one's own imaginings. We see ourselves in the role of celebrated heroes, altering the destiny of our race. Such dreams are part of living.

But the day comes when fantasy is not enough. We become weary of living at second hand, and the hero image then invades our own life. At that moment, the real journey begins.

Each of the 25 chapters concludes with a brief story illustrating its theme. Here is one about heroism in miniature, told by a sensitive girl named Shireen.

Hero

There they were, the neighbour's kids throwing mud on our dog. But he just looked up at them and tried not to be hit. He was so friendly, he only looked for love and warmth from them.

Then my brother came home. "Why are you doing that?" Scott asked them. They didn't know.

"If you were in the dog's position, would you like having mud thrown on you?" said Scott. The neighbour's kids were silent, because they knew the answer was no.

Finally Ian, the youngest of the boys, went up to our dog and had his hand licked. The dog was wagging his tail.

Ian looked at the other two boys. Then they also reached out their hands, and our dog licked their hands too, as he forgave them.

Acting Out the Myths

Using our imagination, we might see that Ian has performed quite an exploit. At first he belongs to the world of his friends, mindlessly tossing mud at the dog. Then, reflecting on what older people say, he advances towards the animal he had attacked.

This brief trip holds dangers, for the dog might wish to bite his tormentor. And the boy risks being condemned by his friends, for following a different path. But he goes forward and wins a kind of prize: self-esteem and the animal's affection.

With vision, we may recognize such moments in daily life, for it is full of them. Many experiences are on such a modest scale, while others loom so large as to transform and lead us into a new stage of life. We'll often replay a mental tape of such events and remember them as the most important of our personal myths.

Sometimes old myths are acted out in a conscious way. This may be beautiful, as when Yoko Ono becomes John Lennon's "Mother of the Universe." But if myths are lived by madmen—as when the rescuing-knight role was played by Adolf Hitler—horrors will happen.

We all act out the myths within and usually in a wholesome kind of way. But we ought to know how they operate in our own lives, and in history. That's what this book is about.

My Longest Journey

Part of downtown Toronto, Ontario

Song

I have made my sky from a cloud
And my forest from a reed.
I have made my longest journey
On a blade of grass in a stream.

From a little plaster, the city;
From a puddle of water, the sea.
From a pebble I made my island
And from an icicle, winter.

Each one of your silences
Is a parting without return
And a moment of indifference
The whole sorrow of love.

Thus it is when I dare
Offer your beauty
A rose, in this rose
Are all the gardens of summer.

GILLES VIGNEAULT
TRANSLATED BY A.J.M. SMITH

Heroic journeys are often taken in mythology. Here the Quebec songwriter Gilles Vigneault goes on a voyage of the imagination.

On a floating blade of grass he takes his longest journey. He discovers an entire city—here is part of Toronto's downtown—in a bit of plaster. He offers a rose, and it holds the promise of many gardens.

A myth is like Vigneault's *Song*—one story giving the pattern of all human life.

1. Beginnings

✳

A strange place it was, that place where the world began. A place of incredible happenings, splendours and revelations, despairs like multitudinous pits of isolated hells. A place of shadow-spookiness, inhabited by the unknowable dead. A place of jubilation and of mourning, horrible and beautiful. It was, in fact, a small prairie town.

MARGARET LAURENCE, *HEART OF A STRANGER*

On Serpent Mountain the Sun is Born *Aztec*

Nature was cruel. Four ages had arisen, and all four perished along with the sun that had upheld it. The first age ended when fierce jaguars devoured the earth's inhabitants. A terrible blast of air swept away the second sun, and fire consumed the third. The fourth age ended in a deluge of water.

Mother Earth, vast and toadlike, swam in the flood waters. Suddenly she was grasped by two gods and stretched until her body split apart. She screamed as the upper part was raised to make a heaven, the lower remaining as dry land.

Other gods, hearing Mother Earth's anguished yells, came down to console her. From her body, they decreed, would come everything needed by the human creatures soon to arrive. Her hair and skin were fashioned into plants, her eyes became springs, her mouth was reshaped into caves where people could dwell.

But Mother Earth also lived on in the person of Coatlicue, who wore a skirt of writhing serpents. She gave birth to the 400 gods of the south and to their sister, Coyolxauhqui, goddess of the moon.

Coatlicue dwelt in the temple on Serpent Mountain. Once at twilight, as she swept the temple, a ball of fine feathers drifted from the sky. She stroked it and placed it in her skirt.

Suddenly, Coatlicue realized that she was pregnant, and her face lit up with happiness.

But her 400 sons, learning the news, were enraged. "Who has shamed us by making our mother pregnant?" they asked.

Coyolxauhqui was the angriest of all. "Brothers," she exclaimed, "because of this disgrace we must kill her!"

Coatlicue felt terror on learning of this menace. But she was calmed by her unborn child, a fearsome male named Huitzilopochli. "Do not be afraid," he said from within her womb. "I know what must be done."

The 400 gods armed themselves for battle, intent on slaying Coatlicue before she conceived. They twisted their hair into ferocious knots, dressed themselves in paper streamers, and tied bells on the calves of their legs. Then the brothers, led by their warlike sister, marched to Serpent Mountain.

Coatlicue now gave birth to Huitzilopochli, already full-grown. He was also well-armed, clutching the terrible Serpent of Fire. The god appeared as living fire—the Fifth Sun that announced a new age.

Up Serpent Mountain the brothers charged, Coyolxauhqui in the lead. But Huitzilopochli wielded the Serpent of Fire with perfect skill. He cut off Coyolxauhqui's head and hurled her body to the mountain's base, where it split apart.

Huitzilopochli's deed utterly confused the gods of the south. He chased them like rabbits, four times around Serpent Mountain. The brothers begged him to retire from the battle, but nearly all were slain.

Huitzilopochli later became the protector of an oppressed people, the Aztecs. He gave them a sign: "I will show you the way to the cactus where the eagle stands. There we shall raise our city and there we shall rule, conquering many different peoples."

The Aztecs came at last to Tenochtitlan. At first, they

were denied any place to settle. But at a marshy island they saw an eagle resting upon a cactus, its wings spread to the rays of the sun. Then the eagle bowed to them in the Four Directions, and they wept for joy.

"How did we deserve such goodness?" they asked; for this was the sign foreseen by Huitzilopochli. Here the Aztecs settled and built a great city. To commemorate their god's birth, at its centre they raised a temple in the shape of Serpent Mountain.

Personalizing the Universe

Where did the world begin? For the Aztecs, on a mountain where a god is born. For Margaret Laurence, in a small prairie town. For all of us, at a place for which we probably feel nostalgia.

We personalize the universe. And it's a good thing we do, or otherwise we would appear as a blip in oceanic space, an eyeblink among the eons.

A myth, many assume, is a story that "explains nature." It would be easy to interpret the Huitzilopochli tale in this manner: "The moon and stars (Coyolxauhqui and her brothers) emerge at night, but are destroyed each morning as the sun (Huitzilopochli) rises from the earth."

But the world's great myths are about more than nature. Mainly they relate to ritual, and support political belief.

Cosmic Calendar		
January 1		universe originates
May 1		Milky Way originates
September 9		solar system originates
September 14		earth originates
September 25		life on earth originates
November 1		sex originates (microorganisms)
December 1		atmosphere originates
December 16		animal life originates (worms)
December 31	10:30 p.m.	human life originates
December 31	11:59:20 p.m.	agriculture originates
December 31	11:59:59 p.m.	Industrial Revolution originates
January 1	00:00:00	Space Age originates

adapted from *The Dragons of Eden* by Carl Sagan

So this origin myth seems to give the outcome of a huge argument. Followers of Coyolxauhqui were opposed by others who embraced Huitzilopochli, it seems, and a struggle for power was won by the latter. This may also signify a triumph of patriarchy.

Huitzilopochli's priests kept alive the eagle-on-a-cactus myth, which found fulfillment when the Aztecs came to what is now Mexico City. Here they built a temple to their god. It represented the universe in symbolic form and the point where the god's powers descend to the earth. The temple also established the "centre," the sacred ground from which the city's four divisions extended.

This was the stage for an early-December ritual called the Raising of the Banners. Paper banners were hung from houses and trees; dough images were made of Huitzilopochli; a footrace dramatized his swiftness—all a repetition of the crisis faced by their god long ago.

On February 21, 1978, as electrical workers dug near the Great Temple's site, they struck a huge engraved stone. Archaeologists saw that it represented, in superb artistic style, Coyolxauhqui's dismembered body. Further excavation showed that the stone lay exactly beneath the west-facing steps of Huitzilopochli's temple.

Today, tourists may penetrate the Great Temple all the way to its grim sacrificial rock. Here from the chests of captured warriors, priests cut out the heart (called "precious eagle cactus fruit"), offered it to the sun, and hurled the body down the temple's westward-facing steps in the direction of the setting sun.

The eagle represents the sun at its zenith. And on the Great Temple's north side, excavation revealed the House of the Eagle Warriors. Any who died in battle were thought to gain the honour of accompanying the sun on its journey to the zenith. (The sun's partners from the zenith to the west were women who died in childbirth.)

The Great Temple of the Aztecs

Even today this great myth lingers, for the flag of modern Mexico shows an eagle perched atop a cactus. The Aztec built their lives around the myth, and through ritual they aimed to return to that moment of the sun's first dawning.

We should take our thoughts about origins all the way back. Back beyond our earliest ancestors, back to that first moment of ascent from the abyss. Then we face the ultimate question: *How is it that anything should have come into existence at all?*

The faces of the past are like leaves that settle to the ground.... They make the earth rich and thick, so that new fruit will come.
                              CHIEF DAN GEORGE

The Happiest Place on Earth *American*

In the spring of 1906, five-year-old Walt Disney first cast sight on his family's newly-purchased Missouri farm. "It was set in green rolling countryside," he later recalled. "I thought it was a beautiful place."

Walt soon gave names to the chickens, ducks, and pigs under his care. The farm's wild rabbits delighted Walt, who burst into tears when a brother shot one of them with an air rifle. But he could share his love of animals with his Uncle Ed, who imitated birds so skilfully that they would come down and perch on his shoulder.

Walt loved to jump into the swimming hole and watch trains passing on the railroad tracks beside it. On the family's horse-drawn wagon he would happily ride into the nearby town of Marcelline. Walking down Main Street, he was always keen to spend a few cents in the general store.

"God will provide," Walt's Bible-reading father would often say; but the farm could not support a large family, and after five years it had to be sold. Walt, who had often sketched the farm animals, took a job drawing cartoons for advertisements shown between movies. In 1923, he went to Hollywood to form a small cartooning company.

After many setbacks, Walt in 1928 won success by synchronizing a cartoon film with sound. It starred a white-gloved rodent, whose high-pitched voice was supplied by Walt himself. This was Mickey Mouse, whose image today ranks with the swastika and the Coca-Cola bottle among the century's best-known graphic symbols.

Walt, gambling that people would sit still throughout a feature-length cartoon, brought out *Snow White and the Seven Dwarfs* in 1937. Its lovable animals and happy-ever-afterward plot have been described as blatantly sentimental, and Walt could not disagree. "We're selling corn," he once said, "and I like corn."

He insisted on total authority over his cartoonists, Hollywood's most underpaid staff. In 1940, they successfully struck for better wages and a mention in the film credits. "I am convinced that this entire mess was Communistically inspired," said the embittered Walt, who now embraced conservative political causes.

A decade later, Walt began evolving plans for an amusement park to be called "Disneyland." It would be dedicated, he said, "to the ideals, the dreams, and the hard facts that have created America."

In 1955, Disneyland opened on a 300-hectare tract near Anaheim, California. Fulfilling Walt's dream of "a family park where parents and children could have fun together," this is the "Happiest Place on Earth," with plenty of smiles beamed by the fresh-faced staff.

NORTH
Fantasyland
Imagination

WEST   Sleeping Beauty's   *EAST*
Frontierland   Castle   *Tomorrowland*
past   future

Main Street U.S.A.
consumption
SOUTH

A bird's-eye plan of Disneyland

Main Street U.S.A. is a re-creation of Marcelline's bygone world, with a steam-train depot and a horse-drawn streetcar. Walt, who saw it as "everyone's home town, the heartland of America," required every brick to be made five-eighths normal size—on the scale, that is, of a child. The consumer also rules here, for the stores offer many old-fashioned items for sale.

At the very centre of Disneyland, we pass through Sleeping Beauty's Castle. Although its towers have only a modest height, they appear to rise higher through tricks of perspective.

In Fantasyland, beyond the castle to the north, we visit Snow White's Grotto and Peter Pan's Flight (a story of a boy who wouldn't grow up). Fantasyland is about the world of the imagination, in contrast to consumer-oriented Main Street.

Technological wizardry is demonstrated in Tomorrowland, to the east. Today a Mission to Mars is offered in place of a mock moon-voyage, which lost its appeal when Yankee know-how actually realized that feat.

To the west in Frontierland, a lake is plied by the steam-powered sternwheeler *Mark Twain*, its lights twinkling at night as on the steamboats of Disney's childhood reading. His New Orleans gives no hint, naturally, of its cruel past as the nation's leading slave emporium.

Disneyland presents America's creation myth, as imagined by Walt. Wilderness outposts figure prominently in the unfolding of its destiny. And native people are shown as bloodthirsty Indians who obstruct the forging of a nation—seen (in European terms) as advanced and progressive.

"Disneyland will never be completed, as long as there is imagination left in the world," Disney foretold before dying (and having his body frozen) in 1966. "Even the trees will keep growing and things will get more beautiful each year."

Lineage

In the beginning was Scream
Who begat Blood
Who begat Eye
Who begat Fear
Who begat Wing
Who begat Bone
Who begat Granite
Who begat Violet
Who begat Guitar
Who begat Sweat
Who begat Adam
Who begat Mary
Who begat God
Who begat Nothing
Who begat Never
Never Never Never

Who begat Crow

Screaming for Blood
Grubs, crusts
Anything

Trembling featherless elbows in the nest's filth

TED HUGHES

To Begin the Journey

Today, our ideas about how things began may derive from science. But mythology offers something equally valuable—an intensely human view of things.

Ancient myths often trace beginnings back to a violent struggle,* and "Lineage" is in this vein. Today we might be more likely to prefer a mild Disneyland-style origin myth, or a scientific one that wraps everything up neatly.

Personal mythology also includes origin tales. In the family photo album or video collection, there we are: coming home from the hospital, displaying rudimentary hair and teeth, taking the first step.

---

*See pages 14,205,266.

Also we have images and stories of ancestors, who brought us to the place from which our own heroic journey may start.

We might ask what stirs people to begin the journey. Is it impatience? The pressure of parents or friends? Simple eagerness? A deathly boredom? Curiosity? Personal calamity? A timely piece of advice? Tidings of greener fields afar? Frustration? Economic necessity? An urge to prove oneself?

When the call comes, it must be answered. There is no other way to fulfill the potential lying within. Then we go, as Glenn tells in the following story, to the holy mountain from which our future may be viewed.

What I Was

I was newly arrived in downtown Calgary, and I decided to see what its night life was like. At once a big man approached me.

Now this guy was big, I mean big. I shook when he said, "GOT A QUARTER BUDDY?"

Well, I knew I had nothing smaller than a five, and I wasn't going to give him five dollars. So I calmly said, "No, I'm sorry but I don't."

I figured that would have been the end of the conversation but no, he looked at me sternly and said, "Hey, want a fight, buddy?"

A fight! I turned around and started walking back the way I came, then eased into a sprint so that he couldn't be bothered running after me.

I got a job which worked out to be only for one or two days a week, and the rest of the time I travelled. Once I thumbed through Crow's Nest Pass alone and climbed a mountain that overlooked a lake. I camped there for three nights, the most peaceful time of my life.

It was then that I decided what I was, how good I was, what I would do and wanted to be. I can still see the lake in my mind, and I still fight for the goals that I set then.

Somewhere...somehow...I want to find a place without any trouble. Do you suppose there is such a place Toto? There must be. It's not a place you can get to by boat or train. It's far, far away behind the moon, beyond the rainbow... somewhere over the rainbow.

J. FRANK BAUM, *THE WIZARD OF OZ*

2. Quest

I Iouston, Tranquility Base here. The Eagle has landed.

FIRST WORDS FROM THE MOON,
BY APOLLO COMMANDER, NEIL ARMSTRONG.

Gilgamesh and Enkidu *Babylonian*

Gilgamesh, He Who Saw Everything, ruled as the king of Uruk. He was the son of the goddess Ninsun, partly divine and mighty enough to wrestle barehanded with lions and wild bulls.

No one could oppose Gilgamesh in combat. He tyrannized the people, making them work long and hard in the fields and building huge walls about the city.

"O gods, give us relief from this work!" they prayed. "Gilgamesh takes even the aged and the very young to do his bidding!"

In answer, the gods created a being as strong as Gilgamesh, named Enkidu. Raised with a herd of wild animals, he looked much like a beast himself, with a long mane of matted hair.

Gilgamesh was told of this shaggy-haired man who behaved like an animal. Cleverly he sent a temple priestess to the stranger. When he saw her, he felt a strange and new emotion and took her in his arms.

For seven nights they were together. Then Enkidu rejoined the beasts, but at once realized that his life had somehow changed. The animals, sensing this difference, backed away from him and raced off across the plains. Bewildered, he returned to the girl.

"Why live with animals?" she asked. "Come to Uruk, a city of human beings." He did, and the people marvelled at his size and strength, which was nearly equal to that of the king.

Gilgamesh had been warned of this rival in a dream. Now he violently charged at the newcomer, who galloped toward him like a bull. At the last moment the king stepped aside, and Enkidu crashed into a doorpost, shattering it. Then the pair grappled with each other, butting like wild rams until the walls of Uruk shook. But finally their rage subsided.

"You are the king, raised up above men," said Enkidu. "Never again shall I oppose you." Vowing to be friends for life, the two men embraced.

One day Gilgamesh told Enkidu, "We must set out to slay Humbaba, appointed by the gods to guard the Cedar Forest."

"That journey could be the death of us," Enkidu replied. "Why go against limits set by the gods?"

"I must establish my name where no other man has had it written," said the king. "Even if I fall I shall have this fame: 'Gilgamesh fell against mighty Humbaba!'"

So Enkidu went with him against the fierce Humbaba, who tried to fix them with his evil eye. But Gilgamesh called on his patron, the sun-god Shamash, who blinded the monster with a blast of white-hot winds. Then the king easily toppled Humbaba with his axe.

On their return, Gilgamesh was wooed by Ishtar, the fertility goddess. She whispered to him, "Be my lover. My house is fragrant, and when you enter, the very threshold will kiss your feet."

But Gilgamesh remained aloof. "I know of your charms," he said. "I know about Tammuz, the lover of your youth. Every year his fate is mourned!"

Rejection made Ishtar so furious that she sent down the sacred Bull of Heaven. But Enkidu managed to grasp the beast's horns, and Gilgamesh was able to give it a fatal sword-thrust in the neck.

Ishtar cried out vengeful words at this insult. Then Enkidu ripped out the Bull's right thigh and flung it in her face, shouting, "I'd like to do the same to you!"

Offense had been given to the gods, and they decreed that Enkidu must die.

Enkidu fell prey to an terrifying sense of weakness. For

nine days he lay constantly losing strength, as Gilgamesh kept sad vigil. Finally, the shaggy man's heart ceased to beat.

His death plunged Gilgamesh into profound sorrow. Now he understood the fate of all people, death. He was tormented by it. "Will I lie down and never rise again, like Enkidu?" he asked.

Gilgamesh learned about a man named Utnapishtim who had won immortality. So now he set out on a long journey to find this fortunate soul.

First the king travelled to a vast mountain whose twin peaks guarded the rising and setting sun. Deep within lay the Road of the Sun, totally black and terrifying. But he travelled its entire length, retracing the route followed nightly by the sun itself.

Gilgamesh eventually reached the garden of the gods beside the sea. Here, among vines spangled by precious gems, Siduri squeezed the juice of grapes into golden vats. The king told her his melancholy tale.

"Enkidu, whom I loved as a brother, has met the fate of men and women," he lamented. "Many nights I wept for him and refused to let him be buried until I saw a maggot fall from his body. Now I fear death, and I search for Utnapishtim who has overcome it."

"Why do you seek immortality?" Siduri replied. "The gods kept it for themselves, and human beings must die. So make every day a time of rejoicing. Fill your belly, dance, wear fresh garments, bathe in soft waters. Look upon your children and embrace your wife, Gilgamesh, for we are given this life alone."

"No," the king answered. "I am going on." So when Siduri told the way, Gilgamesh resumed his travels. He reached the Waters of Death and had to cut 120 poles to push himself across. One touch of these poles, and they could not be used again. Gilgamesh used every one of them and then, to go on, had to use his shirt as a sail. Finally, he reached the island where Utnapishtim lived.

"What can I do to win eternal life?" Gilgamesh asked him.

The old man explained how in the great flood, he had

saved all the animals by building a ship. Afterward he had given thanks to the gods—and for this, was made immortal.

"Beneath the sea is the Plant of Life," Utnapishtim told him. "Find that, and your youth will be renewed."

Gilgamesh, tying heavy stones to his feet, went down into the sea's depths and seized the Plant of Life.

"I will take it to Uruk," he vowed, "so that the aged will find their lost youth." But when he bathed at a pool along the way, a snake devoured the plant.

Gilgamesh, finding only the snake's discarded skin where he had left the Plant of Life, wept bitterly. "Did my labours lead only to this?" he wailed. "A mere beast of the earth has had the good of it!"

And the day inevitably came when Gilgamesh, king of Uruk, lay down and never rose again.

This is the Key

This is the key of the kingdom:
In that kingdom there is a city.
In that city there is a street.
On that street there is a yard.
In that yard there is a house.
In that house there is a room.
In that room there is a bed.
On that bed there is a basket.
In that basket there are flowers.

Flowers in a basket.
Basket on the bed.
Bed in the room.
Room in the house.
House in the yard.
Yard on the street.
Street in the city.
City in the kingdom.
Of the kingdom this is the key.

ANONYMOUS

Crossing the Threshold

Sometimes we are seized by an urge to get up and go, to leave our world behind, to break new ground, to find the ultimate "something." This journey is known as a **quest**. Countless myths tell of the quest: Hercules sets out to discover the Golden Apples, Jason to win the Golden Fleece, Galahad to find the Holy Grail.

Every quest means departure from familiar faces. No matter how excited we are, that last farewell hug or handshake will probably be painful. Yet when the inevitable time comes to open the door, we must still cross the threshold.

Gilgamesh begins his quest simply for adventure, but Enkidu's death spurs him to a more drastic effort. He tries to surpass the boundaries of human life. This time, the hero crosses the threshold on a quest to defeat death.

Gilgamesh reaches the garden of the gods, which may remind us of the Garden of Eden. Humankind's quest begins here, the Bible suggests, and proceeds through a moral wilderness toward a spiritual Eden known as paradise.

The Gilgamesh tale's rediscovery was quite a story in itself. It began in 1839 when an Englishman, Austen Layard, found over 25 000 battered tablets while excavating the Assyrian city of Nineveh. The dozen tablets making up the Gilgamesh Epic were uncovered 14 years later, but their wondrous contents were not revealed to the public until 1872.

"I discovered among the Assyrian tablets in the British Museum," the archaeologist George Smith announced, "an account of the flood." This was the Utnapishtim tale, which amazed the world by its similarities to the Biblical flood story. Today we are more impressed by the strangely modern story of Gilgamesh's vain search for the greatest prize of all, eternal life.

The site of ancient Uruk is in present-day Iraq. It is here that the Sumerians created the world's first civilization. Gilgamesh is listed as Uruk's fifth king, ruling around 2700 B.C. So his story may be an exaggerated account of real events—in other words, a legend.

This myth is told in an **epic**, a long poem dramatizing a hero's adventure and the great themes of human destiny. The Gilgamesh Epic is, in fact, the world's first literary masterpiece. Scholars date it some 2000 years before the next oldest, the *Iliad* of Homer.

The Voyage of Greenpeace *Canadian*

"The rainbow is a sign from Him who is in all things," said the old, wise one. "It is a sign of the union of all peoples like one big family. Go to the mountaintop, child of my flesh, and learn to be a Warrior of the Rainbow, for it is only by spreading love and joy to others that hate in this world can be changed to understanding and kindness, and war and destruction shall end!"

WILLIAM WILLOYA AND VINSON BROWN, *WARRIORS OF THE RAINBOW*

The most horrible destructive force created by human beings is that of atomic bombs. Dropped on two Japanese cities during World War II, they simply vaporized thousands of human lives.

After that war, radioactive fallout from U.S. nuclear tests in the South Pacific produced hideous side-effects on the people of Rongelap atoll. Testing also continued off the Alaskan coast, and it was vigorously opposed by a small group of activists.

The group's leader was Jim Bohlen, an American-born missile engineer who turned against U.S. involvement in the Vietnam War. When his son reached eighteen and could be drafted, the Bohlens moved to Vancouver. There they met others with similar anti-war sentiments. These included several Quakers, who practised a form of passive resistance known as "bearing witness": expressing disapproval by merely being present where something objectionable is happening. During the South Pacific nuclear tests, Quakers had tried unsuccessfully to sail a boat to the explosion site.

To show opposition to the next Alaska blast, the group (of which the Bohlens were now members) wanted to make a decisive gesture. It held several meetings without coming up with a plan, until a suggestion was made by

Bohlen's wife, Marie. "Why doesn't someone sail a boat up there and park right next to the bomb?" she asked. "That's something everyone can understand."

And that's exactly what they tried to do. The organization, now called Greenpeace, chartered a rusting old halibut seiner named the *Cormack*. From Vancouver, on September 15, 1971, it set off for Alaska. Aboard was Robert Hunter of the *Vancouver Sun*, who passed around a collection of Indian myths with the title *Warriors of the Rainbow*.

 **ECOLOGY: HEALTHY WORLD**

GREENPEACE

 **PEACE: WORLD TREE, PERSON**

Greenpeace symbols

In the book there was an old prophecy. The earth would some day be ravaged, it foretold, but then restored after Native Canadians banded with whites to become Warriors of the Rainbow. And when the Greenpeace crew stopped in at Alert Bay to meet with Kwakiutl chiefs, it received a special blessing. This rite, Hunter noted, strengthened a "vague affinity" felt by the group with the Natives.

Unfortunately, a number of circumstances prevented Greenpeace from reaching the test site. The White House received a kilometre-long protest telegram with the names of 177 000 Canadians, but the blast went off as planned.

However, a myth had been created—the story of a tiny boat against a monstrous bomb—and four months later an end to the tests was announced, for "political and other reasons."

Meanwhile in Polynesia, France was still conducting nuclear tests in the atmosphere. In 1972, David MacTaggart, a Canadian-born Greenpeace activist, sailed his ketch *Vega* into international waters near an impending explosion. Despite being rammed by a French military ship, he returned the next year during another test, and this time was severely beaten by commandos. Tests in the atmosphere were then curtailed, but continued underground.

A campaign against the slaughter of whales followed for Greenpeace. Some 23 000 people converged on Vancouver's Jericho Beach one day in 1975, as the *Cormack* and *Vega* set out to the hunting grounds. Activists steered tiny inflatables directly between the harpoonists and the endangered beasts.

From the start, Greenpeace had been media-conscious. This time, a journalist caught the encounter's key moments on film. Later these pictures were broadcast on every major television network in the world. Instantly, it overturned the whale's long-standing image as a kind of sea-monster. "If the mythology of Moby Dick and Captain Ahab had dominated human consciousness about Leviathan for over a century," Hunter wrote, "a whole new age was in the making."

Greenpeace sprouted new branches in Europe in 1977. A timely Dutch grant enabled the organization to buy a derelict trawler, which was rechristened the *Rainbow Warrior*. After playing a role during several campaigns, in 1985, it sailed to the South Pacific on a voyage that would involve Greenpeace in the anti-nuclear struggle as never before.

Again a French nuclear device was the foe. From a New Zealand harbour, the *Rainbow Warrior* was supposed to lead a "peace flotilla" into the Polynesian test zone.

On the way, the ship's crew answered a request from the
people on Rongelap atoll. After the H-bomb blast of 1954,
the fallout drifted upon Rongelap like snow. "Some people
put it in their mouths and tasted it," a reporter was told.
"One man rubbed it in his eye to see if it would cure an
old ailment. People walked in it, and children played in
it." Leukemia, deformities, and miscarriages were the
inevitable result.

The people were evacuated by the Americans and
returned three years later to the atoll, now said to be safe.
But the symptoms of contamination continued to appear.
Their senator, Jeton Anjain, believed that the islanders
should leave for good. When an appeal to the U.S. fell on
deaf ears, he approached Greenpeace.

In Operation Exodus, the *Rainbow Warrior* and its
inflatables were used to ferry the islanders and their
belongings to an uninhabited island. Photographer
Fernando Pereira covered the mission, and his pictures
went out to the world. They whetted a keen appetite for
news of the forthcoming nuclear protest.

Soon afterwards, the *Rainbow Warrior* was in
Auckland. Then on July 10, 1985, two French agents who
had posed as a vacationing couple planted underwater
bombs on the docked boat. Thirteen people were on board
when the first explosion came. Everyone was ordered off,
but Pereira went below and was drowned when the second
blast sank the vessel.

When investigations showed that the French secret service was involved, its chief and the defence minister
resigned. Although the agents were sentenced to ten years
imprisonment, France forced New Zealand to release them
within a year.

The irony of violence used against a ship symbolizing
non-violent protest was not lost on the world. The cause of
Greenpeace, far from being halted, was more widely
advanced than ever before. Among the supportive graffiti
that appeared during this time, one was especially moving. "You Can't Sink a Rainbow," it read.

Flight One

Good afternoon ladies and gentlemen
This is your Captain speaking.

We are flying at an unknown altitude
And an incalculable speed.
The temperature outside is beyond words.

If you look out your windows you will see
Many ruined cities and enduring seas
But if you wish to sleep please close the blinds.

My navigator has been ill for many years
And we are on Automatic Pilot; regrettably
I cannot foresee our ultimate destination.

Have a pleasant trip.
You may smoke, you may drink, you may dance
You may die.
We may even land oneday.

GWENDOLYN MACEWEN

Companions in the Quest

The quest always leads into dangers and uncertainties. However, often we are able to face them with a friend, known in mythology as the **companion**.

Gilgamesh and Enkidu are well-known companions in ancient mythology. Kindred spirits in modern myths include Batman and Robin, Bonnie and Clyde, Tonto and the Lone Ranger. And in personal mythology, a blanket may serve as a friend during childhood, while later we might wear the medal of St. Christopher, patron of travellers.

Advice from one's peers is also helpful in the quest. Students, for instance, will warn one another about the hazards of particular courses and teachers. During the Great Depression, hobos entering a strange town would be guided by messages chalked on fences and walls:

Police harmless	Police hostile	fleas in jail	safe camp	kind woman	tell pitiful story

Hobo language

Supporting the hero, the companion shares similar aims. Each understands what is at stake, each provides a special kind of space for growth.

We all view the quest in a way unique to ourselves. Whatever seems most worth pursuing is the object of our attention. And whether we go alone or with a friend—as Barbara here writes—we show the world who we are.

To Survive on Nothing

In the summertime I was a bad girl. My parents and I had a big fight, and I got kicked out of the house. At the same time, my friend Lori was visiting from Toronto, so I packed my things and we thumbed to TO.

I had no money and I think Lori had a few dollars. She had had this dream earlier, of our going away together, and she told me all of this before it happened. Ironic, huh?

Anyway, we rented a bachelor apartment with a bedroom, kitchen, bathroom, together with Quia the cat, and lots of art hanging around. The first thing we did was spend what money we had on food, and came to the conclusion that we both needed to lose a few kilos anyway.

I spent most of the time watching people, doing watercolours, listening to the radio, playing guitar, going out to dance. It's a shame this all had to end, because of school two weeks later. I have learned a lot about people.

＊

Heated argument—
Then I go out and become
A motorcycle.

KANEKO TOTA

3. Promised Land

And the Lord said, I have surely seen the affliction of my people which are in Egypt, and have heard their cry by reason of their taskmasters; for I know their sorrows; And I am come down to deliver them out of the land of the Egyptians, and to bring them up out of that land unto a good land and a large, unto a land flowing with milk and honey.

EXODUS 3:7-8

Dido and Aeneas *Roman*

In his youth, Anchises of Troy fell madly in love with Venus, the love-goddess. "No god and no man can stop me, here and now, from showing my affection to you!" he declared, and she yielded to this mortal. Their child, Aeneas, grew to manhood enjoying Venus's tender devotion.

Then came the Trojan War.* Although Anchises was too old to battle the invading Greeks, Aeneas fought bravely. More than once Venus came onto the battlefield to shield him from death with her lovely arms.

But finally Troy fell. Through its burning ruins, Aeneas carried Anchises to the boats, and with a number of Trojans he set sail. Anchises died on the voyage, but the fugitives reached the distant city of Carthage. Its queen, the beautiful Dido, welcomed the Trojans with a banquet.

Venus knew that Aeneas was destined to found Rome, the world's greatest nation. To make sure that no harm would come to him from the Carthaginians, she enflamed Dido's heart with passion. Throughout the banquet, the queen remained at his side, asking question after question about his adventures. Afterwards, the image of his face and voice burned in her memory.

---

*See pages 170-174.

34

Juno, queen of the gods, was the protectress of Carthage. She could also look into the future. The city's fate, she knew, was to be destroyed some day by Rome. But if Aeneas were to marry Dido—she hoped—might he be turned aside from his fate?

Juno came to Venus and suggested that the two should marry, so in love they seemed to be. Venus gave her consent, confident that this wouldn't change Aeneas's destiny.

"Then here is my plan," Juno told the love-goddess. "Tomorrow when Dido and Aeneas go hunting in the woods, I'll send them a thunderstorm. They will flee to a nearby cave, and there I'll be to affirm their love."

And it all happened exactly as Juno had planned.

A winter passed. It was a time of happy abandonment for Aeneas, and he became indifferent to his future.

But Jupiter, king of gods, decided that Aeneas should indeed fulfill his destiny. He sternly reminded the hero of his duties and so, reluctantly, Aeneas began secret preparations for his departure.

Dido finally guessed the truth. "Do you intend to leave me by stealth?" she asked one day, confronting him with the truth.

"I never planned to leave you secretly," said Aeneas, "but it is my fate. I must set sail for Italy for I am destined to become the founder of Rome."

"Let the gods look down on me!" Dido cried in despair. "This man was thrown on our shores, and I let him share my realm. What madness!" And she ran from him in fierce anguish. Aeneas, though his heart melted with love for Dido, went to his ships.

Dido's one wish now was for death. She commanded that a funeral pyre be built, and she placed upon it everything that reminded her of Aeneas. To hide her real intentions, the queen said that she was using magic as a kind of relief to her soul.

In the first glow of morning, Dido saw the slim black forms of the Trojan ships sailing away. For a few moments she thought wildly of pursuit. Then she ordered a servant to kindle the funeral pyre.

Climbing to its summit, Dido threw herself against the

blade of her sword. Later Aeneas looked back to see flames mounting to the sky, unaware that they rose from the queen's death-pyre.

The Trojans sailed on to the shores of Italy and landed at Cumae. Here Aeneas climbed to the cave of the Sibyl, who was able to see into the future by consulting her god, Apollo. "Prophetess, Troy has suffered bitter fortune," he cried. "Now that we have reached the soil of Italy, give us our promised home."

The Sibyl's heart pounded as she listened to the words of Apollo. Then the cave's hundred gates flew open and her voice reverberated: "Wars, horrible wars I see. River Tiber froths with blood. Juno pursues you still."

Aeneas spoke again: "My father, Anchises, has gone to the Underworld. Direct me to its entrance, I beg you, so I may see him again."

"Within a tree's thick shade hangs the Golden Bough," the Sibyl replied. "Find it and pluck it out. If Fate intends that you enter the Underworld, the Bough will yield easily to your grasp; if not, there is no metal sharp enough to cut that branch."

Aeneas walked away from the cave, and at once two of Venus's doves descended. He followed them to a forest where they settled—and there, gleaming in the dark, was the Golden Bough. It easily came loose in his hand.

Aeneas took the branch back to the Sibyl, who agreed to lead him into the Underworld. Its entrance was beside Lake Avernus, called the "birdless place" because its sulphurous fumes would suffocate any bird attempting to fly overhead. "Take courage, Aeneas!" cried the Sibyl as she descended into the Underworld, and he quickly followed.

Down to the bubbling swamp of Styx they went and across its waters on the rickety craft of Charon the boatman. Ahead Aeneas saw a region set apart for infants, suicides, famous warriors, those wrongly accused, and victims of cruel love. And there, like a new moon among dim wreaths of clouds, was Dido.

"I swear by whatever is sacred," Aeneas cried to her, "that I left you unwillingly!" But Dido withdrew to the eternal shades, still full of hatred.

The way then divided. On the left was a grim rampart encircled by a rushing river of fire. From within it came moans and the clanking of chains and the sound of vicious lashings. This was Tartarus, where the wicked endured endless punishment.

At this crossroads the Sibyl directed Aeneas to deposit the Golden Bough. Their way was to the right, for ahead shone the Fields of Elysium.

Here the Blessed, under a sun and stars of their own, enjoyed pleasures remembered from earth. In a purplish and more spacious air they could feast, wrestle, sing, and dance. And here Aeneas found Anchises.

Tears poured from the father's eyes. He eagerly stretched out his hands to Aeneas, who rushed to embrace him but in vain. Three times the son reached out to clasp his father's neck, and three times the ghost slipped through his arms.

But Anchises could still speak to Aeneas, passing on his fatherly wisdom. He showed Aeneas another river, the Lethe, its banks filled with countless souls of every nation. "These are souls about to enter earthly bodies once more," Anchises explained. "Drinking these waters, they lose all memories."

"Are some willing to inhabit bodies once again?" asked Aeneas.

"To be alive dulls the sparks of heavenly fire within the soul, of course," said Anchises. "But here in Elysium our souls are kindled again by the spirit that drives the universe. After a thousand years we drink the water of forgetfulness and then long for rebirth."

Then Anchises pointed out the most gallant of all those in Elysium. They would become the great ones of the Rome to be: Julius Caesar, conqueror of Gaul, and Augustus, who would found another Golden Age.

But now in the upper world, the sun was sinking. So it was time for Aeneas and the Sibyl to return. At the Ivory Gate, father and son parted, and soon Aeneas was at his ships again.

Terrible battles followed, as the Sibyl had foretold. But Aeneas had the aid of Venus, who provided strategy in the

wars and lovingly tended his wounds. So after much
bloodshed, he fulfilled his destiny by becoming the
founder of Rome.

Narrowly the path
Fades away into a field
Blooming with flowers.

Fukoku

A New Life

The grass looks greener, they say, on the other side of the hill.
Throughout history, people have set off for other parts of the world
that seemed better, where there is promise of a fresh start and a new
life.

Two thousand years ago, Italy was the scene of bloody civil wars
until Augustus emerged as emperor and brought peace. When the
Aeneid was written by Virgil (70-19 B.C.), Romans had an epic to
glorify their past. Their ancestors had struggled, it said, to reach that
much-favoured site called Rome—their "promised land."

The Golden Bough is a magic plant, similar to the one looked for
by Gilgamesh.* Symbolically, it could mean the unlocking of gates
that hold us from our destiny. For downtrodden souls seeking a
promised land today, this might be a hard-won visa or a plane ticket.

The best-known promised land in the western world was
described in the Bible. The Hebrews, enslaved by the Pharaoh of
Egypt, were led forth by Moses and his vision of "a land flowing
with milk and honey." Throughout the history of the Jewish people,
this place has symbolized a perfect and ideal world, where persecu-
tion would be only a memory.

In a similar way the black people of America, brought from Africa
as slaves, found hope in this Biblical story. Labouring in the cotton
fields of Mississippi, they saw themselves in another Egypt. A great
symbol of release was the prophet Moses, and they awaited such a
leader for their own dream of deliverance. Some saw that leadership
in a minister named Martin Luther King.

---

*See page 26.

Everything has a natural meaning. . . . But this, nevertheless, is inadequate, unless the symbols open the ear ... to the voice of the world, of the universe, speaking in the corn but also the volcano, in the sperm-drop and also the split atom. The pattern of myth, to be living and true, must absorb and relate the dark side of life.

TOM CHETWYND, *A DICTIONARY OF SYMBOLS*

I Have a Dream *American*

King delivers his "I have a dream" speech, Washington, D.C., August 1963.

Martin Luther King, born in 1929, tended towards self-dramatization as a child. Twice he made the same bizarre suicide attempt, leaping from the second-floor window of his home. The first time was when he thought that his grandmother had died, the second after she actually did pass away.

He planned to become a doctor. But while working in the Connecticut tobacco fields during his junior year at college, he felt a call to the ministry. Thus, he followed in the footsteps of his father.

King had become enthralled by the 19th century American essayist Henry Thoreau's notion that "one honest man" might morally regenerate society. When Thoreau refused to pay a poll tax to a pro-slavery government, he accepted a one-night stay in Concord Jail as a form of compensation. This principle of "passive resistance" had been also central to Mahatma Gandhi's mass movement in India, which overthrew English power by non-violent action.

King's motto was an expression used by Gandhi: *satyagraha* or soul force. "From my background," King explained, "I gained my regulating Christian ideals. From Gandhi I learned my operational technique." For a decade this mythology spearheaded black protest with "freedom rides" on interstate buses, lunch-counter sit-ins, and efforts to enroll at white universities.

In 1956, blacks entering any bus in Montgomery, Alabama, were expected to obey a long-established rule: if it became crowded, they must yield their seats to white people. But on Thursday, December 1 of that year, a seamstress named Rosa Parks refused to rise when a white man wanted her seat. "I was just tired from shopping," she later explained. "My feet hurt."

For her crime, Rosa Parks was arrested. Black leaders, feeling it was time to act, decided on a boycott of city buses to take effect on the following Monday. King, then 27, took on the huge task of spreading the word to Montgomery's 50 000 black citizens—75 percent of the bus-riding populace.

When Monday morning came, King's wife, Coretta, stepped out onto the street and scanned the buses. One rolled by with only white riders and then another and another. "They're empty!" she exclaimed to her husband. "They're empty!"

Nearly all of the blacks walked to work, or organized car pools. And the boycott worked. Ten months later, the U.S. Supreme Court ruled against segregated seating on the buses.

So began King's rise to fame. During 1957, he was in such demand as a speaker that he travelled over one million kilometres to deliver 208 speeches. Non-violent resistance was his theme. Again and again he preached this ideal, convinced that it would lead the blacks of America toward the goal of racial equality.

"A man who hits the peak at 27," King observed, "has a tough job ahead. People will be expecting me to pull rabbits out of the hat for the rest of my life." The very big rabbit of 1963 was Birmingham, Alabama, the South's most violent and most thoroughly segregated city.

Eugene "Bull" Connor, Birmingham's burly public safety commissioner, was the immovable white object opposing the irresistible black soul force of King and his followers. But the blacks had a major ally: television. "Television is the medium through which we're going to bring this country face to face with itself," King told his fellow demonstrators.

On April 6, a few dozen men and women marched up a Birmingham street. Some who carried placards—EQUAL OPPORTUNITY AND HUMAN DIGNITY, DON'T BUY SEGREGATION—were arrested and jailed. However, the marches continued, the arrests continued, and King himself was put into prison.

"One who breaks an unjust law must do so openly, lovingly, and with a willingness to accept the penalty," King wrote while in prison. "In our own nation, the Boston Tea Party represented a massive act of civil disobedience. We should never forget that everything Adolf Hitler did in Germany was 'legal'."

When Bull Connor resorted to fire hoses, Americans coast-to-coast saw it on their TV screens. On May 2, nearly a thousand black children marched downtown from the Sixteenth Street Baptist Church. All were arrested. The next day, Connor blundered: he released police dogs, and TV viewers saw them assault black children.

Finally on May 7, U.S. Attorney General Robert Kennedy intervened. Three days later King announced that an agreement had been reached. He told how lunchrooms and restroom facilities would be desegregated, and blacks would be hired on a non-discriminatory basis throughout Birmingham's industrial community.

However, King's hopes for non-violent victory were doomed. The next night white extremists attacked a black neighbourhood. Some blacks, ignoring King's creed, retaliated. President John Kennedy sent a 3000-man "battle unit" to bases near Birmingham and gave a strong statement of warning on television. During the next ten weeks, more than 750 riots broke out in cities and towns throughout the nation.

The emotional peak of King's campaign came on August 28. A quarter-million people joined in a march on Washington, D.C. It surpassed in grandeur anything ever seen in the nation's capital.

The crowd first assembled around the Washington Monument, and soon after 11 a.m., they began strolling toward the Lincoln Memorial. Black and white together, they sang the great anthem of the civil-rights movement, "We Shall Overcome."

At the Lincoln Memorial, protest songs and hymns were performed by Bob Dylan, Mahalia Jackson, and others, and many speeches were delivered. Then cheers broke out as King headed toward the speakers' platform before Lincoln's colossal statue. He gave his prepared address, then went on to deliver an impromptu oration that would be ranked alongside Lincoln's Gettysburg Address in eloquence.

"I have a dream today," said King, his baritone voice rising. "I have a dream that one day every valley shall be exalted, every hill and mountain shall be made low." He continued in the vein of the great vision from Isaiah, his audience roaring with excitement. Then came his moving conclusion:

"When we allow freedom to ring; when we let it ring from every city and every hamlet, from every state and every city, we will be able to speed the day when all of God's children, black men and white men, Jews and Gentiles, Protestants and Catholics, will be able to join hands and sing in the words of the old Negro spiritual, "'Free at last, Free at last, Great God a-mighty, We are free at last!'"

The people expressed their joy in a thunderous ovation, in hugs and tears, in exultant leaps high into the air. "King! King!" they roared. "Free at last!" the crowd chanted again and again. But when King was congratulated on this speech that lifted everyone to the zenith, he quietly explained that he had been moved to utter it by the Holy Spirit.

The March on Washington forced President Kennedy to enact an historic civic rights statute. Yet only three months later, King watched on TV the tragic events of Kennedy's assassination and suddenly confided to his wife: "This is the way I'm going to go. I'll never reach my fortieth birthday."

On July 2, 1964, President Lyndon Johnson signed the Civil Rights Bill, barring discrimination in employment and public accommodation. That summer a voter-registration drive in Mississippi was supported by hundreds of white college youths—three of whom died in the cause—and on December 10, King was awarded the Nobel Peace Prize.

King was able to challenge whites in terms of their own values, merely repeating the creed of "liberty and justice for all." But his ideal of non-violent resistance began to lose its hold. Young activists, weary of the strains of protest, had begun to call him "Dr. Lawd" or "LLJ" (Little Lord Jesus):

> *De Lawd he come,*
> *He seek, he spoke,*
> *De Lawd he go...*
> *We get our asses broke.*

In 1965, King failed to go on a voter-registration drive in Selma, Alabama and was heavily criticized when 50 demonstrators were seriously injured.

The militant Committee on Racial Equality in 1966 rejected non-violence and approved the slogan "Black Power." Also, the message went out that whites were no longer wanted on the crusade.

For King in 1968, one final chance to redeem his philosophy came in Memphis, Tennessee, where he was helping sanitation workers who were striking for modest wage demands. When the press criticized him for choosing a luxurious motel, he checked into the small, black-operated Lorraine.

Opposite the motel stood a nondescript rooming house. An assassin staying here had a clear view of King's balcony, and easily shot a bullet into his neck. Within an hour, King was pronounced dead.

In the book of Exodus, we may read how the ancient Hebrews were led out of slavery by Moses. He received the Ten Commandments at Sinai and from the top of Mount Pisgah, he later saw Israel, the promised land. But sadly, Moses would die before his people could touch its soil.

Martin Luther King, on the night before his assassination, gave a remarkable speech that concluded with these words: "I just want to do God's will. And he has allowed me to go up to the mountain. And I've looked over, and I've seen the Promised Land."

AENEAS	MOSES	KING
Rome	Israel	Washington
Cumae	Pisgah	Birmingham
Troy	Egypt	Atlanta
Carthage	Sinai	Montgomery

Journeys to the promised land

Go Down, Moses

When Moses was in Egypt land,
LET MY PEOPLE GO,
Oppressed so hard they could not stand,
LET MY PEOPLE GO.

Go down, Moses,
Way down in Egypt land.
Tell old Pharaoh
To let my people go.

TRADITIONAL AMERICAN

It's Much Better Out There

Friends, returning from some distant place, might say, "It's much better out there." They tell of new dimensions of life, new pursuits. We think about this, ask questions and then—off we go.

Thus, a personal mythology takes shape. Our adventures are enshrined in memory, passed along to others in story form. They become our own hero myths.

In an earlier day, myths of the tribe were recited or sung by its elders. And in many families, still, stories of its ancestors are told at the dinner table and during family reunions. Somebody survived through lean times to become a big success, another survived a terrible tragedy, someone else was the first to reach a promised land— perhaps the very place where the clan now lives.

Such family myths, often retold, show how pathways through life's uncertainties are found. They help us to give shape and direction to our own existence. The story overleaf is Carrie's stirring tale of a brave ancestor.

Our Heroic Family Myth

The story of my great-great-grandmother has been told again and again, passed down through generations. It has probably been exaggerated through the years, but nevertheless remains a true story. One could say it's somewhat of a myth.

Cathleen Spenser, at the age of 18 in Ireland, became pregnant. Her parents were so disgusted and shocked that they threw her out of the house. All alone, she tried to find work and a home for her future child.

But work in those days was hard to find, especially for a pregnant woman. So she set out on her quest to Canada, travelling on a cargo boat. One sailor, whose name has been forgotten, helped her and protected her from the other sailors.

The boat encountered many wicked storms. Sailors were swept overboard and left there to be devoured by the sea. The boat was infested with rats, and food began to get low. Disease lay waiting around every corner.

But after many months, the boat finally made it to Canada. The young sailor had fallen very much in love with Cathleen and decided to stay in Canada with her and the baby. But before they could live happily ever after, her labour pains started and she did not live through the birth, although the baby did.

It was a boy. And since the sailor had loved Cathleen so dearly, he took care of the boy and raised him like his own son. When the boy was old enough, he told the man about his mother, how she had travelled across dangerous seas to start a new life for herself and for him.

When the son had children, he told them the tale. And when they had children, they were told, and so it became a family myth that we are very proud of, because without her heroism and courage and strength, we would not be living here now.

You have to be careful, ask yourself questions, as for example whether you still are, and if no when it stopped, and if yes how long it will still go on, anything at all to keep you from losing the thread of the dream.

Samuel Beckett, *Molloy*

4. Vision

Two men look out through the same bars:
One sees the mud, and one sees the stars.

FREDERICK LANGBRIDGE

Quest for the Holy Grail *British*

The Knights of the Round Table were the noblest men in all the land. They served King Arthur and took his vows of chivalry: "You must swear never to commit murder or treason, to always show courtesy toward women, and show mercy to all."

One day as the knights sat at the Round Table, a fine-looking youth marched in. He was accompanied by an old hermit, who told the king that this youth wanted to become a knight. Arthur asked the boy his name.

"Sir, I am Galahad."

The great Lancelot felt a shudder, for he realized that this was his son, conceived by enchantment and raised by the nuns after the boy's mother had died of sadness.

Arthur's queen, the lovely Guinevere, went up to Galahad and with a knowing smile—for she knew Lancelot's secret—said: "This must be a noble young man, for so is the knight who fathered him! Never did two men resemble each other more." Yet while Lancelot was a hearty fellow, Galahad would forever appear solemn.

Although everyone who sat around the Round Table was perfectly equal, there was a special seat that had never been claimed. Now the company saw the hermit lead Galahad to this place, the Siege Perilous. "Nobody else has sat there before!" exclaimed Bors, the most faithful of the knights. "Here is the one who will lead us to the Holy Grail!"

47

This was the most sacred of all relics, the golden vessel used by Christ at the Last Supper.

At that moment a miraculous thing happened. Thunder crashed, and a sunbeam seven times brighter than that of day lit up the hall. The knights looking into one another's faces saw a look of youthfulness like that of many years before. All were struck speechless.

Then, covered with a rich white cloth and floating in the air, the Holy Grail itself could be seen shimmering before them. Marvellous food and drink were suddenly placed before them, but only for a few moments—only until the vision had disappeared.

The effect on the knights was stupendous. Many immediately vowed to undertake a quest for the Holy Grail, although this journey would be hard, and the Grail's mysteries might be seen only by those cleansed of their sins.

It was Arthur who expressed the terrible truth felt by all. "Here are the fairest and truest knights ever seen in the world. But never will we all meet together again, for many will die in the quest."

Many paths led to the Grail Castle, Carbonek, all of them difficult. At first the knights went on separate quests.

Lancelot knew Carbonek well, because it was here that Galahad had been conceived. After a long, perilous journey with many adventures he came to the Waste Land, a place of rocks and stunted growth, and there in the midst of it was the castle.

He entered and came to a chamber whose door opened to reveal the Holy Grail draped in red. But suddenly a blast of fire struck him, and he fell to the ground as if dead. When he awoke, servants told him that he had lain senseless for twenty-four days. Lancelot immediately knew that he had been punished for the twenty-four years of committing a grievous sin—adultery with Queen Guinevere.

"Your quest is over now," Lancelot was told. "Being unworthy, you'll never see the Holy Grail again." He left the castle and with a saddened heart returned to Camelot.

Here he learned that many knights, more than half of them, had already lost their lives in the quest.

Three men, however, were especially favoured. One was Percival, the most simple-hearted of knights but a magnificent fighter. Another was the resolute Bors, and Galahad was the third.

These three good knights found themselves on a glorious white ship which, unguided by any sailor, carried them to Carbonek, and they entered the chamber where Lancelot had fallen.

Galahad felt an overwhelming sense of joy. He knew that he was approaching the end of his quest. A door opened, and the three knights saw a procession. Two men carried the Maimed King, Pelles, lying on a couch with his appalling wound clearly visible. This was Galahad's grandfather.

Then came a man holding a spear from which drops of blood fell— the weapon by which a knight had once given Pelles his wound. And finally there was the Grail Maiden, bearing the Holy Grail, which shone as if all the torches of the world were blazing.

"Drink from this vessel," said the Grail Maiden. Galahad came forward, knelt and drank. Percival and Bors did the same, experiencing a sweetness more marvellous than can be told.

"Take the blood of this spear," the Grail Maiden said to Galahad, "and anoint the Maimed King."

Galahad took the spear and allowed the blood to fall onto the king's wound. Miraculously, Pelles sat up and was healed. He stepped down from the couch and stood erect, offering fervent thanks to God.

"I will leave this castle now to become a monk," he said and turned to Percival. "You will guard the Grail, and this woman shall be your wife." The king took the Grail Maiden's hand, joined it to Percival's, and blessed the couple.

Galahad fervently kissed his grandfather goodbye. Then he embraced Percival also and Bors, to whom he said, "When you return to Camelot, greet my father and ask him to remember the instability of our earthly life."

Galahad knelt and prayed before the altar where the Holy Grail had been placed. He looked into its depths, enraptured. Abruptly, his soul departed, and a multitude of angels carried it up to heaven.

Suddenly a green and rose rainbow shafted down into Starvation Ridge not three hundred yards away from my door, like a bolt, like a pillar: it came among steaming clouds and orange sun turmoiling. . . . It hooped right into Lightning Creek, rain and snow fell simultaneous, the lake was milk-white a mile below, it was just too crazy.

JACK KEROUAC, THE DHARMA BUMS

To Pursue a Vision

Three types of Grail are said to exist: those of the mind, emotions, and spirit. Consider the classic story in *The Wizard of Oz*, when Dorothy's fellow-knights follow the yellow brick road. The Scarecrow wins a diploma (brains), the Tin Woodman a heart (feelings), and the Cowardly Lion a medal (courage). Dorothy receives the ruby shoes that make possible her return to Kansas.

To some the Grail is seen as a feminine symbol. Like Mother Earth, this beautiful vessel is the source of fertility, abundance, life itself. In Celtic myth, an ancestor of the Grail is the Cauldron of Plenty with magical food-producing powers. This fabled bowl also has links with the vessel of the sun, holding powers of warmth and renewal.*

In this medieval tale, the knights' first vision of the Grail is brief. To find it again requires a hard and dangerous journey. At its end, Galahad sees the Grail only because he is sexually pure, while Lancelot is blinded to it by his adulterous life.

A central symbol in this tale is the Round Table. It suggests that

---

*See pages 288-292.

everyone was equal in the venture. The circle is regarded as the perfect shape; the Holy Grail is at its centre.

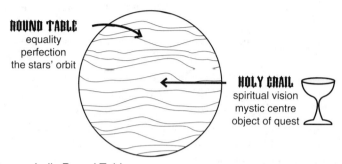

The symbolic Round Table

It would be hard to find a story that has had more influence on our lives than the Knights of the Round Table. Dream can be translated into reality, this myth suggests. The Boy Scout movement was born out of its knightly ideals. The British belief in "playing the game," being pure in the quest, gave strength to our ideas about sport. To pursue a vision shared with others, to involve ourselves in some cause, is to follow in the knights' footsteps.

Saint of the Gutters *Indian*

A hand of friendship takes on the mysticism of a blessing

Agnes Bojaxhiu was born in 1910 into a well-to-do Albanian family. She was mischievous and playful as a girl, but learned from her strong-willed mother to be helpful and kind.

Then her father's death plunged the family into poverty. At 18, Agnes joined the Loretto missionary order, becoming a teaching sister in Calcutta.

She seemed indistinguishable from the other sisters, although delicate in health and so awkward that she couldn't easily light the candles. Then on September 10, 1946, on a long train ride to a retreat in Darjeeling, her life dramatically changed.

"I heard the voice of God," she recalled. "He was calling me to take care of the sick and the dying and the hungry, the naked and the hungry."

From this vision sprang the renown of the remarkable woman known as Mother Teresa.

Without funding, without even a plan, she left the convent several months later and went to be among the downtrodden. "I picked up a man from the street and he was eaten up alive by worms, and nobody could stand him, he was smelling so badly," said Mother Teresa. "I went to him to clean him and he said, 'Why do you do this?' And I said, 'Because I love you'."

Many other stories are told of those first years. One man had a gangrenous thumb which had to be removed, and Mother Teresa cut it off with a pair of scissors. She fainted one way, and her patient the other.

Adapting herself entirely to the Indian way of life, Mother Teresa now wore a sari of white muslin bordered in blue. She ate only what the very poorest souls consumed, rice and salt.

Occasionally help would be offered by an ex-student. One such person was Subhasini Das, who came from a wealthy family. She had a keen desire to devote herself to the work of God. "You must first forget yourself," said Mother Teresa, "so that you can become wholly dedicated to God and your neighbour."

On March 19, 1949, while Mother Teresa was praying, she heard a knock at the door. There was Subhasini, no longer richly dressed. "I have come as you asked me to,"

she said." I have made a decision deep within my heart."
She was the first sister of what became known as the
Missionaries of Charity.

Forty years later, over 350 missions have been established, touching nearly every country in the world. The
Missionaries of Charity must labour for nine years, deny-
ing themselves all comforts, before becoming a fully
fledged member of the order. They receive scarcely any
funding and possess few skills beyond those required to
wash and hug the most wretched people of the earth,
many near death.

Mother Teresa addressed herself to one of the world's
most fundamental needs—the "hunger for love." She
received a Nobel Prize in 1979 and will undoubtedly be
named as a saint. Yet once, when told by an admirer that
nobody could replace her, she replied, "Anybody can."

This "saint of the gutters" takes the greatest joy in the
home for the dying, Kalighat (alongside the temple of
Kali).* Those restored to a kind of health are gently asked
to leave, making room for the ones who are truly dying.

As a devout Roman Catholic, Mother Teresa treasures
the ceremony of the Mass, where bread and wine become
the body and blood of Jesus. But working with the poor
can lend the rite a special significance. "If we can see
Jesus in the appearance of bread," she remarked, "we can
see Him in the broken bodies of the poor."

To help in envisioning the poor in this way, Mother
Teresa devised a simple formula for the nuns. Holding out
a hand, they touch each finger while repeating, "What you
do *to* him; what you do *with* him; what you do *for* him."
This simple utterance holds the power capable of driving
an army of rescuers.

And now here is my secret, a very simple secret: It is only
with the heart that one can see rightly; what is essential is
invisible to the eye.

ANTOINE DE SAINT-EXUPERY, *THE LITTLE PRINCE*

---

*See pages 157-158.

Epiphany

Sometimes, life gives moments of sudden illumination. This may be a "bolt from the blue" or, as Mother Theresa felt it, the voice of God.

An **epiphany**, which means "showing-forth," refers in classical myth to a god's sudden appearance. In Christianity it means the light emitted by a star above the baby Jesus of Nazareth. An epiphany is a revelation, a dazzling vision of the divine pervading mortal life.

Vision is the basis of religion and of literature as well. The Irish writer, James Joyce,* changed the course of literature by his emphasis on the epiphany. Every story, he said, should give a "radiant" glimpse of an event's "hidden significance."

The point of a story, he believed, is found not in a plot twist. It lies in a meaning grasped by the hero, a kind of illumination. Authors since Joyce have followed his example, and the epiphany is so widely found in today's writing that we may not easily grasp its originality.

Among the images of David's vision is a dirty old coffee cup lid. Beauty, he seems to be saying, can be found in simple things, and his "glimpse of perfection" is an epiphany.

---

*See pages 189-192.

Perfection

I just had a glimpse of perfection. Walking out from the grass behind the school, I witnessed the perfect scene. In the parking lot were two parked pickup trucks with students sitting in the back. Somebody had a radio turned up loud, playing Springsteen's, "I'm on Fire."

The sun was shining and there was a warm breeze coming up from the lake. To top off the scene, there was what I saw as the perfect innocence—a German Shepherd pup, as cute and cuddly as can be, playing with an old coffee cup lid.

To see a World in a grain of sand,
And a Heaven in a wild flower,
Hold Infinity in the palm of your hand,
And eternity in an hour.

WILLIAM BLAKE, "AUGURIES OF INNOCENCE"

2 I Recognized The Goddess

STEICHEN, Edward. *Isadora Duncan at the Portal of the Parthenon.* 1921

Dawn

I have held the summer dawn in my arms.

At first nothing stirred on the fronts of the palaces. The water was dead. On the forest road the shadows were still encamped. I walked, awakening live and heated breaths; and priceless stones watched, and wings silently ascended.

The first venture: on the pathway already flooded with fresh and pale light, a flower which revealed its name.

I laughed at the blond waterfall that tangled its hair in the pines: at its silver summit I recognized the goddess.

Then I removed her veils one by one. On the lane, my arms restless. Across the plain, where I denounced her to the rooster. In the big city, she fled among the bell-towers and the domes; and like a beggar I ran chasing her along the marble embankments.

Up the slope near a laurel grove, I wrapped her in her gathered-up veils, touching her immense body. Dawn and the child fell together at the bottom of the wood.

When I awakened, it was noon.

ARTHUR RIMBAUD, *ILLUMINATIONS*

The teenaged Rimbaud discovers the goddess—as all heroes do on the quest. Her spirit animates grove and waterfall, her body is nature itself.

The American dancer, Isadora Duncan, consciously modelled herself after Greek goddesses, and this Edward Steichen photograph shows her dancing in the Parthenon, temple of Athena.

5. Mother

The perfumes of all Arabia wafted into my nostrils as the
Goddess addressed me:
Here you behold me, Lucius, in answer to your prayer.
I am Nature, the Mother of All,
Mistress of Elements,
Primeval Child of Time,
Sovereign of the Spirit,
Queen of the Dead,
Queen of the Immortals,
The single manifestation of all goddesses and gods. My
will directs the flight of stars,
The winds of oceans,
The melancholy silences of the underworld.
I am worshipped in many aspects,
Known by innumerable names,
Served with many rites,
Venerated throughout the world.
I am Isis.

FROM APULEIUS, *THE GOLDEN ASS*

The Healing Wings of Isis *Egyptian*

The god Osiris ruled as king of Egypt, wearing a
feathery crown and grasping the sceptre and flail of
command. His spirit animated the Nile River, which
overflowed its banks each year to spread rich silt that
nourished the crops. Through Osiris, divine spirit acted
upon the land.

Isis, the Mother, was both the sister and wife of Osiris.
As queen she wore a headdress of cow horns signifying the
moon, which was invoked by the Egyptians for the affairs
of love. Mistress of the elements, gatherer of stars,
provider of grain, Isis was revered as *the one who is all*.

Isis

Seth, the brother of Isis and Osiris, personified the scorching desert winds. Jealous of the king, he tried to incite the people to rebellion. But failing, he resorted to trickery.

Seth built a coffin exactly to Osiris's measurements. Then at a party, as a joke, he brought it out. "Who would like this splendid chest?" Seth asked. "I will present it to the man who fits it perfectly."

Of course, it was only Osiris whose body exactly fitted the coffin. Thus Seth captured his brother in it and suffocated him. The coffin was thrown into the Nile, which now dried up entirely, and so drought came to Egypt.

Isis searched a long time for the coffin. It had floated down to the Mediterranean Sea and came ashore at Byblos against a shrub of tamarisk, becoming quite enclosed within the plant as it grew into a tree. But amazingly, Isis did find the coffin and brought her husband's body back to Egypt.

Secretly she buried it, but Seth, hunting when the moon was full, discovered its hiding place. He removed Osiris's corpse and cut it into fourteen pieces—one for every day by which the moon vanishes.

When Isis discovered the empty coffin, she searched for the body once again, taking a basket used for winnowing grain. She retrieved one piece of Osiris's body every day, much as the moon becomes whole each month.

Then, taking the form of a bird, Isis fluttered above these fragments. Her healing wings magically reunited them, so perfectly that Osiris came back to life. He had the strength to impregnate Isis—and at once the Nile rose in flood, spreading its fertile silt upon the land.

Osiris now reigned as god of the Underworld, judging the dead. Those without sin were borne into heaven to live forever in "the great city" of the North Star and its neighbours—the Indestructibles—which never dip below the horizon and never die.

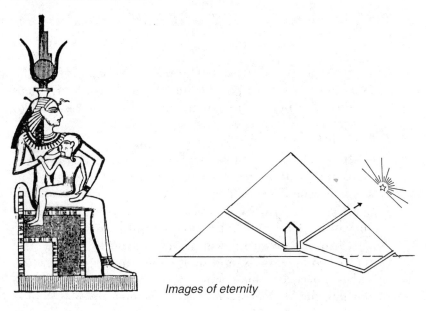

Images of eternity

Isis took refuge from Seth in a marsh, hiding among its papyrus plants, to give birth to her son Horus. Lovingly she raised him into adulthood, when one day the spirit of Osiris came from the realm of the dead.

"What is the noblest of deeds?" Osiris asked his son.

"To avenge one's father and mother when wronged!" Horus immediately replied. And it was time for revenge.

Osiris reappeared several more times to instruct his son in the ways of battle. Horus armed himself with his mother's sistrum, a rattle with a hollow ball containing the four elements: fire, water, earth, and air.

With the sistrum Horus subdued Seth but did not kill him. For nature required both his destructive powers and the rejuvenating force of Osiris and Isis.

After his battle, Horus descended a long passageway into the Underworld. He approached his father and embraced him. At once, vigour radiated from Osiris. Now the grain, newly planted in the rich soil deposited by the Nile, sprouted abundantly.

The god's spirit flowed back into Horus, too, endowing him with potency as the new King of Egypt.

Alleluia

No fanfare of flowers
But an almost inaudible
Clatter of bells
As the last icicle falls
And rivers ride again
And warn their banks
To warn the woods
And the waking worm

Of the coming Passion of our Soil,
An oratorio rehearsed by treble birds
But bursting bass from earth. O hear
The vegetable kingdom swell
And life explode,
The sound upheaved about our ears
By cabbages and cauliflower
And the gangly stalks of freshly risen corn
And radishes newborn
And row on row of cheering lettuces
Proclaiming their authentic green.

ANNE WILKINSON

The Great Mother

The myth of Isis filled all aspects of ancient Egyptian life. In her temples, worshippers were purified by being immersed in holy water, retelling the myth of her search for Osiris's body. Egyptian rites of mummification, too, re-enacted the preservation of Osiris's corpse by Isis.

On sacred lakes seen today in Egypt, like one within the vast temple complex at Karnak, papyrus was grown to represent the marsh where Isis gave birth to Horus. In the myth he quells Seth who, far from being a mere villain, is essential to the land's well-being. He robs the old king of life so that a new one, Horus, can make a fresh start.

Worshippers rattled the sistrum to recall Horus's never-ending battle with Seth. This symbolized, as Plutarch states, that the universe's elements must be "wakened when they fall asleep." But the love and healing power of Isis were vital in maintaining the life of humankind and lifting it to spiritual heights.

During late Roman times, the religion of Isis was widespread throughout the Empire. It lost out to Christianity—one 5th century bishop denouncing Isis as an "odious demon"—but aspects of her ancient worship perhaps did survive. Medieval images showing Mary with Jesus in her lap were much like those of Isis and Horus.

Osiris judged the dead, a responsibility later assumed by Christ. Isis miraculously found her husband's corpse and revived it; similarly, Mary had the power to intercede on behalf of mortals dreading eternity's vast unknown.

If the butterflies in your stomach die, send yellow death announcements to your friends.

YOKO ONO

Yoko and John *British*

When John Lennon was only a year old, his parents' marriage fell apart. Until late adolescence, he was raised in a Liverpool suburb by his Aunt

Mimi. "He was a great big baby," Mimi recalled. "He was no tough nut, never."

Mimi was one of John's anchors throughout his life. Again and again he would go back to her, replenishing his spirit with her solace and wisdom. And at 9 p.m. Liverpool time, he would telephone her every day no matter whether he was in England or the other side of the world.

"I was hip in kindergarten," said Lennon. "There was something wrong with me, I thought, because I seemed to see things other people didn't see." Later his friends' parents disliked John because of his practical joking; Paul McCartney was forbidden to be seen with him. But as soon as John formed his first rock band, at 15, Paul was writing songs with him.

By the time John's band was doing club dates in Hamburg, it had settled for the name "Beatles." Brilliantly managed by a record-store owner named Brian Epstein, the group became so successful that over 200 million of their records were eventually sold.

The group's irreverent wit endeared them to everyone, especially after the 1964 release of their movie, *A Hard Day's Night*. "How do you find America?" a newsman asked one of the Beatles in the movie. "Turn right at Greenland," came the reply.

In 1966, the Beatles went on their last tour. "We were supposed to be sort of 'good'," John recalled. "People kept bringing blind, crippled, and deformed children into our dressing room and this boy's mother would say, 'Go on, kiss him, maybe you'll bring back his sight.'"

On the same tour, John made his infamous remark that the Beatles were more popular than Jesus Christ. It led people to denounce the singer—and also drove him into a political career, as he later embraced dozens of radical causes.

That fall Lennon met a Tokyo-born underground artist named Yoko Ono, at an exhibition of her work in London. "For this whole show everything was in half," Lennon recalled; "there was half a bed, half a room, half of everything, all beautifully cut in half and painted white."

In 1969, John and Yoko, undertaking an anti-war crusade, announced the "Amsterdam Bed Peace." Scores of reporters arrived at their hotel suite in the expectation that they would make love for peace. "We were just sitting in pyjamas saying 'Peace brother'," John recalled, "and that was it."

When their manager, Brian Epstein, died from a drug overdose, it was a devastating blow to the Beatles. "After Brian died," said Lennon, "we collapsed." Paul McCartney started to take over, making John uneasy, and the strains of who was to control the group took their toll.

One cold afternoon in 1970, on the rooftop of their London studio, the group gave a rendition of "Get Back" for the film *Let It Be*. It was the Beatles' last public performance and soon afterwards the group disbanded.

Before the Beatles' breakup, Lennon had released the hymn-like "Give Peace a Chance." Now he reasserted his idealism in the song "Imagine." Although inconsistent in his thinking on social issues, he devoted much of his adult life to a vision of how the world might be.

For a time early in the 1970s, John and Yoko separated. Deeply depressed, John went on an 18-month drug-and-drink "lost weekend," during which he did mad stunts like leaping from moving cars. After their reconciliation, he confessed, "Without her, I'd probably be dead."

John often called his wife "Mother." He described Yoko as his "goddess of love and the fulfillment of his whole life." And Yoko herself wrote "Mother of the Universe," a hymn to the Great Mother.

On December 4, 1980, while John and Yoko recorded "Walking on Thin Ice," they kept asking each other, "Why are we rushing around like this to finish this song?" But only four days later, a schizophrenic youth—"following the instructions of God," he said—murdered John in front of his New York apartment building.

The outpouring of grief was tremendous, much the same as when a major political figure has died. Candlelight vigils were held in cities all around the world and a garden in Central Park was named "Strawberry Fields" after Lennon's popular song.

"John left to become the Great Force," Yoko later said. "He's doing what he can upstairs. And I'm doing what I can down here."

At work you think of the children you've left at home. At home, you think of the work you've left unfinished. Such a struggle is unleashed, your heart is rent.

GOLDA MEIR, FIRST WOMAN PRIME MINISTER OF ISRAEL

Myths of Parenthood

The mythic Isis and Yoko Ono appear as rescuers, but such heroism is regularly shown by everyday mothers as well. They defend loved ones from danger, they banish chaos from their lives. Working mothers, especially, display superheroic powers by fulfilling multiple roles with split-second timing.

To young children, a mother is the source of all good things. Her body provides food and drink, a loving caress, and life itself. She teaches the functions of the body, the first words of communication, the fundamental notions of right and wrong.

An elbow is scratched, and mother is there to patch it up. A nightmare is dreamed, and she arrives again, turning on the lamp to speed reassuring glow. A heroic first bicycle ride is achieved, and she bestows her praise.

The oldest of sculptures, it seems, are tiny stone images of the Mother. All art begins with these statuettes, showing her as hugely pregnant. The male sex claims most of the credit for the world's art and ideas, yet these pale beside the productions of her womb.

Such truths underlie our own myths of parenthood. For children there has always been the enjoyment in playing the role of mother, as Susan recalls.

Good and Plenty

Mainly I remember my sister Cathy, no matter how much we argued, for always being my mom. "Susan, put on your hat or you'll catch cold," etc. She even bought me my first pair of jeans, when my real mom wouldn't buy them.

A twelve-year-old spending her precious money just so her little sister could have a pair of OSH KOSH B'GOSH overalls. Well, she made me wear them six days out of seven, and nicknamed me "Dude" or "Maverick."

"The Dude wants to be a good and plenty box!" my cousins used to scream. Cathy would throw me on my side in her arms and shake me back and forth yelling, "Good and plenty, good and plenty!"

I was always the centre of attention. They would put two kilos of makeup on me and a closetful of clothes. It's amazing I'm not one big zit!

When I couldn't sleep at night, I'd go to Cathy's room. I went through a four-year stage when I woke up at 11 p.m. and couldn't get back to sleep unless I was with Cathy. This was a crucial time in her own life when privacy means a lot to you, but she still took me to bed, her arms wide open for me to snuggle in.

The Mother of Songs, the mother of our whole seed, bore us in the beginning. She is the mother of all races of men and the mother of all tribes. She is the mother of the thunder, the mother of the rivers, the mother of trees and of all kinds of things. She is the mother of songs and dances.

SONG OF THE KAGABA INDIANS, COLOMBIA

6. Liberation

✳

If I seem free it's because I'm always running.

JIMI HENDRIX

Lady of the Wild Things *Greek*

Artemis

I am the mightiest of gods!" Zeus bragged one day. "If you fastened a rope to me and all of you pulled on it, I couldn't be dragged down. But I could haul you up in a moment and hang you from a peak of Olympus."

The other Olympian gods* hated this boasting. Finally, Queen Hera decided to do something about it. That night after Zeus fell asleep, she called the others to his bedside and bound him with a hundred knots.

"I'll punish the lot of you!" Zeus cried on awakening. The others only laughed, having placed his thunderbolts well beyond his reach.

When a sympathetic goddess released him, the other gods fled in terror—all but Hera. The angry Zeus strung her from the sky with golden bracelets about her wrists and an anvil hanging from each ankle. Though she wept and screamed in anguish, nobody could help her. Eventually he released her, but only after the gods had vowed to never challenge his authority again.

Zeus went on to have many love affairs. Hera made as much trouble for her rivals as she could, but there was no stopping him. Although she reigned as Queen of Olympus, she never subdued his heart.

A strange tale is told of Zeus's affair with Metis, the Titaness of Good Council. Zeus was told that their offspring would be wiser than himself, and the great god wondered how childbirth could be prevented. There was only one way he decided—to swallow the mother, Metis.

Soon after, Zeus felt a terrible headache. His skull, it seemed, was about to explode. Finally the pain became so intense that Zeus asked Hephaestus to perform immediate surgery with his axe. Down came the blade, cutting open the god's head.

At once with a mighty shout sprang forth Athena, wearing full armour and holding a spear.

The child proved to be wise indeed, although Zeus's fears of being overthrown were unfounded. Soon Athena took up duties as the goddess of wisdom. She was also well-suited for the task of defending the city of Athens.

Once Zeus fell in love with Leto, a beautiful Titaness.

---

*See page 207.

When Hera learned that Leto would bear him a child, she became so angry that she sent the serpent Python after her. All one night it chased Leto across the seas.

Nobody would give Leto sanctuary, Hera's wrath being so dreadful. Finally Zeus anchored to the sea's bottom a tiny floating island, Delos, and here Leto gave birth to twins.

Artemis, the first child, was born without any pain. The next birth required mighty labour, the soft meadow smiling as Leto dug her knees into it. And with the tiny Artemis helping, into the light sprang her twin brother, Apollo. Both of the twins eventually took their place among the Olympian gods.

When Artemis was three, father Zeus set her on his lap and asked what presents she would like. "Grant me eternal virginity and as many names as Apollo," the child burbled, "and a bow and arrows just like his, a hunting tunic reaching to my knees, sixty young girls for companions, and all the mountains in the world."

Zeus beamed with pride. "This you shall have," he answered, "and more besides." When Artemis grew up, she gloried in being hailed as goddess of the hunt.

Artemis, the Lady of Wild Things as she was called, loved to hunt with bow and arrows. Wilderness was her element, and she was happy to stride the mountains alone, though sometimes her band of young girls, dressed in bear-skins, accompanied her.

As *Giver of Life*, Artemis was keen about protecting the young of all species. But another of her names was *Taker of Life*. Beasts were sacrificed to her, and dark mystery seemed to surround the Lady of Wild Things.

She was a maiden, in the sense that she preferred to remain unwed. No lover would ever be acknowledged as her master.

Artemis wore in her hair the crescent of the moon, her emblem. It ruled the night and represented the mysteries of the goddess, her hidden wisdom and secret knowledge. (For often the moon appears unexpectedly—and most dramatically on evenings when it rises full, silvering the trees and clouds.)

Apollo, by contrast, was seen by many as the sun-god, driving his chariot each day across the heavens. He represented light—the light on earth, the light of the mind.

The god made his home every spring at Delphi, a beautiful mountainside shrine. This was occupied during the winter by the wine-god, Dionysus. Apollo had priestesses to serve as an oracle at Delphi, while Dionysus was served by Maenads, the "wild women." They became possessed by the god's wine while following him in riotous torchlight processions over the mountains.

Artemis also had many women followers, and they would dance in the woods by the moonlight. The largest of her shrines was beside the sea, at Ephesus in present-day Turkey. Here women enjoyed a special freedom, spending entire nights on the hills in mystic dances.

Once while bathing in the woods with other women, Artemis realized that a young hunter was watching her. This was Actaeon, who merely happened to be standing nearby when Artemis arrived. Instantly she transformed him into a stag which his own pack of hounds tore apart.

In Roman times Artemis had a different name, Diana. Readers of the Bible know how Saint Paul opposed Diana's cult, and how her followers wrathfully shouted at him, "Great is Diana of the Ephesians!"

The worship of Diana continued, but in secret. For she was condemned as a demon, with whom witches on broomsticks flew through the night. Often she was confused with Hecate, an ancient Greek goddess of witches to whom living things were sacrificed.

During the witchcraft mania of the late Middle Ages, judges wrung confessions from accused women by any means necessary. Suspected witches in huge numbers, possibly millions, were condemned to death. Deeply-rooted fears are surely behind this crime, and today goddess-worship still meets with suspicion. Such was the unjust fate met by Diana, Lady of the Wild Things.

Sunday Afternoon

After the First Communion
and the banquet of mangoes and
bridal cake, the young daughters
of the coffee merchant lay down
for a long siesta, and their white dresses
lay beside them in quietness
and the white veils floated
in their dreams as the flies buzzed.
But as the afternoon
burned to a close they rose
and ran about the neighbourhood
among the halfbuilt villas
alive, alive, kicking a basketball, wearing
other new dresses, of bloodred velvet.

DENISE LEVERTOV

Sandal-Clad on the Mountainside

Today, Artemis/Diana holds exceptional meaning for women seeking a myth of liberation. Striding sandal-clad on the mountainside, she is at one with its wildness. Her fellow-goddesses in Greek mythology were less free, however, and to understand this we should look at the background.

Many centuries ago, Greece was occupied by food-growing people who worshipped the goddess. Then they were invaded by the Myceneans, followers of the male weather-god, Zeus. When they triumphed, he triumphed.

The goddess cults were not abolished, however, but absorbed. Myth expresses this by saying that Zeus rules with Hera as queen. She had been all-powerful before the Zeus-worshippers overthrew her cults*, but afterwards was said to equal the chief god only in powers of prophecy.

Hera is a suppressed Mother, and so are the many other women with whom Zeus has affairs. He dominates Hera.

Male-chauvinist propaganda appears in the myth of Athena, for she is said to spring from the forehead of mighty Zeus. Myth presents her as an armour-clad maiden, yet she seems to have descended from a great Cretan goddess associated with snakes and trees.

---

*See pages 205-207.

The great temple of Artemis at Ephesus was one of the ancient world's Seven Wonders. But it fell into ruin, finally, as her cult was replaced by Christianity. Indeed all of her shrines were destroyed, or made over into churches, in the wake of Saint Paul's message (*Acts 19*) of male dominance. "Let the woman learn in silence with all subjection," he declared. "And if they will learn anything, let them ask their husbands at home; for the husband is the head of the wife."

In 431 A.D., when Mary was declared to be the Mother of God, the decision was made at Ephesus, where crowds are said to have shouted, "She's the Goddess! Oh yes, she's the Goddess!" But the Lady of the Wild Things met with rejection, and thus died a mythology which had closely linked woman with nature. The image of wilderness journeys lost out to an ideal of patient endurance.

Only recently, largely through efforts by the U.S.-based women's spirituality movement, was her greatness fully reaffirmed. The result has been a renewed respect for the goddess in her many forms.

Women

Women have no wilderness in them,
They are provident instead,
Content in the tight hot cell of their hearts
To eat dusty bread.

They do not see cattle cropping red winter grass,
They do not hear
Snow water going down under culverts
Shallow and clear.

They wait, when they should turn to journeys,
They stiffen, when they should bend.
They use against themselves that benevolence
To which no man is friend.

They cannot think of so many crops to a field
Or of clean wood cleft by an axe.
Their love is an eager meaninglessness
Too tense, or too lax.

They hear in every whisper that speaks to them
A shout and a cry.
As like as not, when they take life over their door-sills
They should let it go by.

LOUISE BOGAN

Both Sides Now *Canadian*

Joni Mitchell wrote her first song, "Day by Day," on the first trip east from her Saskatoon home. Its lyrics matched the beat of the train on the Canadian Pacific Railway's tracks. "I think," she once said, "there is a lot of prairie in my music and in Neil Young's as well." Her mother used to take her out to the fields and teach her bird calls.

Music wasn't Joni's first love. Her "childhood longing" was to become a painter. Learning how to play the ukelele, she earned enough to buy art supplies by strumming it at a Saskatoon coffee house.

A stringent dress code at her high school didn't allow girls to wear slacks, but she flouted it by altering a pair of Bermuda shorts. "It was then and still is," said Joni, "a constant war to liberate myself from values not applicable to the period in which I live." Enrolling in Calgary's Alberta College of Art, she found it too regimented. By then she had discovered herself as a singer and made the decision to head east for the coffee houses of Toronto.

"I remember thinking that if you blew hard enough, you could probably knock her over," Neil Young said of Joni in those days. "She could hold up a Martin D18 [guitar] pretty well, though." Her major undertaking at the start was to earn the $140 needed to join the musicians' union.

Joni met Chuck Mitchell, a folk singer seven years older, married him after a month—and left him within a year. Then off to New York she went, her guitar case full of road maps and song lyrics on scraps of paper.

The gentle mood of her folk-art lyrics struck a chord with her listeners, and at twenty-four Joni recorded her first album, *Song to a Seagull*. She dedicated it to her seventh-grade teacher: "Mr. Kratzman, who taught me to love words." Three years later on a tour, she revisited Saskatoon. "It was a tremendously emotional experience," she recalled. "When I sang 'Both Sides Now,' It was like singing the words for the first time."

Joni became a celebrity when she wrote "Woodstock," often described as the anthem of her generation.* She moved to Los Angeles and lived in a little house cluttered with knickknacks and a grandfather clock given to her by Leonard Cohen.

"We Canadians are a bit more nosegay, a more old-fashioned bouquet than Americans," Joni remarked. "We're poets because we're such a reminiscent kind of people." As a female singer-songwriter she was unique—and destined to remain almost alone in that category for some 20 years, until the emergence of Tracy Chapman and Suzanne Vega.

Joni, with her blue eyes and waist-length blonde hair, attracted a number of well-known men. "When you fall for Joan, you fall all the way," said Graham Nash of the 1970s rock group Crosby, Stills, Nash, and Young.

Fame was also an attraction, but this imposed an ongoing battle with the press. When the rock tabloid, *Rolling Stone*, wounded Joni by publishing a chart of her supposed lovers, she fled to Greece. Her companion was James Taylor, the "bright red devil" of "Carey" on her album *Blue*.

Blue became the first of the era's "confessional" albums. Joni was "just all nerve endings" when the record was made in 1971, soon after her return from Greece, and her producers had to lock the studio doors to complete it.

"Blue" is Nash, Joni's lost lover. She lacked the then current fascination with hell, yet in her music experienced it on his behalf. Again, her listeners identified strongly with the lyrics, which exposed the pleasures and pains of an affluent age with freer moral standards.

Each of Joni's albums provided something new for the listener. Later she developed a style more oriented toward jazz. In 1978, she collaborated with the ailing jazz great, Charlie Mingus, to produce her album, *Mingus*. Because he was dying, she compared the experience to sticking her toes in jazz only to be suddenly tossed into the deep end.

In 1982, Joni was remarried, to record producer Larry Klein. "Insecurity and passion were painful," she recalled. "I'm glad that's over."

---

*See pages 262-264.

Artemis claims me now, calls me to her cruel mysteries with a power I can no longer withstand....Artemis seems to beckon from the future, to call me toward who I am now to become.

CHRISTINE DOWNING, "ARTEMIS, THE GODDESS WHO COMES FROM AFAR"

The Triple Goddess

The young woman, the old woman

This visual illusion, published in a British magazine in 1915, was entitled "My wife and my mother-in-law." Can you see both the pretty woman, in profile at left, and the thin-lipped crone whose nose-tip serves as the other's chin? More important, can you seize both images simultaneously?

We tend to identify people with the age bracket they currently occupy—as if an elderly woman, for instance, never had been a free-spirited girl. But in myth, female figures of diverse ages often appear linked, as the "Triple Goddess."

Women are said to have three ages. They go through a virginal stage, experience a birth-giving time, then attend to the completion of things. These three phases might be termed maiden, mother, matron.

In ordinary life we think of daughter, mother, and grandmother. Males also enter a middle phase (father), and yet this is unremarkable, as they can never show the evidence of pregnancy. But in the female sphere, a special loveliness springs from this flow of generations.

The earth also passes through a three-part drama. Virginal early spring leads to a nesting-germinating phase, which is followed by the calm decay of autumn.

We see this also in the moon, which governs the female menstrual cycle as well as the ocean tides. The moon is feminine, closely allied with love and the irrational. Artemis, like Isis, wore its crescent in her hair.

First of the phases is the virginal new moon, bending her bow toward the sun. The full moon, often with a reddish tinge, symbolizes woman's fertility during her birth-giving years. The old sickle moon, sailing before the sun, is linked with the matron, the essence of female wisdom. Her rounded edge is like a cupped left hand, the "sinister" side since antiquity and thus foreshadowing bad luck.

Artemis is among the oldest of all Greek deities, her powers dating back to a day when humankind lived by hunting. Today as women regain some of those powers, they embrace her image of the self-reliant woman in tune with natural energy. "Because Artemis is at home in the wilderness," Christine Downing writes, "she is comfortable with her own wildness." Jo-Ellen's ritual expresses something of the same spirit.

Our Happy-Dance

One of the rituals that I share with my friend Sarah is a little jig we do when we are very happy. This dance is very private, and only we understand its true meaning. It symbolizes triumph, joy, success, and pure elation.

We began this ritual some time ago. We were both asked out by the guys we wanted to be asked out by. When we got home, we were so utterly happy that we began whirling around the room. Fortunately, no one was home at the time, so the sanctity of our ritual was preserved.

When you're happy, all sorts of extra energy bubbles up inside of you, and dance acts as a release. It's a very spontaneous act, almost instinctive.

Now, whenever something particularly nice happens, we glance sideways at each other and grin. If we're alone, we do our dance, spinning around till we drop laughing to the floor, exhausted. If there are other people around we just do a couple of steps, to show each other we know how happy we are.

Indians have their rain-dances, filled with the symbols of their culture. Sarah and I have our happy-dance, a ritualistic part of our friendship.

Ride a cock-horse to Banbury Cross,
To see a fine lady upon a white horse;
Rings on her fingers and bells on her toes,
And she shall have music wherever she goes.

NURSERY RHYME

7. Sacrifice

✳

Of the myths that were once half-told, half-sung in the igloos, none was more important than that of Sedna. Every [Inuit] knew it & had his own version, all equally true, for this myth was too complex for any single telling.

EDMUND CARPENTER, *OH, WHAT A BLOW THAT PHANTOM GAVE ME!*

She Down There *Inuit*

Sedna was the only child of a widowed father. Many youths courted her, but she refused to wed any of them. Then along came a handsome young hunter in his kayak.

"Come with me into the land of birds where nobody hungers," he sang. "Rest with me on soft bear skins, be assured that your lamp will always have oil and your pot will have meat!"

The youth's first glance had won Sedna, but she hesitated. Then he sang, "Ivory necklaces will be yours, and rich furs!" No longer able to resist him, she was drawn to the ocean and into his kayak.

The young hunter paddled off with Sedna to his home on a rocky cliff. Then suddenly, before her eyes, his arms changed into a loon's wings! This was no man, but a spirit bird.

Sedna fell into despair. She was lonely on that cold cliffside, and although the spirit bird brought plenty of food, it was always fish.

"Father!" she cried. "Come in your kayak and take me back!" He heard this sad plea and came in his kayak to rescue his daughter. Taking Sedna in his arms, he lifted her into the boat and paddled for home.

Her bird-husband flew down and changed back into a man. "Come back, Sedna!" he called after her. "I love you, come back!" But when the father determinedly paddled on, he changed back into a loon and disappeared.

Then came a strange sound. Many birds, beating their wings angrily, raised a violent storm. Sedna's father felt horror as the sky darkened and his kayak tossed on the waves. They were clamouring, he believed, for his daughter.

The terrified man seized Sedna and threw her overboard. Her fingers gripped the boat's edge, but he took his knife and chopped them off. At once, each joint became a seal, a whale, a walrus—for Sedna was now the Great Mother of all sea animals.

"She Down There," the Inuit call her. In the ocean's depths she continues to release the creatures the people depend on for their food. Her belly is the womb from which all life springs.

But sometimes things go out of balance. There is no food. The people are unhappy. Then the shaman, the medicine man for the people, must journey down to Sedna's home.

"I must give of myself, again and again," she complains to him, "and the people are so selfish. Why must I go though this ordeal?"

Gently the shaman combs Sedna's hair, which she could not do because her hands have become flippers. "Yes, the people above no longer do good to one another," he admits. "But they are starving. And now, I know, they will sacrifice their own selfishness for the common good. Please send them the seals again."

Crooning to Sedna, the shaman braids her hair. And when the goddess's spirit is soothed at last, she releases the seals after all.

The great sea
Has sent me adrift
It moves me as the weed in a great river,
Earth and the great weather move me,
Have carried me away,
And move my inward parts with joy.

INUIT WOMAN'S SONG
AS RECORDED BY KNUD RASMUSSEN

The Shaman Goes to the Goddess

Sacrifice is seen today as a kind of choice, as when a batter makes a "sacrifice hit"—being put out, but advancing the team's base-runner.

Sacrifice in a deeper sense appears in Sedna's great deed—giving up her fingers for the people's sake. So it often is in many origin myths, as someone's chopped-up body yields plants or edible creatures. With Sedna it is the classical idea of *Do ut des,* "I give in order that you will give."

To achieve the crop's rebirth, the first farmers realized, some grain must be buried so that a new crop may grow. It must be given to the earth like a corpse. The ancient Egyptian god Osiris's loss and recovery were seen in the same way, like the farmer's seeds.* This may be summed up in the phrase: "No life without death."

In this Inuit myth of Sedna, the people must give of themselves. The shaman goes to the goddess to assure her that this will be so. And he, too, must endure the pain of sacrifice, for his journey is a hard and lonely ordeal.

For wisdom, as one great shaman has said, is only found in the great solitude, and it can be acquired only through suffering.

---

* See pages 58-61.

Shamans hold the most ancient wisdom lying at the root of all mythology. They are the magicians who commune with the spirits of other worlds. They are able to spiritually fly to a time when animals spoke the language of people, an age when all was one—a voyage to paradise.

Sacrifice means looking into the very heart of life and choosing how much must be given, how much received. In a way it is an anticipation of death, the final sacrifice. The shaman makes this journey again and again.

Shamans, since the 1960s, have been given widespread attention. Young people roam the corners of the world, seeking these spiritual guides. Actually, the shaman is everywhere, speaking through the lips of politicians and rock stars, evangelists and entertainers. Think of how the world has been stirred by the charisma of an Elvis Presley or a Joan of Arc.

Normal life is utterly erased on the shaman's far journey to the spirit realm. His body is torn apart, stripped to the bones, before being put back together. That's why in Siberia, the shaman's garment is embroidered with a skelton.

It might seem that this special power resides only in a chosen few. Yet in every one of us, there lives a shaman. A dream, an epiphany, some deeply revealing experience will make us aware of spiritual forces at work in the world, and we may experience the shaman's journey.

When the Siberian shaman gets ready to go into his trance, all the villagers get together and shake rattles and blow whistles and play whatever instruments they have to send him off. . . . It was the same way with the Doors when we played in concert.

RAY MANZAREK, IN JERRY HOPKINS AND DANIEL SUGARMAN'S
NO ONE HERE GETS OUT ALIVE

The Maid of Orleans *French*

Joan of Arc

I was 13," said Joan of Arc, "when I heard a voice from God for my help and guidance." She lived in the village of Domremy during the medieval Hundred Years War, at a time when the French were suffering defeat after defeat. Their prince, Charles VII, had not been crowned, and the country was disunited and lacking the will to win.

In 1429, when Joan was 17, God spoke through the saints, she said. He offered her a mission, and she approached the commanding officer at nearby Vaucouleurs. "The Lord wishes me to see the prince," she told him, "and you must give me a horse and some soldiers for an escort."

"What you need is a good spanking," he replied. But Joan persisted, and eventually she received her horse and escort. Word had spread of this illiterate peasant girl, and several hundred courtiers clustered around Prince Charles as she entered the castle at Chinon. All wondered if she would even know who Charles was. "I recognized him among the others," Joan said, "by the advice of my voice that revealed him to me."

Charles was weak and childish, but he threw his support behind Joan. For four generations the English had ravaged and depopulated the land. Their longbows had ruined the tactics of the boastful French knights, who had failed to learn from their suicidal defeats. Now Orleans, the key to the defence line along the Loire River, was under siege.

Like other walled towns of the time, Orleans was overcrowded and disease-ridden, and was at the point of being starved into surrender. Then Joan, wearing white armour, led a force that penetrated the encircling English forts and entered the town. "And there was a most marvellous press to touch her," an eyewitness observed.

"Whether God loves the English or hates them, I know not," declared the Maid of Orleans. "What I do know is that they will be cast out of the Kingdom of France." She spoke from patriotism—something quite novel for the time—and from religious fervour as well.

Joan's troops crossed the river and made a loop so as to assault the Fort des Tourelles from the south. "Joan was there wounded by an arrow which penetrated half a foot [15 cm] between the neck and shoulder," said an eyewitness. She left the field but returned, at which the English "were seized with sudden fear; our people, on the contrary, took courage."

Tourelles was taken, and early next morning it was found that the enemy had abandoned their other forts. This was the beginning of the end for the English.

What was the source of Joan's astonishing powers? The French followed her because of her courage, certainly, and her military prowess. They also believed Joan's claim to be divinely inspired.

Joan's inner voice demanded two tasks, the first being to free the French. Two months after her triumph at Orleans, she achieved the second by having Charles crowned and anointed king, remaining near his side and holding her standard in her hand.

After the coronation, Joan longed to return home, to be spinning wool at her mother's side. But Charles VII continued to send her on missions, most of them badly-planned. Only a year after Orleans, Joan was captured by the Burgundians, who sold her to the English.

The University of Paris asked that she be tried on suspicion of "several crimes savouring of heresy." The trial was held in 1431 at Rouen, then in English hands, where the Church court accused her of being a "witch, enchantress, false prophet." The English wished to find her guilty in order to undermine the reputation of her protege, Charles VII. This would strengthen their own claims in France.

Joan was permitted no lawyer and denied the Mass. Charles abandoned her, possibly because he was embarrassed by his debt to a simple shepherdess.

The court was headed by Pierre Cochon, Bishop of Beauvais, and he hoped that his work would make him Archbishop of Rouen. The strategy was to find some way of making Joan trip over her words, but she remained shrewd and witty.

"Do you think yourself to be in a state of grace?" Joan was asked.

"If I am not, God will put me in it," she replied. "If I am, God will keep me in it."

On May 24, Joan was given a public hearing. An Act of Abjuration had been drawn up which, if signed by her, would declare that she had renounced heresy. "Do it now."

she was told, "or else you will end in the fire today." And Joan did make her "X," but in a tone of mockery as if it didn't matter what she was signing.

Then on May 27, she withdrew her recantation. After a brief "trial on the relapse," Cochon condemned Joan as a heretic. Because a church court cannot condemn someone to death, she was turned over to the English. On May 30, some 800 English soldiers conducted her to the town square in the executioner's cart.

Joan had loved to laugh, but now she sobbed bitterly. "My body, whole and entire, which has never been corrupted," she cried, "will today be consumed and turned to ashes." The platform had been built high, so that all could see.

"She asked to have a cross, and an Englishman made a little one out of two sticks," an eyewitness said. "And besides, she asked me humbly if I would obtain for her the Church Cross and hold it raised before her eyes until death."

Wearing a pointed hat with the words "Heretic, relapsed, apostate, idolator," Joan clutched the crude cross to her breast. She was bound to the stake, and the fire was ignited. "She continued her praises and devout lamentations to God and His Saints," it was reported. "With her last word, in dying, she cried with a loud voice: 'Jesus!'"

The remains of Joan of Arc were collected and thrown into the Seine, so that relics could not be made of them.

A quarter-century later, the court's verdict was annulled. The reason for this turnabout was that Joan's example, stirring a patriotic spirit, had finally led to the liberation of France. By the war's conclusion in 1453, the English were once and for all driven from the land.

With the English gone, the blame of Joan's death could be placed upon them. And thus, the stain of witchcraft was wiped from the cause of Charles VII. The remains of Cochon (who never did become an archbishop) were then dug up and cast into the sewer.

Joan of Arc became the symbol of France as a nation. This was especially true when it was bled dry by the slaughter of World War I. Her example was cited again and again as all, soldiers and civilians alike, were begged to give themselves up to the cause as Joan had done.

Two years after the war had ended, Joan was made a saint for her martyrdom, but her sacrifice had come to mean other things as well. She died in the cause of individualism, some say. She was the first Protestant, others argue. More recently, Joan's death is cited as the most notorious of all the millions who suffered during the "women's holocaust" of medieval witch-burnings.

The Dying Airman

A handsome young airman lay dying,
And as on the aerodrome he lay,
To the mechanics who round him came sighing,
These last dying words he did say:

"Take the cylinders out of my kidneys,
The connecting-rod out of my brain,
Take the cam-shaft from out of my backbone,
And assemble the engine again."

Anonymous

Sacred Stories

In France, why is there a big annual festival honouring Joan of Arc, who died five centuries ago? Throughout the world, why is a candlelight vigil held each year to remember John Lennon?

All of these rituals honour heroes, whose glory has never died. Their stories have turned into myths, sacred stories, which are reinforced by the sacred acts of ritual.

Joan of Arc's story is sacred to the French, for she once saved their country. John Lennon's story is sacred to those who love his music and peace efforts.* And in both of these myths, a theme of sacrifice may be perceived. Everyday life often entails sacrifice. In a broad sense, it means giving up part of ourselves for the good of the whole. Our little deaths will lead, it is hoped, to a fuller life.

A parent with a hard-earned education, staying home to give children a good start, sacrifices the rewards of advancement. An injury-prone defenceman, going against a bruising team of giants, puts life and limb on the line for the sake of the team. Or as Karl explains, a militia recruit is devoured by his unit for the sake of "the game."

Some Great Beast

"British Bulldog" was often played while I was in the militia. About 20 or 30 would line up at one end of the field and, at the word "British," would try to run past about four others in the middle of the field without being tackled. Once you were tackled, you became a tackler. As the odds of getting through gradually decreased, everyone was finally tackled.

I never liked this game, but always tried, out of pride I guess, to avoid being tackled. However, I was always relieved once I was, as though now I was safe within some great beast.

Except a corn of wheat fall into the earth and die, it abideth alone; but if it die, it bringeth forth much fruit.

GOSPEL ACCORDING TO ST. JOHN, 12:24

*See pages 62-65.

3 THE POWER AND THE GLORY

Senator John F. Kennedy and his wife Jacqueline

After this manner therefore pray ye:
Our Father which art in heaven,
Hallowed be thy name.
Thy kingdom come.
Thy will be done on earth, as it is in heaven. Give us this
day our daily bread.
And forgive us our debts, as we forgive our debtors. And
lead us not into temptation,
but deliver us from evil:
For thine is the kingdom,
and the power and the glory, for ever.
Amen

GOSPEL ACCORDING TO ST. MATTHEW, CHAPTER 6

The Lord's Prayer ends with a formula of praise, honouring the divine "power and glory." On earth the kingdom of God will be established, it is hoped, so that justice may finally triumph.

Such concerns are also found in mythology. Powers vital in the struggle are said to be granted by the gods, who often appear in a fatherly role. John Kennedy (seen here with his wife Jacqueline) had a powerful father who helped him to become president. In this role, Kennedy made his famous vow to "oppose any foe" in defence of liberty.

8. Father

✳

Father and son form the most dangerous and critical animal relationship on earth, and to suppose otherwise is to invite catastrophe.

ANTHROPOLOGIST WESTON LaBARRE

Daedalus and Icarus *Greek*

Europa, daughter of the King of Tyre, was playing one day in a meadow with her brothers. Suddenly they glimpsed a great white bull, grazing near the sea-shore. The bull approached. Europa's brothers fled, but she was mesmerized by his beauty. "What a friendly bull," she thought, "almost as if he were human."

This bull was more than human. Zeus, king of gods, had transformed himself to win Europa's love.

Zeus lowed gently as Europa placed flowers in his mouth and caressed him. The disguised god rubbed his nose against her elbows as she garlanded his horns with flowers and bowed before her feet so that she might reach him more easily. His broad back looked so inviting that the girl could not resist the urge to climb onto it.

At once the bull rose to his feet and ran toward the sea. Europa's brothers ran alongside, laughing. She cried out for help, but the bull galloped all the faster until they were left far behind. Europa clung to the bull's neck as it plunged into the water.

Zeus, still disguised as a bull, brought Europa to the island of Crete. Here he had been raised, in a mountain cave, and this is where Europa gave birth to a son, Minos. He became king of this land, from which the great Minoan civilization later arose.

The craftsmen of Crete were well-known throughout the Mediterranean, and the best of them all was Daedalus. He invented the potter's wheel, a forerunner of the most useful invention of all, the true wheel. But the most famous product of Daedalus's fertile brain was a huge mazelike structure called the Labyrinth.

Minos married the mountain nymph Pasiphae. Like Europa, she fell in love with a bull, but the product of their passion was monstrous, a man with a bull's head, known as the Minotaur. It was kept in the Labyrinth's deepest recesses.

Daedalus, falling into disfavour with the king, was himself shut into the Labyrinth. His son, Icarus, was imprisoned along with him. But Daedalus refused to accept captivity for long.

Discovering some feathers and beeswax, Daedalus fashioned two pairs of wings, then attached them to his son's shoulders and his own. "We shall fly over the sea, but take care," he told Icarus. "Don't skim too low, or the wings will be drenched by the spray. And don't climb too close to the sun, or the wax will melt and down you go!"

Like two great birds, father and son flew up from the Labyrinth's roof, passed over Crete, and soared above the sea. Excitement filled Icarus's heart—how fast he could go! and how high! Intoxicated with this new freedom, he rose still higher and higher.

"Don't fly too near the sun!" Daedalus cried out in alarm. But his son, now only a speck far above, could no longer hear any warning.

Suddenly Daedalus saw the speck growing larger. Icarus's wings had fallen off, and now he was plunging through the sky. Daedalus caught only a glimpse of his son's horror-stricken face as he fell past him. A puff of spray was briefly seen as Icarus splashed into the sea and drowned.

The boy stood on the burning deck
Eating peanuts by the peck;
His father called him, he wouldn't go,
Because he loved the peanuts so.

ANONYMOUS

Father Figures

"Don't fly too near the sun," says Daedalus, voicing the parent's age-old call to headstrong youth.

The Greeks had a word for the fall of Icarus: *hubris*, excessive pride. From a Biblical view, however, it is simply a son's disobedience to his father.

Carl Jung, one of the founders of modern psychology, spoke of two contrasting human types, the *old man* and the *eternal youth*. Caution is all-important for the old man, represented here by Daedalus. Impulse guides the soul of the eternal youth, symbolized by Icarus. The happy medium, as the Greeks thought, is to bring experience and energy together.

"Father figures" are composed of such elements. Too often, the father presents a stern appearance that softens only when his children have left the home. Yet he is front and centre in the son's inner myths—and also in those of the daughter, whose sexual identity he largely shapes.

Father figures have taken many forms. Advertising mythology presents Tony the Tiger, complete with his own family, which he convinces to eat his cereal. Harland "Finger Lickin' Good" Sanders presents the grandfather image, to boost fried-chicken sales. There is also the Voice in the background of a million commercials, approving products in deep, sincere tones.

The father as "klutz" is another well-known father image. It comes from the Industrial Revolution. Until then, the father spent most of his time among his children at home, where income-producing work was to be found. Then the factory began to claim long hours of his time—the home meanwhile turning into a "mother's world."

Thus, the father became somewhat of an intruder in the home, his task being simply to bring home the bacon. Masculinity took on self-destructive forms, governed by a drive to compete and make the grade. So Dad often seemed tough, cold, fearful, remote. Not until recently has the father's nurturing role been revived.

When I am the President
Of these United States,
I'll eat up all the candy
And swing on all the gates.

CHILDREN'S RHYME

One Brief Shining Moment *American*

John Fitzgerald Kennedy hated to lose, and so did his older brother Joe. Once they had a bicycle race, and neither would give way as they approached the finish line, head-on. In the collision Joe was unhurt, but John required 28 stitches.

The boys learned aggressiveness from their father, Joseph Kennedy. As a Catholic in Protestant Boston, he had felt imprisoned by prejudice. Although unable to open all the doors of "Yankee" privilege, he vowed that his children would some day walk through those doors.

Joseph managed to became a millionaire by making shrewd deals on Wall Street. He married an Irish beauty, Rose Fitzgerald, the daughter of a colourful Boston mayor nicknamed "Honey Fitz."

Joseph served in the late 1930s as the U.S. ambassador to Britain, and when the menace of Nazism arose, he favoured the British policy of appeasement.* Believing that the United States should play it safe, he declared that "we would do better fighting in our own backyard." When his son John later became president, he would depart radically from his father's isolationism.

As a youth, John enjoyed reading about the Knights of the Round Table. Perhaps he pictured himself as the youthful King Arthur,** and later as President he jokingly referred to the White House as Camelot. At any rate, in World War II he chose an adventurous role when he became the skipper of motor-torpedo boat PT-109. During

---

*See page 295.
**See pages 47-50.

the night of August 2, 1943, a Japanese destroyer
smashed into the boat, slicing it in two. "This is how it
feels to be killed," he thought at the time.

Kennedy clung with other survivors to PT-109's wreck-
age and then swam to an island. The effort aggravated a
congenital back problem which would cause pain from
then on. He won the Navy and Marine Corps medal for
having "contributed to the saving of several lives"—
although the citation stated that PT-109 was involved in a
"collision," rather than "attempting a torpedo attack" as
Kennedy would have had it.

In 1944, Kennedy's brother, Joe, volunteered for a risky
experimental air raid on German submarine pens. He died
when his bomber blew up in midair. Their father had been
grooming him to become President, but now the torch was
passed to John. "I went into politics," he once said,
"because Joe died."

John Kennedy's success at the polls was guaranteed by
his boyish handsomeness and ready wit. Once, on being
asked how he had became a war hero, he replied, "It was
easy—they sank my boat." He had many political connec-
tions through his father, and more than enough funding
for election drives. The entire Kennedy clan threw their
weight behind him, hundreds of parties being given on his
behalf by Rose. In 1947, he was elected as a Democrat to
the U.S. Congress, and three years later he became a
Senator.

Kennedy's father was a womanizer who had a lengthy
affair with the film star, Gloria Swanson. John inherited
some of his father's attitudes towards women and was also
seen with actresses, notably Marilyn Monroe. When he was
young, Kennedy fell in love with Inga Arvad, a former
Miss Europe, who had been told by Adolf Hitler that she
was a perfect example of Nordic beauty. But his father put
an end to the idea of wedding Arvad.

In 1953, Kennedy married Jacqueline Bouvier. This
beautiful and cultivated society girl (she had once been
named the Debutante of the Year) came from a similar
background. She, too, was the child of a hard-driving Wall
Street financier.

In 1960, Kennedy became the Democratic candidate for the presidency. "I tell you the New Frontier is here," Kennedy declared in his acceptance speech. "My call is to the young in heart, regardless of age."

In the race against Richard Nixon, Kennedy took the advantage during the famous televised debates (the first TV debates of their kind). While Nixon regarded them as just another item on a crowded schedule, Kennedy made careful preparations and appeared clean-shaven and confident while his opponent's make-up failed to conceal a "five-o'clock shadow." At the polls, Kennedy was elected as President in the century's closest election.

So on a bright and bitterly cold January 20, 1961 morning, Kennedy, the youngest American president ever elected, took over from Dwight Eisenhower, one of the oldest. At the Inauguration, the poet Robert Frost heralded "a golden age of poetry and power." Kennedy issued his cold-war challenge in an inaugural address of classic eloquence. "Let every nation know," he vowed, "that we shall pay any price, bear any burden, meet any hardship, support any friend, oppose any foe to assure the survival and the success of liberty."

Bright promise glowed, and it seemed that the world might be changed forever by this youthful leader, destined to become one of the most popular men of the century. John and Jacqueline, patrons of the arts, brought famous artists, musicians, writers, and the great women and men of the day to the White House. Kennedy assembled a staff of anti-Communist intellectuals, many from the ranks of Harvard and MIT. He named his brother, Robert, as attorney-general, and his administration bore the unmistakable stamp of the Kennedy clan, with its mystique of success and power.

Kennedy had many successes and frustrations. The Soviet Union's supremacy in space came into clear focus when Yuri Gagarin became the first man in space. Three days later, Kennedy heard his science and budget advisers debate the costs of a moon-exploration trip, thought to be around $40-billion. Fifteen minutes after the meeting, he announced: "We are going to the moon."

"It will not be one man going to the moon," Kennedy said in a special State of the Union Message, "it will be an entire nation. For all of us must work to put him there." Congress almost unanimously voted for the moon-shot, to be realized "before this decade is out."

Kennedy was not alive, unfortunately, when U.S. astronauts in 1969 became the first to land on the moon. But the space program, spinning off satellite communications and high-speed computers, changed the face of the world.

A Central Intelligence Agency plan to invade Cuba (The Bay of Pigs invasion), was Kennedy's biggest setback. It met with total failure and created tense relations between the two super powers. He accepted full blame, however, declaring, "I am the responsible officer of the government."

Then on October 14, 1962, a U.S. reconnaissance plane spotted Soviet-built missiles being assembled on Cuban soil. Kennedy called together all of his top advisers to the White House. A naval blockade was planned as the U.S. went "eyeball to eyeball" to enforce the missiles' removal. The world moved closer to atomic war until, on October 28, Soviet chairman Nikita Khrushchev promised to withdraw the missiles in exchange for a pledge not to attack Soviet-backed Cuba in the future.

This was not the end of the confrontation, however, as Kennedy hoped still to get rid of the Cuban leader, Fidel Castro. When the Mafia was conscripted in an unfulfilled plot to assassinate Castro, the then Vice President, Lyndon Johnson, complained that Kennedy was running "a damn Murder Incorporated in the Caribbean."

Kennedy, eager to try out new anti-guerrilla techniques, was the first American president to send troops into Vietnam (even though he later spoke of withdrawing every soldier from that trouble spot). Then, in June of 1962, during a triumphal European tour, Kennedy gave his celebrated speech at the Berlin Wall. "*Ich bin ein Berliner,*" he told thousands of cheering German people. "I am a Berliner."

Kennedy's lack of political skill at home made it difficult to deal with Congress, and it meant failure for his civil rights bill. When another presidential election neared, Jacqueline and he went to Texas to gauge the political atmosphere there. On November 22, as they flew to Dallas, John read a vicious diatribe in the morning newspaper. He handed it to Jacqueline, saying, "We're really heading into nut country now."

A large parade had been planned for the President. As the presidential motorcade passed through the Dallas streets, a shot rang out. "My God, I'm hit!" cried Kennedy, clutching his throat. This and a second shot, which fatally pierced the president's head, were allegedly fired by Lee Harvey Oswald, a maladjusted man who resented authority.

Kennedy's body was placed on the presidential jet, *Air Force One*, and brought back to Washington, while the world watched on television. Jacqueline, though in shock, arranged the details of a magnificent state funeral. A black-draped caisson carried Kennedy's body. It was preceded by a company of navy men and followed by a riderless horse, symbolizing the fallen leader.

BOSTON

museum   birthplace

Dallas   PT-109

Berlin Wall   senator

missile crisis   president

space race

WASHINGTON

The hero-cycle, for John F. Kennedy

This was the greatest televised ritual the world had ever seen. At the moment when the church service began, every train and bus in the nation came to a halt, U.S. ships at sea cast wreaths into the ocean, and 21-gun salutes boomed at 7000 American military bases around the globe. But not one detail of all this ceremony pierced the heart as much as the sight of Kennedy's four-year-old son with his hand raised in a final salute.

Mystery surrounds Kennedy's assassination. A commission under chief Supreme Court Justice Earl Warren found a lone gunman responsible, but because many witnesses were not heard, the House Select Committee on Assassinations attacked the question again in 1979. "There was a probable conspiracy," it concluded, adding that the Mafia "had the motive, means, and opportunity" to kill the president.

There have been many other conspiracy theories, usually focussing on Cuba. Castro had retaliated, some believe. Others point to anti-Castro Cubans, who blamed the president for the Bay of Pigs fiasco and also his pledge not to stage any further attacks. Whatever the reason, Kennedy's death remains a mystery—as so often happens when a hero perishes.

Today, the glamour of Kennedy's 1000-day presidency may be recalled at a shrine overlooking Boston Harbour. In the John F. Kennedy Museum and Library are displays evoking the spirit of his times. These culminate in a memorial pavilion, adorned only with a giant U.S. flag.

Americans remained keenly interested in Jacqueline, who had a seven-year marriage with Greek shipping magnate Aristotle Onassis. Though unwilling to talk about her private life, Jacqueline once disclosed her feelings about the dead president. "Now he is a legend when he would have preferred to be a man," she said. "His high noon kept all the freshness of the morning—and he died then, never knowing disillusion."

School of Fine Arts

From a box of woven straw
the father chooses a little paper ball, and before his
curious children throws it in the wash-basin.
Then arises
in many colours
the great Japanese flower,
the instantaneous water-lily,
and the children are silent
with wonder.
That flower can never fade
later in their memory,
that sudden flower
made for them
at a moment's notice
before their eyes.

JACQUES PREVERT
TRANSLATED BY ANTHONY HARTLEY

A Dog Pound of Daddies

Fathers forever try to inspire awe by a display of wondrous powers. In a political campaign, similarly, voters look for candidates who best seem able to draw the rabbit from the hat. "All this bit about electing a President," John Lennon once reflected. "We pick our own daddy out of the dog pound of daddies. This is the daddy that looks like the daddy in the commercials."

Our earthly fathers, counterparts of the heavenly fathers in myth, always seem immense to their children. They give encouragement in the quest, magnifying whatever skills their offspring show. But in time, they inevitably appear to diminish in size.

Eternally the fathers fret about how the sons will "measure up"; eternally the sons fear they will remain in Dad's shadow. Such anxieties generally originate in relation to the father figures of one's life. The principal of a school, as Mike shows, may become someone to criticize, surpass, dismiss.

Who I Was

His voice was awash with emptiness and sterility. The only thing interesting about it was that it buzzed like a power transformer.

My mind floated away from real time, responding only with uh-huh or mmmmm. For the grass was dancing, swaying in the wind, each blade blowing in unison. As the clouds slowly rearranged the light I was amazed to see a pretty girl walk past, throwing her head to one side.

Far away the principal was telling me who I was and what I think.

A boy wants something very special from his father. You hear it said that fathers want their sons to be what they feel they cannot themselves be, but I tell you it also works the other way.

SHERWOOD ANDERSON, *MEMOIRS*

9. Tests

"It is hard to be brave," said Piglet, sniffing slightly, "when you're only a Very Small Animal."

A. A. MILNE, *WINNIE-THE-POOH*

The Labours of Hercules *Greek*

Hercules

Two huge snakes slid toward the cradle. The baby inside awoke to see them hovering over him, poised to strike. With a gurgle, he reached out and grasped their necks.

This tiny infant's hands tightened their grip. The snakes began to writhe and jerk, coil and uncoil, but they couldn't escape. The baby, bouncing happily in his cradle, held fast until the snakes' bodies became limp ropes.

Hercules, a mere eight months old, had killed them.

Such an infant must have had remarkable parents. The mother of Hercules was a princess, Alcmene; the father was Zeus, the chief of all the gods.

Hercules quickly grew to a great height, with a powerful frame to match. His aim was deadly, and he could easily kill any man or beast. Once, while hunting a lion near the palace of a king, he was attended to by the monarch's fifty daughters. They took turns waiting on him, each princess being given a full day with Hercules, so that it took him more than seven weeks to catch the lion.

Hercules eventually married, and happily raised a family.

But trouble was on its way—for Hera, Zeus's wife, nursed a lasting resentment toward Alcmene's illegitimate son. The snakes' visit had been plotted by her. Now she thought of a far more terrible plan.

One day, as Hercules was watching his sons playing, the sky swiftly darkened, and his mood abruptly grew black as well. Foaming at the mouth, he took up his bow, notched an arrow, took aim at one of his sons, and let the arrow fly. Again he shot at his offspring, and again and again until all were dead, including their mother.

Hera had sent this fit of madness, and this time she had gained her revenge.

When the slaughter ended, Hercules regained his sanity and realized with horror what he had done. Almost mad with grief, he went to Delphi to ask the oracle how to atone for his crime.

"Go to Tiryns," the priestess pronounced. "Serve King Eurystheus. For twelve years you will perform labours. In reward, you will be granted immortality."

Thus began the Twelve Labours of Hercules.

His first six tasks were carried out not far from Tiryns. The Nemean Lion, whose skin could not be pierced, was throttled by Hercules. From then on he wore the hide as a fine suit of armour.

The Hydra of Lerna had nine heads, and although Hercules easily sliced off one of them with his sword, two sprouted in its place. This went on and on, the Hydra simply growing more heads all the time. Finally Hercules took a flaming branch and seared the wound left by each head as it was removed. Soon the beast was dead.

The Cerynean Deer, said Eurystheus, must be brought back alive. So Hercules shot an arrow neatly through its forelegs, pinning them together so that he could deliver it to Tiryns with ease. Similarly, the Erymanthian Boar was pursued through snowdrifts until it became exhausted, allowing Hercules to carry it back to Tiryns.

The fifth labour required a clever solution. The Augean Stables, occupied by three thousand cows, had not been cleaned out for thirty years. Hercules devised a plan of diverting a river, so that its cleansing waters flowed into one end of the barn and out the other. This was close to Olympia, where Hercules paced off a stadium for games that are still being played in various places around the globe.

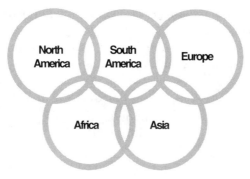

The symbol for the modern Olympics

Next on the agenda were the Stymphalian birds, who killed people by shooting metallic feathers at them, and then swooped down to eat the bodies. Hercules used his bow to destroy as many as he could and shook a huge rattle to scare away the others.

Halfway through! Now Hercules had to travel far, first to capture the Cretan Bull and the Thracian Horses. Then he went on to the land of the Amazons, a race of women who maintained control by breaking the limbs of all boys born to them. Their queen wore a wondrous girdle of solid gold, and it was the ninth labour of Hercules to steal it away from her.

The tenth labour sent Hercules all the way to Spain, to seize the cattle of Geryon. He then drove Geryon's cattle back to Tiryns.

At her wedding Hera had received a tree bearing golden apples, and it was Hercules' eleventh labour to steal these wonders. But having no idea where they might be, he went to ask mighty Atlas.

Bent under the weight of the sky which he carried on his shoulders, Atlas was happy to set out to find the apples if only he could gain a moment's relief from his burden. Hercules readily agreed, bending to take this incredible weight as Atlas set out.

"What a load!" cried Hercules after only a short time. "Atlas had better be back quickly or my spine will snap for sure!"

Soon he was ready to call Atlas back, apples or no apples. But just then he saw the giant happily whistling and returning with the golden treasure.

"That was easy enough," said Atlas, "and now if you'll stay there just a while longer, I'll deliver these to your master."

Hercules, who didn't like the sound of this at all, made a quick decision. "Fair enough," he replied. "But I'm not too comfortable in this position. Perhaps you could show me a better grip."

"So you're straining yourself!" laughed Atlas, who wasn't the smartest fellow in the world. "Here, let me show you how *I* do this job!" and he bent down to take the sky. At once Hercules snatched up the apples and was on his way, Atlas bellowing a torrent of curses.

The twelfth labour was by far the most hazardous, as it

called for a descent into the underworld. The three-headed watchdog, Cerberus, had to be caught without any weapons and brought to Tiryns.

Following the dank tunnel that led into the Underworld's depths, Hercules crept downwards to the river Styx. The boatman Charon transported him to the other side, and here he met the shaggy monster, Cerberus. Its snapping heads met only the impenetrable hide of the lion-skin, so Hercules was able to hoist the beast onto his shoulders.

Hercules travelled across the Styx once again, up through the twisting tunnel, and back to Tiryns. The final task of all was over, he thought. But Cerberus rushed about so fiercely that Eurystheus cried out, "Take it back at once!" And again Hercules made the descent, allowing Cerberus to remain as before at its old post.

And so his trials were finally over.

Now that he had atoned for the murders, Hercules was eager to settle down. He fell in love with Deianeira, a mortal daughter of the god Dionysus, and they were soon married. But as he still continued to perform heroic deeds far from home, his new wife looked for some means to prevent any other woman from winning his heart.

Here is the strange tale of how Deianeira succeeded.

Once when she travelled with Hercules, a flooded river barred their way. He prepared to carry her across on his back, but along came Nessus the centaur—a horse with the upper part of a man for a head.

Hercules arranged to have Nessus carry Deianeira across the river while he swam behind. But the centaur, entranced by her beauty, began to run away with her as soon as they reached the opposite bank. From midstream, Hercules managed to send an arrow into Nessus's leg, toppling him over.

But the creature, even in his dying moments, plotted revenge. "To prevent Hercules from falling in love with anyone else," he told Deianeira, "you need only to smear some of my blood on his shirt." She foolishly believed him and quickly collected some of the centaur's blood even as the beast was dying.

Soon Deianeira had a reason to carry out Nessus's plan. Hercules had won victory over a northern town, and a lovely princess was said to be among his captives. Preparing to do sacrifice to Zeus, he sent for the special shirt worn on such occasions. Now Deianeira, suspecting that her husband might be unfaithful to her, smeared some of the centaur's blood on his garment.

Hercules received the shirt, put it on, and set the wood ablaze to begin the sacrifice. But the blood of the shirt now bit into his flesh. He tore at the garment, yet it still clung to his body. He plunged into a stream, yet the fiery pain still tormented him. He stumbled about in agony, tearing up trees by the roots, yet nothing could provide relief.

"Carry me to the mountaintop," he said at last. "Prepare another pyre and place my body upon it." When he lay down, thunderbolts crashed down to ignite the wood.

The hero's mortal parts were consumed by the fire. Then a cloud enclosed the scene, a chariot drawn by four horses descended, and Hercules was carried up to Mount Olympus, where he served as the guardian of its gates. For eternal life, as the priestess of Delphi had foretold, was to be the hero's reward.

Rush Hour

The streets are busy changing gears
under mechanical eyes
dispensing time fragments
democratically to all.
Despite our nervous throttling
and meaningless mastery
that we slave to preserve,
we rush from one red-eyed giant to another
and turn the schizophrenic pavement
into our daily devils.
Lanes rise into joustings.
Dragon tongues set fire to our fleeing heels.
Home is a shadowy castle in quiet forests,
the quest of all our erratic rushings.

OWEN NEILL

Meeting the Challenge

Hercules kills the lion and then wears its wondrous skin. Similarly, we might don driving gloves and cool shades for a spin in our accessory-laden car—but only after learning how to handle all the challenges of the road.

Gaining a driver's licence is among the big initiation rites of today. More severe are those in tribal life, at which initiates are given scars or have teeth knocked out as proof that they will be brave when danger arises.

Nevertheless, meeting the challenge is part of life at any age. As newborn babies we gather our strength to take a first breath, and a billion other tests must be passed en route to the paradise of our dreams.

The famed labours of Hercules are tests on the mythic level. Such trials are always given to the great heroes—Gilgamesh, Jason, Arthur—who thus prove their readiness to become kings. Their adventures, told long ago in an exaggerated way, have come down to us as myths.

"Without heroes we're all plain people and don't know how far we can go," writes Bernard Malamud in *The Natural*. "It's their function to be the best." The best in every sphere of athletics sets a new standard, every four years, at the Olympic games.

Myth credits Hercules with founding the games, but actually they began with a festival of Zeus. Every fourth year during the August moon, wars ceased and athletes from everywhere in the Greek world gathered at Olympia for five days of sport.

There was glory only in victory, none in merely being chosen to perform. No bronze nor silver medals were awarded. Winners were often crowned even as they perished from wounds, and losers on their return suffered another kind of death—humiliating shame.

First Practice

After the doctor checked to see
we weren't ruptured,
the man with the short cigar took us
under the grade school,
where we went in case of attack
or storm, and said
he was Clifford Hill, he was
a man who believed dogs
ate dogs, he had once killed
for his country, and if
there were any girls present
for them to leave now.
                              No one
left. OK, he said, he said I take
that to mean you are hungry
men who hate to lose as much
as I do. OK. Then
he made two lines of us
facing each other,
and across the way, he said,
is the man you hate most
in the world,
and if we are to win
that title I want to see how.
But I don't want to see
any marks when you're dressed,
he said. He said, *Now.*

GARY GILDNER

The Sultan of Swat *American*

Babe Ruth in action

The Gate of Heaven cemetery in New York State is near two communities named Valhalla* and Mount Pleasant. It is the resting place of a baseball player named "Babe" Ruth. Although he died in 1948, so many people still come here that every few days, someone must go out to remove baseballs left on Ruth's grave. "MAY THE DIVINE SPIRIT THAT ANIMATED BABE RUTH TO WIN THE CRUCIAL GAME OF LIFE," says the inscription, "INSPIRE THE YOUTH OF AMERICA."

Baseball is a game for anyone, young and old alike. They can play it just about anywhere, even on city streets, but the regulation grass-and-dirt field is called a "park." We associate this game with green open spaces; outfielders shag fly balls "out in the daisies."

Baseball expresses the great North American myth of individual effort, of opportunities seized by those who "hustle." Yet it is played by people who are boys and girls at heart. Baseball history is full of players with nicknames like "Peewee" and "Pepper," "Yogi" and "Shoeless Joe," "Buster" and "Babe."

George Herman Ruth, while growing up on the Baltimore waterfront, was often beaten with a billiard cue by his saloon-keeping father. At seven, his brutal father dragged him through the gates of St. Mary's Industrial School for Orphans, Delinquent, Incorrigible, and Wayward Boys. Ruth remained there most of the time until 1914, when he was 19.

"It was at St. Mary's," Ruth would often recall, "that I met and learned to love the greatest man I've ever known." In Ruthian mythology this was Brother Mathias, the school's huge and fierce prefect of discipline. (At various times, though, Ruth would give the names of four different brothers.) In St. Mary's, he developed awesome skills as a left-handed pitcher.

Jack Dunn, owner of the Baltimore Orioles (then a minor-league club) brought him to its training camp for the 1914 season. "Here comes Dunn with his newest babe," someone remarked, and the sport's most famous nickname was born.

---

*See page 268.

That same year, Ruth went up to the majors to the Boston Red Sox. He was the winning pitcher in his first major-league game—the first he had ever seen! Even though he was a superb pitcher, he was proud of his hitting skills. He angered the veteran players by trying to take his place in batting practice, something a pitcher never did at that time, and one morning, he discovered that his bats had been sawed into sections.

Ruth was so brilliant as a pitcher that he set a World Series record for consecutive scoreless innings, 29, which wasn't broken for over 40 years. But his hitting proved even more impressive, and in 1919 the Babe was made an outfielder so that he could come to the plate more often. That year, he slammed 29 home runs—a figure regarded as freakish, never to be duplicated.

Then in 1920, having been traded to the New York Yankees, Ruth hit the amazing total of 54 home runs. The centre of media attention, he was called the Bambino (Italian for "Babe"), Wizard of Whack, Behemoth of Biff, Sultan of Swat, King of Clout.

And each home run was a spectacle, as Ruth ominously waved the bat at the plate, connected in a perfect picture of grace and power, laughed at the pitcher while rounding the bases on his pipestem legs, and tipped his cap to the fans as he entered the dugout. Even his strikeouts were stupendous, as he would twist himself twice around, sometimes right off his feet.

Baseball is a game of innocence. But that innocence was tarnished back in 1920 when eight members of the Chicago White Sox, including the great Shoeless Joe Jackson, were suspended for life for trying to fix the previous World Series.

Pessimists feared that the "Black Sox" scandal, as it was called, would ruin public confidence and empty the ballparks. But this never happened, because baseball had a saviour—the spindly-legged marvel known as Babe Ruth.

Over the winter, club owners waited anxiously to discover whether spectators would return to the stands in 1921. They did in droves, paying less attention to the scandal than to the burning question: would Ruth's big bat repeat the wonders of 1920? That season, he hit 59 homers and set records for total bases and extra-base hits that stood for many decades.

After each game, Ruth would be swarmed by fans hoping to get his famous signature, and he would always oblige, calling every boy "kid." Ruth himself remained boyish (childish, to his critics) for during a slump in 1922, he reacted to the fans' booing by swearing at them and once leaped into the stands to chase a heckler. Meanwhile, the Babe was gaining notoriety for his womanizing, even though he was married.

That fall the Baseball Writers Association invited Ruth to be the guest of honour at its annual dinner. New York senator Jimmy Walker, the featured speaker, rose and delivered the famous "dirty-faced kids of America" speech, lambasting the slugger for his sins. "On every vacant lot where the kids play baseball," the senator remarked, "they think of you, their hero."

Ruth is said to have been sobbing by the time Walker asked, "Will you not, for the kids of America, solemnly promise to mend your ways?"

"So help me, Jim, I will!" the King of Clout cried. Ruth never disgraced himself again—that is, in public. And next spring, when Yankee Stadium opened, he was proud that it became known as The House that Ruth Built.

Ruth had a measureless appetite. For breakfast he would devour a steak, fried potatoes and four eggs, washed down by a pot of coffee and a pint of bourbon and ginger ale. During spring training in 1925, Ruth was struck by a serious ailment, rumoured to be indigestion. Concern grew in the heart of nearly every baseball fan.

Sports writers knew, however, that the hero had contracted what was politely called "a social disease": syphilis. The problem was, what to tell the fans. It was after consuming a dozen hot dogs and eight bottles of soda pop, the official explanation went, that the Babe had come down with "the stomach ache heard round the world."

During the 1926 World Series, the Ruth myth was further embellished by the story of a young boy, Johnny

Sylvester. He had been kicked in the head by a horse and lay dying in hospital from the injury. The Babe came to the hospital and the visit was recorded by sportswriter, Paul Gallico:

"It was God himself who walked into the room," he wrote, "straight from his glittering throne. God with a big flat nose and little piggy eyes and a big grin, with a fat, black cigar sticking out the side of it."

Johnny received a baseball as the slugger declared: "I'll hit a home run for you in Wednesday's game." And he did, clubbing not one, but three. Then Johnny miraculously bounced back, becoming the most celebrated invalid in the country. But only a year later, after the boy's uncle had dropped by to offer his thanks, the Babe had to inquire, "Who the hell is Johnny Sylvester?"

The Yankees' golden year, in 1927, elevated to almost divine status the deadliest of batting lineups, called "Murderer's Row." It led the league in every offensive category except doubles and steals, while Ruth blasted an unprecedented 60 home runs (in 154 games). His record stood until 1961 when Roger Maris hit Number 61 in his 162nd game—and instead of being praised, was maligned for dethroning the Bambino.

The supreme moment in Ruth's story, many believe, came in Chicago in 1932. The Babe was loudly booed by Chicago Cub fans in the huge crowd of 50 000. When he came out in the fifth inning with the score tied, even the Chicago players joined in.

Ruth swung at hurler Charlie Root's first pitch, missed, and held up one finger—supposedly to indicate the first strike. The crowd roared with contempt. When Root threw another strike, the Babe held up two fingers—and then pointed, it seems, to dead centre field. The hero swung at the next pitch and it sailed right into the centre-field bleachers.

If Ruth did indeed prophesy his homer, it was the only "called shot" in baseball history. Ruth himself referred to it as such. But the idea infuriated Root, who would fume, "If he'd really called his shot, that next pitch would have been nowhere near the plate!" And what about seeing the replay, by viewing film footage of the game? No film record exists to mar the event's mythic aura.

At 38, Ruth was still a force in the game. Against the Red Sox near the end of the 1933 season, he was put in as pitcher and won the game, going the full nine innings.

Ruth retired from baseball in 1935. Four years later, at the upstate New York town of Cooperstown, he was inducted into the game's Valhalla, the Hall of Fame. During World War II, Japanese soldiers confirmed his exalted stature by shouting what they believed to be the ultimate insult: "To hell with Babe Ruth!"

But death was a only a year away when "Babe Ruth Day" was held at Yankee Stadium on April 27, 1947. He stood once again at home plate, the starting point of so many circuit blasts. And although the Babe's vocal chords were almost ruined (he was suffering from throat cancer), he managed to make his sincere feelings heard. "The only real game in the world, I think, is baseball," he said. "If you're successful, and you try hard enough, you're bound to come out on top."

WHAM! WHAM! WHAM!... WHAM! WHAM! WHAM!... WHAM! WHAM! WHAM!... POP! POP!

BATTLE CRY OF THREE-TIME HEAVYWEIGHT CHAMPION, Muhammed Ali

Passage Rites

When baseball needs a star to maintain the game's prestige, Babe Ruth rises to the occasion. He does so again by knocking a homer to calm a sick child's dread. The greatest test, to hit one on cue, is also the most moving because it comes when his talents are fading.

Each stage of life presents a challenge. Tying shoelaces can be a puzzle in childhood; in old age comes the problem of remaining hopeful despite infirmity.

To help people move ahead, society provides a series of passage rites. Thus we have marriage ceremonies and christening rites, promotion celebrations and retirement banquets. Formal initiation rites, such as the Jewish Bar Mitzvah, are becoming uncommon, however, and youths are likely to invent an ordeal—attempting a feat of endurance, doing something on a dare.

Learning to bake was once a traditional passage rite for teenage girls. Today, writing a computer program or achieving a physical goal might be preferable tests. Native people in the American southwest still have Blessing Way as an initiation rite for girls. Just as "Changing Woman" and the earth undergo changes throughout the year, the girl also must mature and later become aged. So at one point she runs in a circle around a cane—to help her to have a long life—and later dances beneath a tepee symbolic of her future home.

Perhaps some day, coming-of-age rites of comparable beauty will be re-invented for modern times. Until then we have our personal mythology which, as Lisa shows, holds moments when we discover our strengths, great or small.

Mom's Line

I'm babysitting and the kid says, "May I have a cookie?"

Now what will I tell him? "No," I say, "it is almost dinner time." So he agrees, and finds something else to do.

I can't believe it. I've used one of the lines my mom always used on me. And it worked! Wow, it's a power I never knew I had.

A passage rite is like knocking at the door of a house, opening the door, and stepping over the threshold. The threshold is the boundary between one state and another, and to cross it is dangerous.

FRANCIS HUXLEY, *THE WAY OF THE SACRED*

10. Trickster

The Rabbit

The rabbit has a charming face:
Its private life is a disgrace.
I really dare not name to you
The awful things that rabbits do.

They have such lost, degraded souls
No wonder they inhabit holes;
When such depravity is found
They only can live underground.

ANONYMOUS

Hare's Mischief *Winnebago*

When Hare's mother died giving birth to him, he was raised by his grandmother. The rabbit was very mischievous and unruly, and his grandmother decided to make him do some work.

"Get some arrowheads from Flint," she said, and off he went to get them.

When he asked Flint for one of his arrowheads, he said: "I give you one from my wrist, one of great value." But Hare knew that these were the fellow's poorest ones, and he chased him about, finally clubbing him to death.

Picking up all the arrowheads, Hare returned to his grandmother and told her what had happened.

"Oh, you ugly, big-eared creature, surely you didn't kill him!" she exclaimed.

"That I did, and I'll go after you with my club, too!"

"Grandson, I said that only in fun!" She gave Hare the bow she had made, and he soon left with this and several arrows he had fashioned.

Hare promptly shot an elk in the belly, then trailed the elk to the lodge of Sharp-Elbow. This was an evil being, but Hare knew how to handle him.

Knowing that Sharp-Elbow would try to jab him in the elbow, he placed a whetstone there. Sure enough, the oaf did try but broke his own elbow instead. When Hare shifted the whetstone to the other elbow, the same thing happened. Then he placed it on his knees, making Sharp-Elbow break both of his own! Finally, Hare shot him with an arrow.

"Burn all of Sharp-elbow's wives and children!" said Hare to the people, and they did. Then he told his grandmother what he had done.

"Oh, you ugly, big-eared creature, surely you didn't kill that evil spirit!" she cried.

"That I did, and I'll shoot and burn you as well!"

"Grandson, I only said that in fun!"

Later Hare came upon a man with a bandaged head, who invited him to a meal. "Kettle, get some water and hang over the fire," the man said, and the kettle obeyed his command perfectly.

"Plate, put bear-ribs in the kettle," said the man, "and then put it on yourself and come to Hare's place." The plate did just that, and the rabbit dined well.

Then the man said to Hare, "Go across the ocean to retrieve my scalp, and I'll give you powers like mine!" So Hare crossed the ocean on a beaver's back and managed to steal the scalp.

Returning to the bandaged man, Hare threw the scalp at his head, and the two were perfectly bonded together. "I will give you my power," he told Hare, "but you must never ask for the same thing more than three times."

That night in his lodge, Hare commanded: "Let me have a pretty girl to be with." Along came a very attractive one, but he didn't care for her. Twice more he used his power to get replacements—and thus he used it up.

Suddenly the lodge began to roar, Hare ran out, and when he looked back it had disappeared.

He came back to tell his grandmother what happened, but this time she whipped him with a poker.

"Ouch!" Hare cried. "OUCH!"

Hare had never done anything to please Earthmaker, the creator, but now he thought of something. He prepared a vat of oil and called together all the animals.

"Everyone willing to be eaten by the people, bathe in this oil!" Hare commanded. Many jumped in, and the bear rolled about for a long time—which is why he became so fat. Even the skunk bathed in the oil, though some animals jeered him because of his bad smell. "No, that's fine," said Hare "because any sick people eating the skunk will be able to get well."

When Hare was finished, he said, "Now the people will never be hungry, and they'll live forever!"

"No," said his grandmother, "everything comes to an end. You must have seen how trees fall to the ground and rot. So do the people, or else they would fill up the earth. Then the suffering would be even greater than now!"

Hare thought about this for a long time. "Now you've spoiled everything," he said. So sad was Hare that he wrapped himself in his blanket, went into the corner, and wept for the people.

That was when Hare thought of the Medicine Rite, which he taught the people how to perform, just as they still do today.

Heroes are put on pedestals and worshipped. The trickster is here on earth with us, and we can laugh or cry with him or her, depending on the situation. The trickster is a more democratic way to deal with the world.

OJIBWA PLAYWRIGHT DANIEL MOSES

Before Heroes

Long before myths of heroes were told, it seems, there were tales about tricksters. They are among the oldest of all mythic types. Cunning and full of pranks, tricksters repeatedly play the clown.

But unlike heroes, tricksters are not necessarily to be admired—as the tale of Hare demonstrates. Yet although often deceitful and greedy, tricksters are also wise and capable of doing good.

Among nearly all forest-dwelling peoples, there is a trickster. In the East he is known as Nanabush or Manabozho, on the Plains as Coyote or Old Man, and on the Pacific Coast as Blue Jay or Raven. And everywhere he is up to much the same stunts. He rebels against authority, breaks the rules, and often displays violence.

For native North Americans, a spirit or manitou is thought to live in every stone and blade of grass, every beast and person. There is also the Great Spirit, Gitche Manitou, and the trickster serves as an intermediary between him and the people. The trickster even today is central to the spiritual beliefs of native groups, as their link with the energies of the Great Spirit—who is higher, being a god.

Suffering, however, is often the trickster's lot, as the story of Hare shows. We note also that he assumes responsibility, for he bestows the Medicine Rite. The trickster might stand, in fact, for the free-wheeling aspects of the shaman* who is also unpredictable, buffoonish, full of magical stunts.

The trickster aids in creation and is a provider, the theft of fire being his best-known deed. He also steals tobacco, and through the rites of smoking, Indians gain harmony among themselves and contact with the Great Spirit.

The trickster is a rebel against authority and the breaker of all taboos. He is what the best-behaved and most circumspect person may secretly wish to be.

RICHARD ERDOES, *AMERICAN INDIAN MYTHS AND LEGENDS*

Wascawwy Wabbit *American*

The Warner Brothers studio in 1938 saw the birth of Happy Rabbit, a cute little fellow with buck teeth. But his godfather, Mel Blanc, didn't care for his name and gave him a new one, Bugs Bunny.

On with the show, this is it!

The world first heard Bugs's Brooklyn accent (lent by Blanc) in the 1940 short, "A Wild Hare." He grew into a sophisticated young performer, simply superb (or "supoib"). Yet according to Elmer Fudd, he was a "wascawwy wabbit" who used dastardly means to defeat his foes. Didn't he drop a piano once on Yosemite Sam, when both were trying to win the hand of a wealthy widow?

Bugs did his bit during World War II, appearing in several cartoons promoting the sale of war bonds. He also had a brief operatic career, memorably recorded in the classic cartoon, *What's Opera, Doc?*

*See pages 78-81.

Bugs is in direct line of descent from Hare. Rabbits, after all, are ridiculously weak little fellows who survive by being constantly vigilant and smart. Also, their buck teeth, long ears and powers of reproduction are sources of amusement. And to the native peoples, few creatures were more vital as sources of food and clothing.

One of Bugs's ancestors came from southern Africa, a Hare trickster who became known in America as Br'er Rabbit. In Joel Chandler Harris's "Uncle Remus" stories, we read about an ongoing battle of wits between him and Br'er Fox, who set a tar doll in his path one day. As the figure seemed insolent, Br'er Rabbit butted it and became hopelessly stuck in the goo. "All right, you've got me," said Br'er Rabbit, "and now you can chop off my head if you like but don't, please don't toss me in the briar patch!" With a mean grin Br'er Fox did just that—and in the thorny briars, of course, he was perfectly safe once more.

Bugs reminds us that tricksters are still very much with us. Cool and in command, always ready with a one-liner, he forever wins out, whether it means impersonating a sheep or plugging Elmer's shotgun with his fingers.

Although Bugs retired from active cartoon-making in 1963, he appears in reruns every Saturday morning. The mythology of this buffoonish bunny is most reassuring, showing us how easy it is to outwit oppressors and bask in the sun, munching carrots.

Well, th-th-th-th-that's all f-f-f-folks.

Bugs Bunny

TV interference caused by copper-wire bras
White cliffs of Dover turning green
Scientists seek iceberg that sank Titanic
Welshmen disappear in Llandudno Triangle
Bumper spaghetti harvest in Switzerland

APRIL FOOLS' DAY GAGS, BRITISH MEDIA

The Spirit of Play

We have one occasion, April Fools' Day, when anyone may live out a fantasy of telling lies without punishment. The world is often too serious, but on that day it is invaded by the spirit of play. And isn't play the basis of all great accomplishments?

So it is with the trickster. Cree playwright Tomson Highway notes that "he stands at the centre of our dream life, as opposed to the European context where the central figure is an agonized individual. European mythology says we are here to suffer; our mythology says we're here to have a good time."

Playfulness takes the trickster into trouble, then out of it by a lightning feat of shapeshifting. He has an animal nature and can be as slick as an otter, as cheeky as a squirrel. When Jamie tells of howling like wolves, we're in the world of the trickster.

Howlin' at the Moon

On the first night of our camping trip the moon was full and sounds of the night abounded. The tent was set up and we made tea on Rob's campstove. It was around one in the morning when the wolves first started.

AROOOOOOO. AROOOOOOOOO!

Their howling was unbelievably loud. All the other night noises disappeared except for the Canis Lupi baying at the full round moon.

AR. AR. AR. AROOOOOOO!

It was incredible. From another side of the mountain another wolf pack joined in the exchange. Gerry attempted a howl of his own.

ARF. ARF. ROWOOOOL!

We all tried to howl like the wolves. That night in the woods Rob, Gerry and I talked with them, but we have no idea what they said.

Ritual grew up in sacred play; poetry was born in play and nourished on play; music and dancing were pure play. Wisdom and philosophy found expression in words and forms derived from religious contests. The rules of warfare, the conventions of noble living were built up on play-patterns. We have to conclude, therefore, that civilization is, in its earliest phases, play.

JOHN HUIZINGA, *HOMO LUDENS*

Passages: A Photo Essay

Torn posters on an Athens wall (*right*) show a beam colliding with two chained human forms. Does this mean truth against error? Freedom against bondage? Good against evil?

We interpret such images in terms of our feelings. Making a discovery, or becoming liberated or purified in some way, we will read our emotion into the posters. Whatever is within, we apply to the outer world.

So it is with the myths. We make an emotional response to the drama expressed in them. Then we find their themes everywhere—in a relationship, on the TV screen, out in the street.

Turning to the cover photo, we find a Paris bridge with the new day's sun blazing in its heart. Seen literally, this is a matter of statistics—size, weight, age, use.

We may also view the photo in symbolic terms. Then it speaks of passages—two shores joined, loss and gain, deep waters below. It suggests danger and discovery, fear and eagerness, the old and the new.

Myths belong to the realm of symbol. They take us away from literal viewpoints into a world of associations, one thing suggesting another. Thus many feelings are expressed.

This is why poems are presented alongside the myths. Direct statement is not enough. Only poems can express the power of myths, which themselves are poetry.

Literal and Symbolic		
(Literal)		
SUN	WATER	BRIDGE
temperature: 6 000°C	formula: H_2O	iron; built in 1830's
(Symbolic)		
SUN	WATER	BRIDGE
rises and sets	voyage; peril; baptism	passage; joining

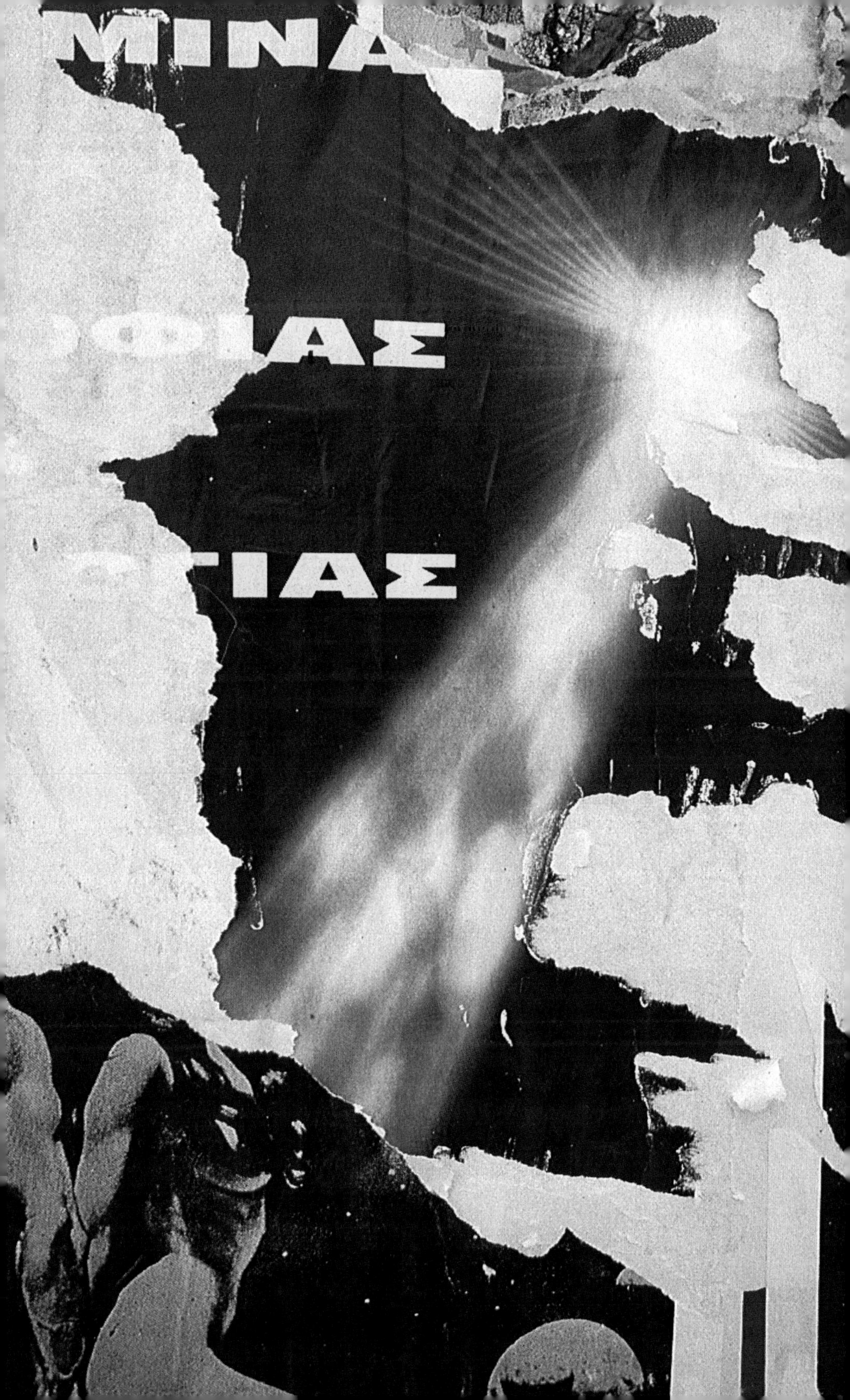
MINA
ΙΑΣ
ΤΙΑΣ

JOSEPH CAMPBELL, *THE HERO WITH A THOUSAND FACES*

1 My Longest Journey

Life calls on us to take a journey, leaving safety behind. Myths tell about Gilgamesh braving many dangers,and knights passing through the Waste Land in quest of the Grail.

This Montreal sanitation worker (*left*) appears in the context of high adventure. Here we see the magic vehicle, the moon of dream and aspiration—and the hero, poised and ready.

A Promised Land might lie ahead, or special powers gained at the end of this Yellow Brick Road—actually, a Manhattan sidewalk (*above*). Such mythic images suggest a wish to find the right path in life.

Campbell states that the path leads into a "zone unknown," a realm that is new and unfamiliar. Strangeness is avidly sought in fantasy films, yet may actually be found anywhere. All we need is to cast away dread and dreariness, and take the journey's first step.

She is the ship, on which we sail the waters of the deep self, exploring the uncharted waters within. She is the door, through which we pass into the future.

MIRIAM STARHAWK, *THE SPIRAL DANCE*

2 I Recognized the Goddess

We know the goddess first as Mother, our portal into life. She represents comfort, love, wisdom, idealism—but also sacrifice, for all life comes out of death.

All mythology comes from the goddess. Able to weave within herself the body's tissues, she seems responsible for the web of life itself. Without that magic, nothing human would exist.

Three phases make up the traditional female life-span: maiden, mother, matron. We see the first during a pause in a splash-battle at a Munich fountain (*above left*). A family threesome (*below left*) in an old train carriage represents the child-bearing years. And an image from New York's Little Italy (*below*) suggests the third phase, of wise age.

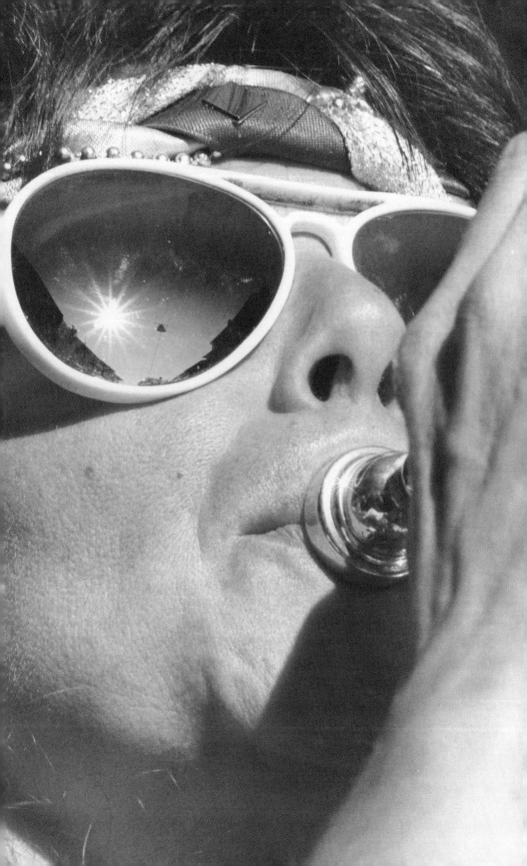

In the beginning, God gave to every people a cup, a cup of clay, and from this cup they drank their life.

OLD DIGGER INDIAN (AS QUOTED BY RUTH BENEDICT)

3 The Power and the Glory

Sooner or later, we discover powers within. We learn to use our talents, to seize the moment.

Here is youth giving its energies full tilt. The trumpeter (*left*) was found at a Swiss wine festival, and the exuberant street dance (*above left*) occurred during London's Notting Hill Carnival.

Gods, in myth, grant wondrous skills of agility and strength. Fathers upon earth bequeath powers, too, helping us to become what we are meant to be. Father and son are shown marching in a parade at Villena, Spain (*above right*), during its annual week-long re-enactment of the medieval struggle between Christians and Moors.

By the very acknowledgement of our darkness and our pain we are saved, that is, healed. By refusing to cover up the cosmic despair and the cosmic anguish that life rains on us we make healing possible.

MATTHEW FOX

4 After Great Pain

This scene, at a racing event near Toronto (*above*), might only imply an over-enthusiastic worship of the wine god, Dionysus. But a dark side appears when this becomes a flight from pain, leading only toward more anguish.

Mythology depicts the pain of life as a fearsome monster. Its defeat by the hero symbolizes conquest over evil—within society, and within oneself.

In Zurich every April, on the third Monday, a figure representing winter is placed on a huge pile of brushwood, to be set ablaze as riders gallop wildly around it (*right*). Within minutes, the figure blows itself into flaming bits. Old Man Winter in that moment is slain, rent apart, sent to the winds.

The late winter was once seen as a time of crisis. Magic was needed to defeat darkness, restoring the sun's power. Accordingly, the Celts would build a giant wicker man to contain people who were burned to death. This dramatized the death of the year, the pain of seasonal advance.

Let the word go forth from this time and place, to friend and foe alike,
that the torch has been passed to a new generation of Americans...

5 King of Kings

The hero's triumph is a mythic moment. Every Mardi Gras in New Orleans, the community greets an amazing king-figure. This is the Big Chief, seen here perspiring under the weight of a costume weighing as much as himself (*right*). He has spent the entire year making it.

"I might dream of a design and wake up with it on my mind," one Big Chief said, "and I'll make it just as I dreamed it. I build some outfits so beautiful that I just cry."

Because Big Chief must always dismantle his costume, this task represents an end as well as a beginning. So it is with any new season or new generation—the torch of triumph serves to burn down what is used up.

When communism triumphed in Eastern Europe, many were hopeful of better things. But it collapsed, whereupon the infamous Berlin Wall (*below*) was torn down in a renewed atmosphere of hope.

> What we learn, if we stay at it long enough, is some facility for that most delicate and enigmatic balancing act of all: the art of giving to another while still maintaining a lively sense of self. Or, to put it another way, the capacity of intimacy.
>
> GAIL SHEEHY, *PASSAGES*

6 Lovers Meeting

What is the mysterious force that hurls the sexes together? Science explains it with biological and behavioral theory, while myth speaks of the love-goddess.

Venus does not stand above it all, remote from love's turmoil. She experiences both its ecstasy and anguish.

Two hearts beating as one, our notion of romance, is rooted mainly in medieval legend. This moment at a Notting Hill Carnival sound stage (*left*) expresses, perhaps, the intimacy of two lives in balance. But street-art graffiti on a Paris wall (*below*) suggests a darker side of relationships.

I give you the end of a golden string;
Only wind it into a ball,
It will lead you in at Heaven's gate,
Built in Jerusalem's wall.
WILLIAM BLAKE

7 Till We Have Built Jerusalem

Everyone hopes to find a happiness known, in mythic terms, as paradise. Blake's golden string might suggest the thread of life and also the wholeness gained by bringing all strands into harmony.

A holy city at the world's centre, Jerusalem, serves as a symbol for paradise. Here stands the Dome of the Rock, said to be the world's loveliest building. Steps on four sides (*below*) lead to its exterior, octagonal to suggest the material world—the inner colonnade being round to symbolize paradise.

Paradise is often viewed as something due to appear at the end of time. But with vision, we may glimpse it at any moment. In the Lisbon flea-market amid old clocks, leaves reflected within a mirror (*above*) imply a deep well of life.

ETHEREAL
COSMOS
ASTRAL
GALAXY
STAR
CLUSTER

MASS

MOUNT

HILL
GEM
MOUND
JEWEL
ISLAND
QUARTZ
SAND
CRYSTAL
TIME
ICE
AGE
AGE
AGE
AGE
AGE
AGE
AGE

The Pattern of Myths

This mural in Glasgow offers a huge overview of existence. The language might seem scientific at first. But it is actually close to that of myth— which also attunes us to AGE AGE AGE AGE AGE AGE AGE..., and directs us toward the ISLAND, the MOUNT, the ETHEREAL.

Myths document the big moments of life. They give a chart of human experience and show a clear path.

Sometimes we feel alone in a confusing world. Our problems seem unique to ourselves. But the same ones recur through the ages, as mythology shows. And it inspires us, by showing how heroes confront perils.

Knowing the world's great myths, we may put our own into perspective. Experiencing depression may then appear as an underworld descent. Fighting for a cause, the odds stacked against us, becomes a monster-battle. Winning a trophy may be seen in terms of a grail quest.

Thus personal mythology provides dramatic roles, all of them old. When big stories unfold in our lives, we file them for future reference: The Fight, Falling in Love, Taste of Success. These are the myths within—ancient stories that have become one's own.

Myths are stories that give meanings in compressed form, much as scientific formulas do. We might assume that science offers more truth, being based on the clear-cut 2+2=4 of mathematics. Yet myths are every bit as true and hold a firmer grip on the human heart.

People sometimes fear the power of myth. It appears as "dabbing in the occult," telling mysteries which science ought to solve. But always it relates directly to life.

Myth offers not an escape, but a grip on fundamentals. And there is a tragic dimension not found in fairy tales: prince and princess do not live happily ever after.

Grasping the pattern of myths is not an easy task. Because they raise the ultimate life questions, our minds are pushed to the limit. Entering its primeval world, we burst into brand-new patterns of thought.

4 After Great Pain

Sigurd battles the dragon Fafnir

After Great Pain a Formal Feeling Comes

After great pain a formal feeling comes—
The nerves sit ceremonious like tombs;
The stiff Heart questions—was it He that bore?
And yesterday—or centuries before?

The feet mechanical
Go round a wooden way
Of ground or air or Ought, regardless grown,
A quartz contentment like a stone.

This is the hour of lead
Remembered if outlived,
As freezing persons recollect the snow—
First chill, then stupor, then the letting go.

EMILY DICKINSON

Sometimes we are quite incapacitated by a painful experience. It makes us go about with no regard for the present, the heart wondering how it could have endured the pain.

Myth presents this dark time as the hero's struggle with a monster. Here is Sigurd* in the throes of combat, as visualized by Arthur Rackham. We like to see the monster-struggle in dramatic terms, with decisive action by wrestler, or private eye, or politician. On a deeper level, such anguish may be seen as a force by which the spirit is refined and purified.

---

*See pages 144-148.

11. Monster

The Spirit of Windigo *Ojibwa*

A hunter named Windigo lived with his family on the shores of Lake Nipissing. They were very happy, until a time when the animals became scarce and people began to starve.

Windigo's family was reduced to making soup from the inner bark of trees. So he went to a medicine man, who gave him a potion that would bring success in the hunt. It was a kind of tea, and he drank some before going to bed.

The next morning, Windigo woke up and was amazed at how quickly he could walk—from Nipissing all the way to Temagami in a few strides, and then to Temiskaming. He had become a great giant.

Windigo gave a shout, and people nearby were struck by such a fear that they changed into beavers. He reached down and killed all of the beavers, then plunged them into his mouth. "Himself only for himself," was his cry. Windigo quite forgot all else. Indeed, this is what his very name meant: *ween*, himself; *digo*, for himself.

Windigo now had a terrible longing to eat the flesh of human beings and to drink their blood. Once more he gave the cry of death and feasted—then a third time and a fourth. The more he ate, the more hunger he felt, so that he grew until his head pierced the clouds.

126

Whenever Windigo came near his old home, he would
return to his previous form and forget what had happened. But again the hunger would return, again
Windigo's terrible bellow would be heard, again he would
feed to excess before returning to normal.

All the Ojibwa tribes dreaded Windigo. Then the Great
Spirit spoke to another hunter, Big Goose, telling him to
challenge Windigo by changing also into a giant. He did at
once, receiving the name Missahba.

The people gathered about their champion with fresh
hope. "You must prepare huge amounts of goose oil,"
Missahba commanded. And they worked very hard to do
what he asked, not knowing how the oil might be used.

One night the people saw two fires in the sky, and they
knew that Windigo had come again. "I will protect you,"
Missahba promised. "And even though many will fall at
his cry, I will restore you to good health."

When Windigo's feet shook the ground and he gave his
deafening yell, all the people fell down—all but Missahba.
Every bit as large, he attacked using a tree as a club.
Windigo fought back in the same way, and then they used
mountains as weapons. They battled all across the Great
Lakes, breaking the ice as they clubbed and punched and
kicked each other with all their might.

And finally, Windigo himself fell dead on the ground.

Then Missahba returned to his normal size, and became
Big Goose once more. But he felt sick, having inhaled
some of Windigo's bad ice during the fight. Big Goose
drank goose oil, and immediately vomited forth the bad
ice. Then he poured the oil into the mouths of the fallen
Ojibwa, bringing them back to life.

The people thanked the Great Spirit for their deliverance. But sadly, the spirit of Windigo endured.

And still today it enters people so that they also "turn
windigo." They shout and murder, they eat and drink to
horrible excess without thought of others. Yet the Ojibwa
have a protector, Missahba, and he provides hope of even-
tual triumph over this terrible evil.

Listen to them . . . creatures of the night. What music they make!

BELA LUGOSI IN *DRACULA*, 1931

Booing the Bad Guys

Monsters personify life's agonizing problems. They do violence upon us, as when Windigo in this grim myth inflicts hard blows on Missahba.

Monsters are loathsome, but take us into the heart of the human struggle. So we boo the bad guys of the wrestling rings and hockey rinks with a special affection. They represent the cruelties of life in play form, leaving us free to release our hatred.

But the monster figure is only too real in the Windigo tale, for it means the grinding horror of having no food. When Windigo turns into a monster, this is part of an effort to feed his family.

A monotonous job may appear as a monster—although the powerlessness of being unemployed is even worse. Monstrous above all is experience of death, worst if it is by violence and within the home.

...I am in blood
Stepped in so far that should I wade no more,
Returning were as tedious as go o'er.

WILLIAM SHAKESPEARE, *MACBETH*

Uncle Joe *Russian*

Joseph Stalin, Russia's leader from 1925 to 1953, had twinkling eyes and a warm smile. A pipe was often tucked beneath his bushy mustache. He somewhat resembled Santa Claus, and was affectionately known as "Uncle Joe."

Stalin, forever wearing an ordinary soldier's uniform, was described by Winston Churchill as Russia's "great warrior." U.S. President Harry Truman once remarked, "I like old Joe. Joe is a decent fellow."

But Vladimir Lenin, founder of Russia's Communist state, had held a different view. "Comrade Stalin, having become General Secretary, has concentrated unreasonable power in his hands, and I am not sure that he always knows how to use that power with sufficient caution," he wrote. "Therefore I propose to the comrades to find some way of removing Stalin from his position."

A massive stroke prevented Lenin from achieving this end. And after Lenin's death, Stalin built up the role of General Secretary into one of unprecedented strength. So this former theology student emerged, at the 1925 Soviet Congress, as the supreme leader.

Lenin had been a thinker as well as a doer. But Stalin reduced all theory to one goal: industrialization through terror. In 1928, he launched the first Five Year Plan with its emphasis on heavy industry, and thanks to the policy of terror, it succeeded. For the plant manager or worker who fell short of target, there was always the threat of labour camp or firing squad. "I trust no one," said Stalin, "not even myself."

A quarter million collective farms were created, and peasants were torn from their private plots to fill them. They opposed Stalin at first, by slaughtering their livestock. Then he starved the people into submission.

To Churchill, Stalin once gave the number of his victims as 10 million. Later estimates suggest a figure closer to 14.5 million, most of these dying in the Ukrainian famine of 1932-33. During this time there was enough grain to feed everyone, but Stalin went on exporting it to the West. This was a calculated act of genocide, ranking with the Jewish Holocaust in infamy.

By 1937, Stalin had liquidated the independent farmers (*kulaks*), and ninety-nine percent of all grain-yielding farms had been collectivized, with half of the sowing and reaping done by machines. And it was a stupendous failure. For farm output fell so low that the state had to rely on food imports, causing a colossal drain on the country's hard currency.

Then at the 1934 Soviet Congress, "The Great Terror" began. Of the 1966 delegates, 1108 were arrested and accused of being counter-revolutionaries, and 98 of the 139 members of the Russian Central committee were executed.

What became known as the KGB (Committee for State Security) did the job of execution. For Stalin's henchmen, the most effective method was the "conveyor": interrogation by relays of police, for days, until fatigue "poisons" the victim. The total of those killed by the security police is believed to be about 25 million.

Meanwhile, undoubted advances were made. Illiteracy under the Czars had been at around 79 percent, but in Stalin's day it dropped to 10 percent. There were also the triumphs of technology, duly hailed as the Communist Party's work. But factory managers were unwilling to risk trying out new technologies, under the strain of meeting production quotas.

In 1941, Russia suffered the Nazi assault,* the most awesome the world had ever seen. But Stalin lacked nearly all of his top generals because they had been eliminated in his purges. "We have only to kick in the door," Hitler boasted, "and the whole rotten structure will come crashing down."

And indeed the Germans won success at once, capturing three million Russian soldiers. This came in part from the low prestige of Stalin, for in many places the Nazis were hailed as liberators. But Hitler, with victory in his grasp, made an error as costly as Napoleon's**: he delayed taking Moscow—Russia's political and military nerve centre—and insisted on a broad line of advance to the north and south. He sacked the field marshal who argued that Moscow be taken at once.

And so the Battle of Moscow was not fought until the end of 1941, in the early winter before the Germans had dug in. Stalin ordered a counter-attack, and they were rolled back.

There was agony in Leningrad, where 632 000 Russians starved to death during the Nazi siege. But the

---

*See pages 150-154.
**See pages 176-179

defenders' triumph at Stalingrad was a decisive turning point of the war. The Russians began an advance that went on for two years, and eventually gained them an empire in Eastern Europe.

At the Yalta conference in 1945, Churchill and U.S. President Franklin Roosevelt agreed to give Stalin Poland and East Germany. Later at Potsdam, the fate of Hungary and Czechoslovakia was handed over to the Russians, as Eastern Europe became shut off behind an "Iron Curtain" of Stalin's Communism.

Russia had helped to win the war by the slimmest of margins and at the cost of some 20 million lives. But it turned her into a great military power, with a true sense of direction. Then the Stalinist idea of "capitalist encirclement" was sounded, and between the two "super-powers" of Russia and America, there grew a nightmarish nuclear race.

After World War II, there were some 14 million people in the 100-odd camps of the Gulag Archipelago (Labor Camp Administration). During Stalin's time, at least 12 million died in these "Auschwitzes without ovens." Decades later their population still remained at around 2 million.

Russia in the early 20th century was in the forefront of modern art. But the doctrine of Socialist Realism snuffed out experimentation in art, turning it into propaganda. Karl Marx's ideal of a classless society had come to this. "The truthfulness and exactitude of the artistic image," declared officialdom, "must be linked with the task of ideological transformation, of the education of the working man in the spirit of socialism."

Stalin had dissenting artists murdered, and only the lucky survived. Composer Dmitri Shostakovitch gained favour for his Seventh Symphony because of its so-called "invasion theme," thought to represent the Nazi assault. But this was not so. "I was thinking of other enemies of humanity," the composer disclosed in his Memoirs, meaning Stalin. As Shostakovitch explained, "Stalin liked to put a man face to face with death and then make him dance to his own tune."

Stalin reviewed parading troops from atop the Lenin Mausoleum. There was something eerily primitive about this rite, the chieftains standing above where the Soviet Union's father lay in his crystal sarcophagus.

Stalin died in 1953, and his body was placed beside that of Lenin. But in 1961, it disappeared after State authorities finally disclosed the cruelties committed in the name of Stalin.

He may well be history's greatest tyrant.

When Howitzers Began

When howitzers began
    the fish darted downward
to weeds and rocks,
    dark forms motionless
in darkness, yet they were
    stunned and again
stunned
    and again and
again stunned, until their
    lives loosened, spreading
a darker darkness
    over the river.

HAYDEN CARRUTH

Demons and Devils

"The devil made me do it!" we might say, blaming all on this horned fellow with a pointy tail. His origins have to do with the word demon, from the Greek *daimon*, meaning a personal spirit hovering nearby like an angel. When the church used the term in a negative sense—to condemn ancient deities such as Artemis—demons became assistants of a totally evil spirit called the devil.

This word's root is also Greek: *diabolos*, "slanderer." It was taken as equivalent to the Hebrew term "satan" meaning "adversary"—as when he appeared in God's heavenly court to state the case against a person. Thus the devil is full of malice, infinitely skilled at deceit, often destroying trust with his polished slander.

Although monsters are usually portrayed in such simple good-versus-evil terms, the hero often finds a kinship to them. Lurking within us, too, are bad spirits threatening to gobble up all of our goodness.

"You must get to know your personal devil," says a character in the Robertson Davies novel, *Fifth Business*. "You must even get to know his father, the Old Devil."

Monsters always appear as dark forces. Often we meet them at night, in our dreams. And as Kim shows, they have a mind of their own.

His Head Stood Out Above Them

When I was six, I had a dream about walking with a friend along our street. We dawdled, but finally we were opposite the park.

Suddenly the ground began to shake. It was a huge Tyrannosaurus Rex. The trees were tall enough to hide the body, but his head stood out above them.

The monster came down the street toward us. His teeth were bared. We stopped, too frightened to move.

That was all. And once every year this dream comes back, just like that. I'm still six years old, and I'm still scared.

Pierre is in his bed. He sees threads that move around. He watches them. He touches them and they form balls. When he begins touching them again, they form shapes "like head shapes." He begins to touch them and they make "all sorts of things," and then "a big monster." Pierre goes outside. He climbs on the car. When the monster touches water, he dies. And his blood creates another monster.

CHILD'S DREAM RECORDED IN DENYSE BEAUDET,
ENCOUNTERING THE MONSTER

12. Underworld

I got the dark night blues,
I'm feeling awful bad.
That's the worst ol' feeling
that a good man ever had.

"Dark Night Blues"

The Descent of Ishtar *Babylonian*

Fertility goddess

Ishtar was the goddess of love, gleaming with celestial light. Her resplendent planet, the Evening Star, led all the other stars in their nightly dance.

On earth, Ishtar brought fertility. "I turn the male to the female, the female to the male," she said. "I adorn the male for the female, the female for the male."

Every year, Ishtar joined with the king in Sacred Marriage. "When he has made love to me," she said, "I shall make him a good destiny, I shall make him shepherd of the land."

Ishtar belonged to the heavens, the Great Above. But one day she opened her ear to the Great Below, earth's inner depths. Resolving to plunge into those depths, the goddess gathered seven adornments to serve as protection.

Down went Ishtar to the House of Dust, the Underworld, where clay is food and feathers serve as garments. She had abandoned heaven to descend to the underworld.

"Gatekeeper, open up!" she cried. "Quickly, or I'll smash the door and raise up the dead!"

"Admit Ishtar," commanded Ereshkigal, Queen of the Underworld. "But at each gate, she must leave a part of her clothing."

So Ishtar at each portal left one piece of raiment: her gleaming crown, pendants from her ears, her glittering necklace, jewels from her breast, her girdle studded with birthstones, bracelets from both hands and feet. Finally the Queen of Heaven shed her last garment and was naked.

Ishtar entered the presence of Ereshkigal. And at once, powerless, she was seized. So great Ishtar became a mere corpse, hanging from a stake.

Upon Earth, the bull no longer leaped on the cow, the man no longer impregnated the maiden. There was sterility among humankind and deep sorrow among the gods.

For three days Ishtar did not return. Then the god of wisdom, Enki, took dirt from beneath his fingernails and made a sexless being who went down to Ereshkigal.

"Give me the life-water skin," he demanded. Ereshkigal cursed him, loud and long.

But finally Ereshkigal's fury was exhausted. "Sprinkle Ishtar with the water of life and bring her back to life," she ordered. "Then let her go, but if she fails to provide the ransom-price, summon her to return."

So Ishtar, now resurrected, went back through the Underworld's seven gates, recovering an item of apparel at each. So she returned to heaven once more. Tammuz, the queen's son, would also have to go down heroically into the Underworld. But he too was destined to return.

Where, O Where?

I need not die to go
So far you cannot know
My escape, my retreat,
And the prints of my feet
Written in blood or dew;
They shall be hid from you,
In fern-seed lost
Or the soft flakes of frost.
They will turn somewhere
Under water, over air,
To earth space or stellar,
Or the garret or cellar
Of the house next door;
You shall see me no more
Though each night I hide
In your bed, at your side.

ELINOR WYLIE

Into the Depths

The Underworld is the monster's pit, the valley of the shadow of death. It symbolizes the sense of being lost, trapped, suffocated.

Heroes journeying into the Underworld's depths will suffer a kind of death, like that endured in initiation rites. The descent is a time of crisis, panic, disorientation.

Even great Ishtar descends to the Underworld. Probably the greatest goddess in history, she held power based on the magic of childbearing. In her time and rule, Babylonian women could own estates and serve as judges, and anyone sinning against a mother would suffer banishment. But this was not to last: Gilgamesh's defiance of Ishtar expresses deep male opposition to the goddess's cult.*

The Sacred Marriage rite of ancient Babylon vividly dramatized the facts of life. On New Year's Eve a bed of cedar and rushes would be prepared atop the seven-tiered ziggurat,** and here king and priestess made love so as to ensure the fields' fertility.

But beneath the ziggurat was a pit of seven levels, each with its own gate. And this also holds great significance.

When Ishtar opens her "ear" (which also means "wisdom"), she acknowledges a deeper part of herself. She casts off her fine garments—much as the waning moon is gradually fragmented—and yields to the Underworld.

So Ishtar, Queen of Heaven, by stages forfeits her status not only as queen, but as woman. In the presence of Ereshkigal, a kind of dark sister, she dies. Now, no demands may be made of the goddess, who is connected only to her depths.

Ishtar's myth gives the pattern for underworld journeys made by all of us. We all put on a special appearance for the world and then, one day, withdraw from self-display. We feel naked to a bone-chilling grief. Hung up on our terror like Ishtar in the Great Below, we suffer a darkness of the soul. But finally the journey resumes as we climb back into the world, into a new state of being.

A man who has not passed through the inferno of his passions has never overcome them. They then dwell in the house next door, and at any moment a flame may dart out and set fire to his own house.

CARL JUNG, *MEMORIES, DREAMS, REFLECTIONS*

The Roads to Zelda's Sanitarium *American*

At Montgomery, Alabama, during the summer of 1918, local army officers were invited to a country club dance. At one point, a 17-year-old girl performed the "Dance of the Hours." Her name was Zelda Sayre, and she had long honey-gold hair.

*See pages 71-72.
**See page 198.

To a 67th Infantry first lieutenant, Scott Fitzgerald, Zelda was the most beautiful girl he had ever seen.

Scott went up to her, introduced himself, and they danced. He was handsome in his officer's uniform, and she well remembered her feelings. "There seemed to be some heavenly support," she said, "that lifted his feet from the ground in ecstatic suspension, as if he secretly enjoyed the ability to fly but was walking as a compromise to convention."

Conventional he was not, nor was she. Scott, who craved hectic fun and escapades, for the first time had met a girl with the same exuberance. Zelda was the epitome of the Southern belle, but also a hellion who had once phoned the fire department to report a stranded child, then climbed onto the roof and kicked away the ladder. The two were alike in body and soul; people said that they appeared to be brother and sister.

Scott, like Zelda, had aristocratic ancestors. But ever since his father had been fired as a salesman, he had suffered deep anxieties about money. "Dear God," Scott had prayed during that crisis, "please don't let us go to the poorhouse." An inheritance provided enough to allow Scott to attend Princeton University, however, and to apply for the army commission that was destined to lead him to Zelda.

Zelda was the girl of Scott's dreams—beautiful, rich, socially prominent. The two fell in love at once and soon became engaged. But at the time he was vainly trying to become established as a writer, and she backed off, unsure of his prospects.

Then Scott had *This Side of Paradise* published and won her back again. "We're building our love-castle on a firm foundation," Zelda told him. "We're going to marry and live happily ever afterward."

After the wedding in New York City on April 3, 1920, Zelda and Scott honeymooned at the Biltmore Hotel, but were asked to leave for disturbing other guests with their hilarity. At the Waldorf they danced on the tables; at the

Commodore they spun around in the revolving doors for half an hour; at the Plaza they made midnight plunges in the fountain outside its doors.

Both were gifted writers, and Zelda received an offer to have her diaries published. Scott overruled this, however, asserting that he needed parts of them for his own work. It would be hard for him, indeed, to keep up with the writing necessary to maintain their prosperity.

Scott meanwhile was writing what would become his most acclaimed novel, *The Great Gatsby*. He based the character of Daisy Buchanan largely on Zelda's, and Jay Gatsby's mainly on his own. Both Scott and Jay come out of the Midwest, win prestige in the army, and storm the bastions of wealth to claim the princess—as suggested by a memorable phrase from the novel: "High in a white palace the king's daughter, the golden girl."

The couple went to the French Riviera to give Scott a chance to write. But here Zelda grew bored. She sought release in strenuous swimming—and eventually in a relationship with a French aviator that enraged Scott. "I was locked in my villa for one month," she later claimed, "to prevent me from seeing him."

Then Zelda's behaviour grew erratic. At a Riviera restaurant, Scott noticed the aging Isadora Duncan,* and went over to talk with her. When she began running her fingers through his hair, Zelda impulsively threw herself down a stone staircase.

"So we beat on, boats against the current, borne back ceaselessly into the past," states the famous last sentence of *The Great Gatsby*. So it was with this gifted couple, unable to go forward.

Late in her 20s, Zelda decided to become a professional ballet dancer. She would always be the first at her morning class, with a bouquet for her beloved teacher, "Madame." But when Scott grew concerned about neglect to their daughter, Scotty, she gave it up. "If I couldn't be great, it wasn't worth going on," said Zelda, "though I loved my work to the point of obsession."

---

*See pages 162-162.

In 1930, Zelda went into hospital suffering from acute anxiety. Again and again she repeated the same phrases: "It's horrible," "What's going to become of me," "I must work and I no longer can," "I have to see Madame." When she was persuaded to take psychiatric treatment in Switzerland, Scott wrote pot-boilers to earn enough to give her the best treatment. But money was in short supply.

In only six weeks, Zelda wrote *Save Me the Waltz.* Scott, who objected to his portrait in the book and also to her use of his materials, tried unsuccessfully to block its publication. "My books make her a legend," he complained, "and her single intention in this somewhat thin portrait is to make me a nonentity."

Then, in 1934, Scott brought out the book on which he had laboured for seven years, *Tender is the Night.* It described the breakup of a marriage resembling his own under the strains of alcoholism—for which he was now taking treatment—and insanity. Though praised by the critics, it sold fewer than 12 000 copies.

Scott had pinned all his hopes on the novel. With its failure, he went to Hollywood and wrote movies to pay for his mounting debts. "I left my capacity for hoping," he remarked, "on the little roads that led to Zelda's sanitarium." At a Hollywood restaurant in 1940, Scott died of a sudden heart attack.

Zelda struggled, between bouts of illness, to find happiness in life. She enjoyed the countryside around the Tennessee sanitarium where she lived, and was cheered on March 9, 1948, by news of her first grandchild. "Today there is promise of spring in the air and an aura of sunshine over the mountains," she wrote to Scotty. "I long to see the new baby."

But the next night the sanitarium caught fire. Zelda was trapped on the top floor and perished in the flames.

Do you expect to enter the Garden of Bliss without trials, such
as came to those who passed before you?

THE KORAN

Turn Left Into the Labyrinth

The underworld in myth is sometimes represented as a labyrinth.
This ancient symbol suggests the twists and turns of Mother Earth.
Babies must find their way out of the labyrinth, and tribal initiation
rituals require youths to re-enter it—coming to terms with mortality
so as to be reborn as adults.

The labyrinth's path offers a full vision of life and death. The dead
go back into their Mother's coils, to be utterly transformed as the
soul goes into new realms. In much the same way, a seed has to journey into and out of the darkness to become a plant.

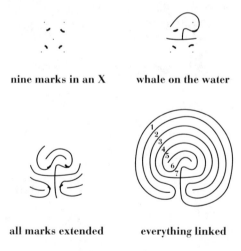

nine marks in an X   whale on the water

all marks extended   everything linked

How to draw a labyrinth

The labyrinth's coils go in and out, following a continuous spiral.
To travel its twists and turns, we can only go toward its centre, as
seen in this basic design found at many places throughout the
world. Passage is always to the left, against the path of the sun, thus

implying a person's passage toward death. The return is in the opposite way, implying renewal of life.

Present-day labyrinths of the soul include depression, which may bring a form of mental and physical paralysis. The term comes from the Latin, *deprimere*, to press down. Psychologists say that "being pressed down" should make us stop and go into the meaning of our sadness, until something comes of it. When Kirstin "has a good cry," better days may be presumed to lie ahead.

Tears of a Fool

As I lie in the dark tranquility of my bedroom, a tear rolls down my cheek. Then another. No, I can't let myself do this. I shouldn't but I do.

My body begins to shake with uncontrollable sobs. I bury my face in the pillow to eliminate the sound. All I want is to be left alone to cry by myself.

Why am I crying? Everything has piled up and I can't take it any more. Crying is a release. It lets everything out.

I feel much better now. The calm after the storm. I roll over away from my tear-stained pillow. As I fall asleep one last tear escapes.

We're all in the dumps,
For diamonds are trumps;
The kittens are gone to St Paul's!
The babies are bit,
The moon's in a fit,
And the houses are built without walls.

ANONYMOUS

13. Betrayal

A Word of Encouragement

O what a tangled web we weave
When first we practise to deceive!
But when we've practised quite a while
How vastly we improve our style!

J.R. Pope

Sigurd and Brunhild *Scandinavian*

Sigurd and Brunhild

Sigurd the Volsung had a perilous childhood. Even before being born he lost his father, who was slain in battle. As a young man, he had the blacksmith Regin as a tutor.

Regin urged him to slay the dragon Fafnir. This was actually a person, who stole the elves' treasure-hoard and assumed a dragon's face to guard it.

So Sigurd took a fine sword, forged from fragments of his father's, and steeled himself to attack the dragon. When its immense scaly bulk came near, he thrust with his sword right up to the hilt.*

Blood gushed from the gaping wound in a flood, pouring over Sigurd's body. Absently, he licked from his finger some drops of blood from Fafnir's heart. Birds had gathered above him, and at that instant he understood their language.

"Now you must seize the treasure!" a bird warbled.

"Then journey to the mountain where Brunhild sleeps and learn wisdom from her!" another one sang.

Sigurd entered Fafnir's den. Here was the elves' treasure, stolen long ago by the gods. He grasped the great ring, wonder of wonders, and put it on his finger.

Sigurd loaded the gold onto his horse's back and set off in search of Brunhild. She had once been the leader of the Valkyries. These armour-clad warrior maidens, whose spears flashed sparks, rode their winged horses across fields of battle to choose the greatest heroes from among the dead. These worthies were taken to Valhalla, their hall of reward.

Brunhild had been the favourite daughter of Odin, king of the gods.** But once she had defied him, by awarding victory to a king who had been condemned to death by her father. Odin banished Brunhild and placed her on a rocky height, surrounded by a wall of fire.

There Brunhild would lie, slumbering, until the first mortal broke through the flame and won her for his own. She would then be able to live like any other woman on earth, suffering its trials, united in love with her rescuer.

After a long journey, Sigurd saw the ring of flame high

*See page 124.
**See pages 266-268.

on a mountaintop. He urged his horse up the slopes and
fearlessly broke through the fire. Here he came upon the
figure of a warrior, seemingly dead. Sigurd dismounted
and removed the helmet of the fallen soldier. At once the
maiden's golden hair tumbled loose. Then with a kiss, he
awakened her.

Brunhild smiled and asked, "Who are you, riding
through the flames to bring me to life again?"

"I am Sigurd, and I ask that you teach me your wisdom." This she did, and as the days past by, they grew
more and more fond of each other. Finally, the two fell in
love.

For many days and nights, Sigurd and Brunhild stayed
together on the mountaintop. But then it was time for him
to continue his adventures. Tenderly he placed the gold
ring on Brunhild's finger.

"One day," Sigurd declared, "I will return to be your
husband." "You will be mine," she said, "and I will be
yours forever." She gave Sigurd some magic charms,
which would allow him to alter his shape to that of any
other man, should the need arise. Then he went on his
way to the land of the Nibelungs.

Sigurd was made welcome at the court by King Giuki
and his queen, Grimhild, a sorceress. She saw at once that
Gudrun, her pretty daughter, was falling in love with their
guest. But when he spoke of his devotion to Brunhild,
Grimhild used her devious arts to prepare a special drink
for him.

Sigurd drank. Immediately he forgot Brunhild and
instantly felt his heart going out to Gudrun. He asked for
her hand in marriage, which was eagerly given. This drew
him close to Gudrun's brother, Gunnar, and they
exchanged a pledge of eternal friendship.

Grimhild's schemes, however, were not at an end.
"Gunnar, now that your sister is happily married, you
should turn your thoughts to the same," she said. "I have
just the bride for you, the warrior maiden Brunhild."

Gunnar agreed and rode off to Brunhild's mountain. He
was accompanied by Sigurd, who had no recollection of

the time he had spent there. When they arrived, Gunnar tried to gallop through the ring of fire, but he was stopped by the ring of flames. So Sigurd, out of loyalty to his friend, assumed Gunnar's shape and easily leaped the flames.

Brunhild saw this figure appear and was overwhelmed with dismay. "Who are you?" she asked.

"I am Gunnar, and I have come to make you Queen of the Nibelungs."

Silently Brunhild cried out to Odin for help, but knew that the god's will was otherwise.

"Odin requires that you marry whoever can ride through the flames," said the man, "and this I have done!" He seized Brunhild's hand and placed a ring on her finger after drawing off the great golden one. Unhappiness was soon to follow.

Sigurd went back to Gunnar, reported success, and returned to his true shape. When Brunhild crossed through the flames at last, she saw that Sigurd was the companion of her husband-to-be. Her heart filled with bitterness, as he gave no sign of recognition.

Brunhild accompanied the two men to the Nibelung castle. Here she met Gudrun, and her anger grew when she learned that Sigurd had married her.

Then Brunhild saw the great golden ring that Gudrun was wearing. "Who gave you that ring?" she asked.

"My husband," said Gudrun. And immediately Brunhild realized that Sigurd must have changed his shape to woo her as Gunnar. That was how he had acquired the ring!

Brunhild was plunged into grief and locked herself in her chamber. After several days, the kind-hearted Sigurd came to inquire about her sadness.

"How can you ask me this?" she cried. "It was not Gunnar who rode through the flames, but you!"

Her furious words shocked him, and suddenly he remembered. Grimhild's spell was broken. He bowed his head in sorrow. "I loved you," he said, "but we have been betrayed!"

"And I once loved you, too," she said, "but now my heart is cold. My only wish is to die. And for you to die as well."

Nothing more could be said between them.

Then Brunhild went to Gunnar and told him the truth, "You were not the man who wooed me, but Sigurd!" she told him. A look of shame came into Gunnar's face. "And now he must die!"

"But we have sworn eternal friendship!"

"All that matters to me," Brunhild went on, "is that Sigurd should die!"

Gunnar could not carry out this deed. But he went to his younger brother, Hogni, who was not above such treachery. "If Sigurd should die, we will have his gold," Gunnar told him. "You must kill him." And Hogni easily agreed, deciding to murder Sigurd when they all went on a boar hunt.

Hogni went to Gudrun, hoping to learn of something of Sigurd's vulnerability. As they talked, she told him how Sigurd had killed Fafnir, the blood pouring down upon him. "Wherever it touched his body, no weapon can ever harm him," Gudrun revealed. "But the leaf of a linden tree fell just at that time and stuck beneath the shoulder blades, keeping this spot dry. I fear that if he is ever wounded there, he will die."

Shortly after, Sigurd and the two brothers rode off on the hunt. At a stream, when Sigurd bent to drink, Hogni hurled his spear. It struck in the back, at the very place Gudrun had told him about. Within moments, the hero was dead.

Sigurd's corpse was carried to the castle. Gudrun wept as the brothers told how an accident had taken his life, but Brunhild revealed the truth. Then she told of the terrible bloodshed that would soon afflict them all—for with Sigurd's death, they had taken Fafnir's gold. "It will only end," she said, "when this treasure is hurled into the river where it came from!"

A funeral pyre was built, and Sigurd's body placed on top. Soberly Brunhild held a dagger to her heart. "I will go

with him to Valhalla!" she cried. "We will be together in
Odin's hall!" And she thrust the sharp blade into her
heart.

So as the flames began to roar, Brunhild's body was
placed beside her lover's, and they were side by side once
again.

On Top of Old Smoky

On top of old Smoky, all covered with snow,
I lost my true lover by a-courting too slow.
Now courting is pleasure, parting is grief;
But a false-hearted lover is worse than a thief.

A thief he will rob you and take what you have,
But a false-hearted lover will take you to your grave.
The grave will decay you and turn you to dust,
But where is the young man a poor girl can trust?

They'll hug you and kiss you and tell you more lies
Than the cross-ties on railroads or the stars in the skies;
They'll tell you they love you to give your heart ease,
But the minute your back's turned, they'll court who they please.

On top of old Smoky, all covered with snow,
I lost my true lover by courting too slow.
Bury me on old Smoky, old Smoky so high,
Where the wild birds in heaven can hear my sad cry.

ANONYMOUS

Stabbed in the Back

The pain of betrayal is the sharpest of all, for it destroys trust, the
absolute essential to harmony among people. In the myth of Sigurd,
blood is spilled to atone for an ancient blood-guilt, and betrayal is
piled on betrayal.

When Richard Wagner undertook to compose a vast music drama on the Sigurd myth, he called it *The Ring of the Nibelungs.* Wagner's message in the opera is dark, as its true hero is the Odin figure, Wotan, who wants only the peace of nothingness. "We must learn to die," said Wagner of Wotan's role, "and die in the most complete sense of the word."

Originally Wagner intended to indicate that the body of Siegfried, the Sigurd figure, is conveyed to Valhalla. But he showed Valhalla being destroyed by flames from his pyre, and thus the gods go to their doom. So ends *The Ring's* fourth part, *Die Gotterdammerung*— the twilight of the gods.*

Because the gods are doomed, this mythology is steeped in fatalism. More positive are the personal merits trumpeted by the myth: courage, loyalty, contempt for death. The figures of this old North-European mythology nobly struggle on, despite being aware that they will lose in time.

Adolf Hitler saw the Germany of his day in terms of Sigurd, stabbed in the back by his betrayers. When people feel betrayed, revenge is sure to follow, and this became Hitler's scenario in the events that brought on the horrors of World War II.

Thus he groped his way forward, like a blind seer, led and sustained by the mysterious common will.

THOMAS MANN, *MARIO THE MAGICIAN,* 1929

I go the way dictated by Providence, with the assurance of a sleepwalker.

ADOLF HITLER, 1936

---

*See page 277.

The Thousand Year Reich *German*

"The most evil man in history"

The film shows a trimotor plane among billowing cumulus clouds. Wagnerian music swells. And through a rift appear the spires of a medieval German city, Nuremberg, where columns of men march through the streets.

The plane lands, tumultuous cheers erupt. The door is flung open and out steps *der Fuhrer*, Adolf Hitler, the new Messiah descending to the earth. So begins one of the most effective propaganda films ever made, Leni Reifenstahl's *Triumph of the Will*.

Hitler was born in 1889, the son of a stern Austrian official named Alois and his third wife, Klara. He hoped to be a painter, and after quarrelling with his father over this ambition, he went to Vienna in hopes of entering the Fine Arts Academy. Twice refused, he had to eke out an existence painting postcards and shoe-polish advertisements.

In World War I, Hitler joined up on the side of Germany, a nation then only 43 years old. The initial German advance seemed almost certain to bring a swift victory, but France turned the advancing army back and four years of brutal trench warfare followed. Hitler rose to the rank of corporal, and was temporarily blinded from a British gas attack when an armistice ended the war.

The peace treaty was signed at Versailles. It required Germany to pay huge reparations and limit her army to 100 000 men. And even though nearly all of Europe was responsible for starting the war, the treaty's infamous Article 321 placed the entire blame upon "the aggression of Germany and her allies."

The "dictate of Versailles" became Hitler's chief complaint. He despised the parliamentarians who agreed to it. This gave Germany's World War I generals, he declared, a "stab in the back" like the one that killed Sigurd.

Living in Munich after the war, Hitler joined the small German Workers' Party, a "socialist organization led only by German leaders." Later it was called National Socialism, or "Nazi" for short. Links were forged with the Thule Society, named after the supposed homeland of the Germanic race. "Remember that you are a German! Keep your blood pure!" was the slogan of its 1500 influential members.

In a Munich beer hall on November 9, 1923, Hitler declared himself dictator in a new government. He marched with his followers to seize command, but the police broke up this "beer-hall *putsch*." Later, the Fuhrer was arrested and briefly put in prison, where he began writing his autobiographical *Mein Kampf*—"My Struggle."

Hitler finally won political success in 1933, with the Nazi party's victory at the polls. Under him for the first time in their history, Germans focussed all of their energies on the state. "You are nothing; your nation is everything," said the slogan. And in a mood of self-sacrifice, the nation went out to meet its destiny.

Deeply-rooted myths governed these events. Nazi art portrayed Hitler as a knight in shining armour, come to rescue the nation from failure. Another key image was the swastika, an old symbol used in India and many other lands.

Sanskrit: su asti - good, he is
means
good luck, power of sun

white disc = racial purity

red background = blood

HARAPPA, 2ND MILLENIUM   **Germany, 1920s**

The swastika symbol

The Nazi calendar had pagan holy days—the winter and summer solstice celebrated the sun's rebirth and climax—but otherwise imitated the Church's calendar of feasts. Hitler's birthday fell, luckily, on April 20, close to the time of Easter. "Just as Jesus saved people from sin and hell," said a school dictation exercise, "Hitler saves the German Folk from ruin."

Nazism also developed the idea of a "Thousand Year Reich," borrowed from *Revelation* in the New Testament. This book tells of a battle between good and evil fought at Armageddon, the Biblical town of Megiddo. Afterwards Satan is cast into a lake of fire and chained for the thousand years of the Millenium.

This end-of-the-world story was merged with the ancient myth about a Twilight of the Gods. Hitler often attended the annual Wagner festival at Bayreuth, and for him the supreme moment came at the fiery climax of

Gotterdammerung. He would reach back at this moment to kiss the hand of the festival director, Wagner's daughter-in-law.

"The new age of today is at work on a new human type," said Hitler in 1937 at the opening of Munich's House of Art. "Men and women are to be more healthy, stronger." Hitler, who liked chaste Aryan nudes, loathed modern art. That year the Nazis mounted an Exhibit of Degenerate Art, presenting great 20th-century works with mocking labels. This dealt a terrible blow to German art, as most of the 16 500 modern works confiscated for the show were auctioned off and the rest burned.

The next year Hitler engineered the infamous Munich Agreement.* It allowed Hitler to occupy the Sudeten region of Czechoslovakia, where a large German population lived. "I have no more territorial demands on Europe," he promised. But five months later he proclaimed a protectorate over all of Czechoslovakia, which had been the only democracy left in Europe. "Our enemies are little worms," Hitler told his generals. "I saw them at Munich."

In 1939, with Germany's invasion of Poland, World War II began. Hitler's will was backed by the most dreaded military force the world had ever seen, and it came close to accomplishing what had never been done before—the total conquest of Europe.

Imagine an armoured force directed toward France, stretching in three columns for 160 kilometres east of the Rhine, then unleashed in the *Blitzkrieg* that won victory in only 43 days. One year later, the mightiest army yet seen—153 divisions, 2740 planes, 3580 tanks—was hurled the other way against Soviet Russia. But even this was not enough to gain victory. **

Meanwhile the Nazis had set up twenty concentration camps and interned some 18 million people. Of these, 11 million were executed. In 1942, Hitler ordered the "final solution of the Jewish question": the extermination of all Jews in Europe. Six million Jews died.

---

*See page 295.
**See page 130.

But by now, the United States had entered the war. On June 6, 1944, history's greatest amphibious force smashed against Hitler's Atlantic wall, and thus began a long triumphant march toward Germany.

A month later, several German army officers planned to assassinate Hitler. They put a bomb in a briefcase and placed it in a conference room. He walked away from the room only moments before the explosion, enabling him to boast of a real act of "Providence." Hitler decreed a horrifying execution for those who had tried to stab their Fuhrer in the back.

Providence dictated that German civilians would suffer horribly, too, as their cities were swept by massive Allied air raids. Over 100 million tonnes of rubble were created in Berlin alone by 363 bombing raids, and by the apocalyptic Russian artillery barrage that finally ended the assault in April, 1945.

By then Hitler had retreated to his bunker vowing a scorched-earth policy. "If the war is lost, the people will be lost," he raved. "It is not necessary to worry about what the German people will need for elementary survival." In the Twilight of the Gods, Hitler imagined, the flames consuming Valhalla would destroy all.

Hitler ended his life on the afternoon of the 20th, his birthday, apparently by shooting himself. He had finally married Eva Braun, his mistress for many years, who took cyanide to join him. Their bodies were placed in a gasoline-filled depression near the bunker, burned for three hours, and let down into a shell hole. On May 5, the Soviets found what was "presumably Hitler's corpse."

Hitler and all that he represents have since been rejected in Germany, showing the world how well a nation might rise from ignominy. His evils, in a sense, have been atoned for. And so are those of the Versailles Treaty—for in 1948, a massive U.S. economic-aid program was offered to all European countries, including Germany.

From the moment of birth, when the stone-age baby con-
fronts the twentieth-century mother, the baby is subjected to
these forces of violence, called love, as its mother and father
have been, and their parents and their parents before them.
Those forces are mainly concerned with destroying most of
its potentialities.

R. D. LAING, *THE POLITICS OF EXPERIENCE*

The Worst Possible Evil

In Dante's *Inferno,* punishments for all varieties of evil are
described. At the very lowest circle is Satan, endlessly devouring
the worst of sinners. Their names are Brutus and Cassius and Judas,
who brought about the deaths of Julius Caesar and Jesus Christ. All
three of these villains had committed the worst possible evil: betrayal.

In everyday life we might find ourselves betrayed by friends, dis-
respectful of our feelings or rights. Spouses might betray each other,
whereupon the entire family pays. The ultimate betrayal is said to be
that of child abuse—horror and pain originating in the very place
where refuge should be found.

Again and again in myth, we find betrayal. A roll-call of its victims would include such names as Dido, Ariadne, Osiris, Hercules.
And even on the scale or ordinary life, as Jason shows, betrayal
hurts.

No Trust

Although I've had my share of accidents, which included totally writing off my parent's Cadillac, they still kept their trust in me. If I need wheels, it's always "There son, take the station wagon but remember, be careful." Through this I acquired a feeling of trust for my friends—for a while anyway.

One day I was studying at my friend Mitch's house when I heard a shout from outside. "Hey Jason, are you in there?" said Mitch, who was eyeing my one-month-old Honda, one of the hottest bikes on the road.

Well, Mitch was a good friend and I trusted him. I also owed him a favour. It's ironic how I joked, "Hey, if you smash up my bike tell them you stole it, so the insurance will cover it. And phone my mother before you phone me, so I don't have to tell her I've had another accident."

Not ten minutes after he left, the phone rang. "Jason, I've had an a-a-accident, your bike is ruined."

And I'm thinking, this guy must be some sort of comedian, ha ha. He told me to come down the street where the accident had happened, and I did. There sitting beside the road was a bike, tank bashed in, handlebars bent, forks cracked, the list goes on and on. Mitch survived it with a sore hand.

Well, that was the end of my bike, the end of my days of riding the twisted roads, 160 kph on the QE, the looks people gave me as I pulled up at a red light. I don't know whether it's good or bad, but I don't have the trust any more. And although I'm still friends with Mitch, the jerk owes me 75 bucks for the insurance.

In Adam's Fall
We sinned all.

NEW ENGLAND PRIMER

14. Destruction

If all the seas were one sea,
What a *great* sea that would be!
If all the trees were one tree,
What a *great* tree that would be!
And if all the axes were one axe,
What a *great* axe that would be!
And if the *great* man took the *great* axe,
And cut down the *great* tree,
And let it fall into the *great* sea,
What a splish-splash *that* would be!

CHILDREN'S RHYME

The Last Night of the Age *Indian*

Hindus believe that there are four ages. Beginning with the Golden Age and ending with our own wretched one, they add up to a Great Age of 4 320 000 years. Yet this is nothing, for a thousand Great Ages make up a single day of Brahma, the Creator, and his life lasts 108 years.

Brahma is the creative agent of Vishnu, the Preserver. They stand opposed to Siva, the Destroyer, who gets rid of everything worn-out and old.

Siva is Time itself, dancing the cosmic dance that ends each age and integrates everything into the World Spirit. The source of his power is meditation. Wearing beggars' rags, he sits on a mountain in the Himalayas, deep in thought.

The Great Mother, Siva's wife, had the task of spurring him into action. Awesome in her powers of fertility, she has had many reincarnations.

Once, the Great Mother became Sati, daughter of the wise man, Dakshi. He hated Siva's untidy and abnormal ways, and would not invite him to a feast at which Sati was to choose a husband.

But Siva was Sati's overwhelming choice. And at her cry, he came at once to marry her.

Dakshi offended the god once again, by inviting all the gods except Siva to a festival of fire. But Sati appeared, and to vindicate the god's honour, she flung herself onto the flames. Siva embraced her charred body and performed a dance of mourning.

Vishnu dreaded that Siva might dance the world into destruction. So he took Sati's corpse, carved it up, and flung the pieces across the face of the earth. Siva once more returned to his meditations in the Himalayas.

The Great Mother was again reincarnated, this time as Parvati. She did her utmost to distract Siva. When she finally had won his affection, he took her in an embrace that made the entire world tremble.

But Siva quarreled so much with Parvati that he eventually left her. So he resumed his thoughts with even more concentration. Now when the time came for him to do his dance of destruction—for the world was becoming stagnant once more, turning into a junkpile—he paid no heed.

The Great Mother now appeared as Kali, fearsome in her necklace of skulls. Killing many demons and lapping their blood with her huge tongue, she gained the god's attention utterly.

Siva begged Kali to stop, but her divine madness was so complete that she didn't even notice him. Soon she was trampling on Siva himself—thus earning her name: Kali, Conqueror of Time.

When Kali finally came to her senses, she was ashamed. Siva, excited by Kali's rage, now recognized that the last night of the age had indeed come. And so his dance began.

The dance of Siva made the worlds fall from their courses, to become mere sparks and ashes receding into the farthest reaches of space. And when this ended, Kali gathered the seeds of the next creation.

The Great Mother

In the beginning, the Great Mother looked at herself in a mirror. Then she looked at a second mirror and at a third. In this way all mothers came into being. The Great Mother had eyes like the depths of an abyss, but those of the other mothers were as blue as the sky.

In the ancient city of Amber, next to the Temple of Kali, a priest wearing a red tunic and with feet covered with the blood of sacrifices, explained these things to me. And so I came to know that I had not one mother but many.Since my life seems to have been so much like an abyss and to be more and more like one, I am trying to look within myself to discover the coffin of the original Great Mother. I will open it and inside I will probably find that she has taken the form of somebody else. Perhaps she will be the Queen of Sheba; possibly even Jesus Christ. Whatever form she takes will be the form of my soul.

Of course when one opens a coffin, one destroys it. Nevertheless a delicate odour of cedarwood will come forth.

MIGUEL SERRANO
TRANSLATED BY FRANK MCSHANE

Burning Out the Ego

The Western world is concerned with the problem of becoming an individual. People become absorbed in matters of "personality" and "getting ahead." This self-assertion finds its myth in the tale of the rebel Prometheus.*

But in Hinduism, individuality is something to be erased. Burning out the ego is the initial step to reaching the Highest Self, a principle of Being.

Hindus consider existence as a painful thing. The world is seen as a prison, an eternal circle of birth and death. This is the tyranny of time, and its liberation does not lie in the triumph of the individual person. The Highest Self is reached through the endless reincarnation of "selves" in a multitude of bodily forms.

---

*See pages 208-209.

Hinduism flourishes in India, a land of intense heat where nature acts in cruel ways. But at least nature never casts one out, for it is all-embracing.

Kali lends her name to the teeming city of Calcutta. At her great temple in that city, goats are sacrificed to the goddess—who licks up the blood, in the sense that sand absorbs it and is then buried to make the land fertile. The Mother's vast destructive powers are symbolized by the lapping Kali tongue, emblem of the Rolling Stones.

The Siva absorbed in meditation, utterly calm, is divinity as the West knows it. Less familiar is the Siva who dances with untrammeled violence. While doing so he shows neither sadness nor joy on his face, but a tranquility beyond what the world knows. For although his dance means destruction, it also invites us to enter with equal zest into the game, *lila*, of life.

Siva's dance

In the image of Siva as Lord of the Dance, every detail has mean-ing. One hand raised in a palms-out posture states "Fear not," because all forms that flash in and out of existence are divine. Each of them manifests the god.

The Hindu perspective of time is vast. Trillions of years are imag-ined, in contrast to the Biblical counting of generations back to Adam and Eve.

An offshoot of Hinduism is the religion of Gautama, the Buddha. When Buddha was assaulted by the demons of Death and Desire, he held firm and thus achieved the bliss of Nirvana: being "blown out" into Nothingness. "To live is to suffer," the Buddha preached; a per-son must gain release from the self by following the eight phases of the Path of Enlightenment, ending with meditation.

Cup of Tea

Nan-in, a Japanese Zen master, received a university profes-sor who wished to be taught.

Nan-in said nothing, but filled his guest's cup with tea. It began to overflow, running across the table and onto the floor. But still he kept pouring.

"It is all filled up," the professor objected. "No more will go in!"

"You are like this cup," Nan-in said. "You are full of your own opinions. How can I teach Zen to you until you first empty yourself of them?"

ZEN BUDDHIST MASTER

Opening the Door of Death *American*

I have noticed," Isadora Duncan once remarked, "that all the great events of my life have taken place by the sea." Born in San Francisco in 1878, as a child she loved to dance beside the Pacific. "The sun danced on the waves," she recalled. "The movement of the waves rocked my soul."

Isadora's father founded a bank, but it collapsed when she was five months old. Perhaps because of this failure, he abandoned his family. His wife had to raise their four children from her small earnings as a music teacher.

Isadora took three ballet lessons and then stopped, declaring that the tiptoe poses were "ugly and against nature." This was the start of a revolution whereby she created a new form of dance—free movement that expressed inner emotion. She meant it to be a "divine expression of the human spirit."

What Isadora called a "gypsy opportunism" now governed her life. The family, living from hand to mouth, drifted east and then went by cattle boat to Europe. Isadora's dancing first became a sensation in Budapest, where her interpretation of Strauss's Blue Danube thrilled the audience.

In a day of whalebone corsets, Isadora danced barelegged, wearing a filmy tunic adapted from those of ancient Greece. Her spontaneous skips and bounds left some viewers unimpressed, but most were exalted. (When she danced in Munich, students unharnessed the horses from her carriage and drew it themselves.)

Isadora amazed her admirers by giving her entire body to the music. She moved, she said, "as if in a trance." Her neck and shoulders formed a soft curve, her hands making gestures that seemed to leave a ripple in the air. Sadly, there are no films showing her in action, and she never wrote down her techniques. But this freedom of movement, based on the body's normal activity, transformed modern dance.

In 1904, Isadora met theatre designer Gordon Craig, who shared her excitement for simplicity in all things artistic. They became lovers, so absorbed in each other that for two weeks they forgot all else. "As flame meets flame, we burned in one bright fire," Isadora wrote. "Here at last was my mate; my love; myself, for we were not two but one."

A daughter, Deirdre, was born from this affair, which ended when career pressures tore it apart. By then Isadora had established a school for children, teaching them "to breathe, to vibrate, to feel, and to become one with the general harmony and movement of nature." Six talented girls from her school, the "Isadorables," became famous in Europe and America.

In 1905, her visit to Russia made dance history. It gave "an irreparable jolt to the classic ballet of Imperial Russia," Sergei Diaghileff wrote. "She was the first to *dance* the music and not dance *to* the music."

Having suffered from her father's desertion, Isadora distrusted marriage. Yet she was on the lookout for a gallant knight who would solve her financial problems, as it had become difficult to maintain the dancing school she had established. "I must find a millionaire," she kept repeating.

Then one afternoon in 1909, as Isadora sat in her dressing room, she received a calling card with the name "Paris Eugene Singer." This was a millionaire indeed, heir to the Singer sewing-machine fortune.

Singer gave Isadora not only security, but luxury as well. The affair began with a Mediterranean tour on his yacht. "I can see it all," she later wrote; "the broad deck of the yacht, the table set with crystal and silver for lunch, and Deirdre, in her white tunic, dancing about. Certainly I was in love and happy."

She and Singer had a child which they called Patrick. It seemed that now Isadora had everything. But in 1913, a terrible freak accident shattered her life. She had sent her children for a drive in Paris. Automobiles at that time were started by turning a crank in front of the car. The driver of their car had not set the hand brake properly. When the man cranked the motor, the car rolled into the Seine, and both of the children were drowned.

Isadora was nearly crazed with grief, yet she performed a solemn death dance for her children. "I want to be brave enough," she said, "to make death beautiful."

Then in 1917 came the end of her relationship with Singer. At a gala dinner for Isadora, he was going to announce that he would purchase Madison Square Garden for her use as a school. For some reason, Isadora doubted his motives. "I suppose you want to advertise prizefights with my dancing," she told him.

Singer, so angry that his hands shook, silently got up from the table and left the room. He never returned.

When she went back to Russia in 1921, just after the Russian Revolution, she was filled with the revolutionary excitement that had just swept the nation. "Adieu, Old World!" she cried. "I would hail a New World!" In her performances, she draped her body in red and mimed the conquest of the old order by Communism.

Such destruction is in the nature of things, Isadora believed: "Death is but a door that leads to the Eternal Harmony of the Universe. The fearsome appearances of physical suffering and matter are merely an illusion."

A Russian poet, Sergei Essenine, inspired such passion in Isadora that she married this man, fifteen years her junior, quite impulsively. No doubt somewhat crazy, he would wreck their hotel rooms and run naked down the corridors. "God bless him," she once wrote, "but he's no good for a husband."

Soon after their marriage came her disastrous 1922 tour of the United States. In Boston, finding the audience unresponsive, Isadora waved her red scarf over her head. "This is red! So am I! It is the colour of life and vigour!" she exclaimed. "You don't know what beauty is!"

According to a newspaper account, Isadora then "tore her tunic down to bare one of her breasts and cried out, 'This—this is beauty!'" The students cheered, but proper Bostonians quickly left the theatre. The mayor banned her from making any further appearances in the city, and many other engagements in the tour were cancelled.

Afterwards, her marriage to Essenine ended in divorce. Then, tragically, he booked a room in a hotel in which they had once stayed, wrote her name in blood, and hanged himself.

On September 14, 1927, beside the sea in Nice, France, Isadora accepted the offer of a drive in a handsome open sports car. Around her neck she looped the long shawl which had become her trademark, and waved goodbye to a group of admirers. "Farewell, my friends," she called out. "I go to glory." As the car sped off, the shawl caught in the rear wheel, tightened around her throat, and instantly killed her.

The smallest living cell probably contains over a quarter of a million protein molecules engaged in the multitudinous coordinated activities which make up the phenomenon of life. At the instant of death, whether of man or microbe, that ordered incredible spinning passes away in an almost furious haste of those same particles to get themselves back into the chaotic, unplanned earth.

LOREN EISELEY, "THE SECRET OF LIFE"

Violent Energies

Destruction in the Western world is often presented as a form of evil. Yet violence is a fact of nature, wherein creatures are destroyed in countless numbers.

Whenever there is creation, something is destroyed in the process. Autumn ruins summer's greenery, only to replace it with gold. Then this is swept away by winter—which promptly prepares a new world of crystal.

A teenager will discard a beloved teddybear in the process of growing up. An army conscript at boot camp will abide the destruction of any weak traits, in order to be toughened. A dancer will suffer poverty and defamation in the pursuit of greatness.

The term "agony" derives from *agon*, a Greek word meaning "contest for a prize." Professional sport grinds athletes up, and the public responds deeply to it. For as Andrea shows, the human race has violent energies which cannot, and must not, be blocked.

Yell at the Top of My Lungs

Sometimes I look down a long, empty hallway and I feel like just forgetting where I am and turning cartwheels, all the way to the far end. Or when I'm in a crowded place, I want to be where I can throw back my head and yell at the top of my lungs.

When I hear certain songs and feel their power, I wish I could express my emotions in that way. I throw things around my room because something inside me wants to be let out, but can't.

Butcher Shop

Sometimes walking late at night
I stop before a closed butcher shop.
There is a single light in the store
Like the light in which the convict digs his tunnel.

An apron hangs on the hook:
The blood on it smeared into a map
Of the great continents of blood,
The great rivers and oceans of blood.

There are knives that glitter like altars
In a dark church
Where they bring the cripple and imbecile
To be healed.

There is a wooden slab where bones are broken,
Scraped clean:—a river dried to its bed
Where I am fed,
Where deep in the night I hear a voice.

CHARLES SIMIC

5 King Of Kings

Napoleon Bonaparte

Ozymandias

I met a traveller from an antique land
Who said: Two vast and trunkless legs of stone
Stand in the desert. Near them, on the sand,
Half sunk, a shattered visage lies, whose frown,
And wrinkled lip, and sneer of cold command,
Tell that its sculptor well those passions read
Which yet survive, stamped on these lifeless things,
The hand that mocked them and the heart that fed;
And on the pedestal these words appear:
"My name is Ozymandias, king of kings:
Look on my works, ye Mighty, and despair!"
Nothing beside remains. Round the decay
Of that colossal wreck, boundless and bare
The lone and level sands stretch far away.

PERCY BYSSHE SHELLEY

Victories occur in everyone's life. But we must learn to accept the brevity of those triumphs, no matter how impressive they might seem.

Mythic heroes cap their exploits by winning the kingship. Yet even the Egyptian "king of kings," Rameses II, is unable to prevent his works from falling into dust.

Napoleon Bonaparte, after scoring great triumphs as Emperor of France, loses his touch and is sent into exile. He escapes only to lead the French to an even more calamitous defeat at Waterloo.

15. Justice

The Trojan War *Greek*

Embarrassment on Mount Olympus! When the gods held a great banquet they made a terrible mistake. Eris, the goddess of discord, had not been invited.

Spitefully, Eris appeared at the door and did her worst. Into their midst she rolled a golden apple inscribed, *For the Fairest*. Discord resulted at once, for the prize was claimed by three goddesses: Hera, Athena, and Aphrodite.

Zeus decided that the matter would be decided by a beauty contest. The judge would be Paris, prince of Troy.

Hera was the first to step forward. Turning slowly to allow Paris full appreciation of her regal beauty, she said, "Choose me, Paris, and you shall have power over all of Asia."

Now Athena paraded her well-proportioned form before the prince's gaze. "If I am chosen," she told him, "I will give you supreme wisdom."

Finally it was Aphrodite's turn, and Paris marvelled at the perfection of her beauty. With a dazzling smile, she said to him, "Give me the apple, and I'll win for you the loveliest of mortal women."

The choice was easy. Aphrodite held out her hand and received the prize from Paris. Hera and Athena glared angrily at them, then strode away. Discord had begun in earnest.

The world's most beautiful woman was Helen, Queen of Sparta. Paris wasted no time eloping with her, and all of Greece was thunderstruck by the news.

When Helen had been growing up, she bedazzled every nobleman in Greece. Many would feel dismay when she chose a husband, and it was feared some might unite to attack him. So it was decided that every suitor must swear an oath on behalf of the man Helen chose—that anyone who tried to steal her would be brought to justice.

Helen had selected Menelaus, and heroes from all over Greece now kept their vow to him by gathering a company of troops. His brother Agamemnon, king of Mycenae, became their commander. The impending conflict would be known as the Trojan War.

On the Greek side, the greatest hero was Achilles, stronger and swifter than any other man. Also, his skin was impermeable to wounds. For Thetis, his mother, had dipped her newborn son in the River Styx, making all parts touched by its waters immune from harm.

The Greeks' ships gathered at Aulis. But here, contrary winds prevented them from sailing on to Troy. Artemis* had been offended, said a prophet, and could be appeased only by the sacrifice of Agamemnon's daughter, Iphigeneia.

Sorrowfully, Agamemnon wrote a false message to his wife, Clytemnestra, who was the sister of Helen. "Send Iphigeneia to Aulis," it said, "so that she can become the bride of Achilles."

Clytemnestra dressed Iphigeneia in wedding garments and brought her to Aulis. Here Agamemnon, to his wife's horror, carried out their daughter's sacrifice. Then the winds dropped, the Greek ships set out toward the enemy's land, and the Trojan War began.

But hopes for an early triumph soon faded. For although the Greeks set up a blockade, the Trojans could

---

*See pages 67-70.

easily break it to bring in food. A stalemate was the result, and it lasted for nine long years.

Then the Trojans received a lucky opportunity. Apollo had asked Agamemnon to return a female captive to her Trojan father. As compensation, the king demanded Achilles's mistress. An inevitable quarrel broke out between the two men, and Achilles angrily withdrew from the battle. His mother came to his aid by persuading Zeus to let Trojans stream out of their walls at last. The Greeks were driven back, and Achilles had the pleasure of knowing that Agamemnon regretted his offence to him.

Not until Achilles suffered the loss of his best friend, Patroclus, did he rejoin the battle. Patroclus had been slain by Troy's greatest warrior, Hector, and Achilles killed him in revenge.

Then Achilles did a terrible thing. He slit the tendons of Hector's feet from heel to ankle and bound them with leather straps to his chariot, driving across the plain with his foe's head dragging in the dust.

The battle of Troy continued. As Achilles led the Greeks in rush after rush, he boasted that even the gods of Olympus were powerless against him. At that very moment, Apollo directed a Trojan arrow into Achilles' heel.

The hero fell, wounded fatally. For despite his mother's precautions, he was not immune from death after all. When she had dipped him in the protecting waters, she had held him by the heel. This part had not been made invulnerable.

And so the battle raged on, until one day a wooden horse as high as a hill was found outside Troy's walls. The Greeks had gone the night before, and on the horse's flank were these words: *For their safe return, the Greeks dedicate this offering to Athena.*

"Bring it within the walls!" many cried.

But the priest Laocoon asked, "Are you mad? How could anyone trust Greeks, even bearing gifts? This wood conceals our enemies!" And he hurled a spear, making a hollow echo.

Then two monstrous snakes slithered toward Laocoon and his sons, coiled about them, and crushed out their lives.

"Bring the horse to Athena's temple!" cried the mob, certain that Laocoon had been punished for profaning this offering to her. So the walls of Troy, which for a decade had turned back the Greeks, were opened to receive the wooden horse.

The Trojans rejoiced over the retreat of the Greeks. They feasted and celebrated long into the night, until sleep overtook them. So there was no one awake when the Greek warriors concealed within the horse emerged and set the city on fire.

Agamemnon and the fleet of the Greek warships were hidden behind an island. When the leader saw the flames, he gave the command to assault Troy, and they destroyed the city until it had been reduced to ashes. All of the Trojan women were herded together and assigned to Greek masters, while those males who had not escaped were murdered.

Even the Trojan priestess of Athena, Cassandra, was dragged from her refuge in the goddess' temple. Athena became enraged by this sacrilege and vowed to bring disaster to the Greeks on their return to their homeland.

This brought grief to Odysseus, King of Ithaca—from whose fertile brain had come the hoax of the wooden horse—for he would suffer from years of wandering.*

But it was Agamemnon who met the most terrible fate. Clytemnestra, having seen him treacherously place their daughter on the altar of sacrifice, plotted her revenge.

At Mycenae, Clytemnestra lavishly welcomed Agamemnon on his return. Then she skillfully carried out her plan. In the palace she caused a net to fall on the king, and then it was easy to stab him to death.

Agamemnon's death, too, had to be avenged, and it was the duty of the oldest son to seek justice for his slain father. This was Orestes, who was encouraged by his sister, Electra, to murder their mother. To help him in his resolve, he consulted the oracle at Delphi. "Appease the

---

*See pages 181-187.

horror of this act," said Apollo, "for whoever hears not the cry of the dead will roam the world without refuge."

So Orestes came secretly to Mycenae, and with his sister's blessings, killed Clytemnestra.

Such a disgusting act as this could not fail to arouse the wrath of the Furies, three hags pledged to punish those who murder their kin. This act of Orestes was only one of several bloody deeds in the history of his clan, the house of Atreus.

At Apollo's bidding, Orestes went to Athens, where the ancient court of Areopagus would decide his fate. Did a father's murder justify the son in slaying his own mother? When the jury's vote turned out to be a tie, Athena was called upon to decide.

"I am for the father," Athena declared. Thus Orestes was acquitted, and an end came to the age-long curse on his family. The Furies were renamed the Eumenides, Gracious Ones, and given a new home below the Acropolis. And Athena proclaimed a new law: not that of unbending tradition, but of persuasion—as in the democratic Assembly of her city during this classical age.

God's mill grinds slow, but sure.

GEORGE HERBERT

A Just War

War, during the tribal period of humankind, was conducted as a ritual. Often it re-enacted the myth of creation.

Heroic battle came about from the growth of a nobility. Its deeds during the Trojan War are memorably told in a great epic poem, the *Iliad*. The author, presumed to be a man named Homer, is concerned especially with the hero's response to death and its inevitability.

Homer also shows the brutalization of all who are caught up in the war. This is much worse today, when soldiers are conscripted from the masses. And since the invention of the machine-gun and chemical weapons, war has turned into a horror like nothing before.

Today a question arises whenever a conflict breaks out: Is this a just war? Traditionally the standards for a just war are these: started by a legitimate authority, fought with right intention, waged as a last resort, and achieving a good that outweighs the resulting evil.

The last is the most difficult to judge. But Agamemnon's bloody inheritance is gauged, over a lengthy span of time, in an ancient Greek play cycle called *The Oresteia*. Its author, Aeschylus, shows that a moral order may be perceived in fate, higher than the gods. The suffering is immense, but at the end comes justice.

Aeschylus's three-part tragedy ends with the trial of Orestes in Athens, soon after the ancient Council lost its powers. These were transferred to the popular Assembly, open to all males over eighteen. Essentially a mass meeting with no rules of order—the world's first democracy—it provided grounds for faith in a truly equitable system of justice.

The trial of Orestes was held in a place that tourists often visit today. This is the hill called Areopagus, beneath the Acropolis on the northwest side. And underneath that rocky hill, as well, may be found the Cave of the Furies.

Mycenae was excavated in the 1870s by Heinrich Schliemann, who had been captivated by Homer's tale of the Trojan War. Here he found six "shaft graves" cut into the rock, the fifth one occupied by an extraordinary corpse. "The round face, with all its teeth, had been wonderfully preserved under its ponderous gold mask," wrote Schliemann, who announced in a feverish telegram, "I have gazed on the face of Agamemnon." The mask is now known to be from around 1600 B.C., four centuries before Homeric times, yet it holds immense fascination still.

Code Napoléon *French*

Whether or not it is clear to you, no doubt the universe is unfolding as it should.

MAX EHRMANN, *DESIDERATA*

Napoleon Bonaparte's star rose during 1795 in Paris, when the French Revolution ran into trouble. Its boldest feat had been the execution of the king, Louis XVI, but monarchists now were determined to install a new king.

Napoleon was called upon to prevent them. Although outnumbered six to one, he loaded his guns with grapeshot—small iron balls fired in murderous clusters— and stopped the monarchists in their tracks.

So afterwards, Napoleon was able to boast, "I saved the revolution, which was about to perish."

For his timely "whiff of grapeshot," Napoleon was rewarded by receiving command of troops ready to go against Austrian soldiers in Italy. At the same time, he married Josephine de Beauharnais, a graceful Creole widow. So the general spent most of their honeymoon poring over maps before embarking on this campaign, considered one of the most brilliant in military history.

Then in 1799, when he returned home, he carried out a coup to seize power for himself. Soon a constitution was concocted to set up Napoleon as dictator of France.

In only four months, the *Code Napoléon* was framed. This civil code, printed in pocket-sized form, could easily be consulted by any citizen concerned about his or her rights. Still operating in France, it is the most widely copied legal system since Roman times, used from Egypt to Japan to Chile to Quebec.

Napoleon's propaganda promoted advancement based not on birth, but on ability. That is, there were "careers open to talent." His army marshals were drawn from the people and were often very young. They were gifted in a new kind of warfare—huge armies attacking each other in swift bayonet attacks.

Napoleon was ambitious, and his ambition was to conquer all of Europe. In 1805, he assembled a huge force to cross the English Channel and strike Britain, which had opposed his expansionist plans. But when the Austrians joined the fight against him, he redirected his army toward them and easily triumphed.

Only 42 days later, Napoleon at Austerlitz (in present day Czechoslovakia) faced the Russians, who unwittingly fell into his trap. It was his greatest victory. Other generals had won decisively—notably Julius Caesar over the Celts—but never had such mastery been shown over peoples at the same level of technology.

The next year, Napoleon conquered Prussia, and all of western Europe was his.

Liberals throughout Europe saw religion and monarchy as so much mumbo-jumbo.* Its myths should be squashed, they felt, so that reason might prevail. Two new myths were destined to come out of this new age—that of progress, supported by science and industry; and nationalism, founded on military power.

Napoleon pointed the way to a new kind of unity, based on the idea of the nation. The French had achieved it, as had the Americans. In time so would other peoples, notably the Germans and Italians. He saw himself as the Soldier of the Revolution as he spread—on the tips of bayonets—the ideals of liberty, equality, and fraternity.

Yet at home in France, there was no freedom of the press, few restrictions on the greed of the rich, and little brotherhood beyond that found in his army. Napoleon's ambition for Europe, in fact, was to turn it into a huge colony providing raw materials for French manufacturing. To achieve this end he placed his enemy, Britain, under a blockade.

In 1812, Czar Alexander declared that he would no longer help Napoleon by keeping up the blockade. So Napoleon invaded Russia with 600 000 men. "Perhaps he will yield at the sight of my unprecedented weapons," he said. "If not, well, let destiny be accomplished."

The 67-year-old Russian commander, Michael Kutuzov, was slow to act but full of wisdom. "Moscow," he said, "will be the sponge that will suck him in."

After a ferocious battle before Moscow, Napoleon realized one of his loftiest dreams by taking the Russian capital on September 14. But almost immediately, arsonists set Moscow on fire. "To burn one's own cities!" Napoleon exclaimed. "What savage determination! What a people! What a people!"

---

*See page 208.

Napoleon waited for Alexander to sue for peace. But the Czar would sooner "eat potatoes with the lowliest of my peasants in the depths of Siberia." Napoleon for the first time was unsure of what to do. He took five weeks to order a retreat, and by then his men faced one of the coldest winters in memory. Their famous retreat in the snow took the incredible toll of half a million lives.

Meanwhile in Spain, another disaster was unfolding for Napoleon. Off Trafalgar in 1805, the British had been saved by the decisive victory of their navy, under Lord Nelson. Then on land, they persevered to discover many of Napoleon's military secrets, and defeat him, together with help of Spanish guerrillas.

In the east, Prussian and Russian armies dealt Napoleon such crippling blows that, in 1814, they entered Paris and took him captive. They sent him into exile on the Italian island of Elba.

Then came the most fantastic adventure of all. Boldly, Napoleon escaped from Elba, and with a tiny force again took all of France. Now, having been declared an outlaw by the European community, he saw that his only hope to prevent an alliance of his enemies was by defeating them separately.

This very nearly happened. But on a soggy field near the Belgian town of Waterloo, the British held back wave after wave of Napoleon's cavalry, until the Prussians arrived and his era was at last ended.

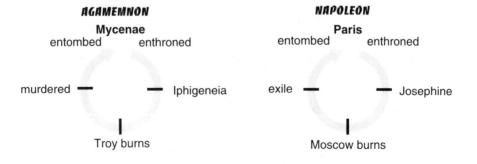

Wheels of justice

Napoleon had spread revolutionary dreams. People longed to be rid of unjust laws, and the fear of dungeons and the gallows. They wished to belong to genuine nations, not lands that were ruled by foreign powers. They wanted the freedom to share in their own government—applying reason to political choice, then voting accordingly.

But the Congress of Vienna killed these dreams. It forged a medieval-style union of states, defending Europe against the "moral gangrene" of liberalism. Traditional order took precedence over liberty, nationhood, and the vote. Central Europe stagnated, and refugees from its oppressive regimes began flooding into North America. Both Germany and Italy were left in fragments, not to become true nations for another half-century—whereupon their fiery nationalism would upset Europe all over again.

After Waterloo, Napoleon was sent to the remote Atlantic island of St. Helena. Here he dictated his memoirs before dying in 1821. Later he was reburied in Paris, with this inscription on his tomb: *It is my wish to have my bones rest on the Seine's banks among the Frenchmen I loved so much.*

Humpty Dumpty sat on a wall,
Humpty Dumpty had a great fall.
All the king's horses,
And all the king's men,
Couldn't put Humpty together again.

NURSERY RHYME

Balancing Everything Out

Is there justice in the world? Is some divine force at work, balancing everything out? The Biblical view is that God, though often full of wrath, is ultimately fair. So the bitter wars described in the Bible were felt to be just.

Today, aggression finds its outlet in sports. Campaigns fought on football fields substitute for those once waged with guns. Wrestling bouts are blood feuds in which the fans hold passionate loyalties.

The spirit of battle might extend, as Dave shows, even to the age-old friction between general and soldier. His story might illustrate a kind of symmetry in which two wrongs make a right.

An Argument

I play juvenile baseball, just about any position except for catcher because I'm left-handed. Also, I hit .387 this season. But apparently my stats weren't good enough for my coach, because he only played the guys he liked.

You probably guessed it, during the championships I was collecting splinters the whole tournament. Finally the coach said to the four guys sitting out the game, "Hey, you guys, warm up, stay loose."

I wasn't paying attention, and said, "What?"

I heard him repeat his request and I slowly made my way up to my feet. The coach then said, "What's wrong, don't you want to play?"

"Yeah," I replied, "but I'm always sitting and I get quite STIFF, coach."

Well, that started quite an argument. I called the coach names that I should not have—but then again, it made him think. I was benched for five innings, until the top of the ninth when I pinch-hit for the third baseman.

After the game I was immediately taken off next year's roster. But my yelling at the coach had made other players look up to me, as their leader. They had the same thoughts as I did, but were too afraid to express them.

Tulsi Das, the Hindu poet, created the tale of Hanuman and his army of monkeys. Years afterwards, a despot imprisoned him in a stone tower. Alone in his cell, he fell to meditating, and from his meditation came Hanuman and his monkey army, who laid low the city, broke open the tower, and freed Tulsi Das.

RICHARD BURTON, *THE BOOK OF FANTASY*

16. Return

I would have run to him, only I was a coward in the presence of such a mob—would have embraced him, only, being an Englishman, I did not know how he would receive me; so I did what cowardice and false pride suggested was the best thing—walked deliberately to him, took off my hat, and said:

"Dr. Livingstone, I presume?"

HENRY M. STANLEY, *HOW I FOUND LIVINGSTONE*

Odysseus and Penelope *Greek*

Penelope harassed by suitors

Odysseus, king of Ithaca, gained high renown in the Battle of Troy,* for it was he who devised the trickery of the wooden horse. But its aftermath brought many ordeals to Odysseus, and not for a long while would he return to his island home and to his wife, Penelope.

For Poseidon showed his displeasure, and Odysseus and his crews were swept far off course soon after departing from Troy. They first came ashore in the realm of the Lotus-eaters, who taste only the honeyed fruit that drugs them. Odysseus had to exert brute force to drag his sailors back to the ships.

At the next landing, Odysseus, with a dozen men, entered a cave to wait for the owner's return. It was a Cyclops, Polyphemus, who herded his sheep inside and then closed the door with a massive boulder. This oaf, discovering visitors, began to devour them in pairs, but Odysseus managed to blind the beast. He then lashed his men beneath the thick-wooled rams and curled himself under another. At dawn the Cyclops released his flock, unaware that they carried his tormentors to safety.

Odysseus and his sailors met a more gracious welcome at the floating island of Aeolia. Here the king gave him a magical bag of the winds, which imprisoned every breeze but the favourable ones. Odysseus sailed all the way back to the waters of Ithaca, but his men, looking for treasure, opened the bag, and the wrong winds blew him right back to Aeolia.

After many more adventures, they reached the wooded island of Aeaea, and an exploring party came to a stone house. At the doorway appeared Circe, the beautiful enchantress. All entered but the group's leader, who suspected a trap. And sure enough, she touched each of them with her wand and their bodies sprouted bristles, hooves, and curly tails. The men had become pigs—but still with the minds of men, for they wept real tears.

When their leader told Odysseus what had happened, he set out to rescue his men. On the way he was lucky enough to meet the god Hermes, who provided a milk-white flower and invaluable advice. "When Circe offers

---

*See pages 172-173.

food you must sniff this herb as an antidote," said the god. "When she strikes you with her wand, draw your sword and threaten her with her life."

Everything happened as the god had predicted, and the enchantress fell sobbing at Odysseus's feet, quite within his power. She promptly obeyed his demand for the release of his men and even made them taller and more handsome than before.

Then she begged him to draw his ship onto the land and return with the rest of his men. He did, and she proved to be so charming a hostess that they stayed for an entire year.

When Odysseus spoke of returning to Ithaca, Circe arranged for him to hear a prophecy by the blind prophet, Tiresias. For this, Odysseus had to sail into the Land of the Dead.

Across the sea went Odysseus to a foggy realm of eternal night, where two rivers poured into the Underworld. He dug a trench and filled it with the blood of two sheep. Up came the spirits of the dead to drink, in a wailing multitude. With his sword, Odysseus held them at bay until he saw the ghost of Tiresias.

"Poseidon still intends harm toward you," Tiresias warned, "but you must especially avoid offending Helios, the Sun-Titan. When you come upon his cattle, let them not be touched!"

On his return journey home, the first peril Odysseus faced was the Sirens' Isle. "None has heard the voice of the Sirens and returned to his home," Circe had warned him. "For the song bewitches them into coming ashore to certain death." Yet he hoped to hear the Sirens' song and live. So the hero had his sailors tie him securely to the mast, and ordered them to fill their ears with wax.

Even as this was done, a strange misty calm fell on the sea. Out of the haze appeared the Sirens' Isle. And as the ship drew closer, the men could see that the island was littered with corpses, skin still drooping from the bones.

Meanwhile Odysseus heard the Sirens' song, a melody of indescribable loveliness. What a horrible torment it was—to be shackled, unable to go toward the women who made such music. Even though he begged and pleaded with his men, the crew released him only after the danger had passed.

But more danger awaited the men ahead. On one side of a strait was the monster Charybdis, who made a violent whirlpool by swallowing the water and spouting it forth. Within a cave on the other side lurked Scylla, a horrible creature with six heads. It was able to pluck and devour six sailors—like fish whipped from the sea by an angler's rod—before Odysseus could get the ship through.

When the men came ashore for the night, they heard the lowing of cattle. "Those are the sacred cattle of Hyperion," said Odysseus. "You must swear not to touch them." The sailors obeyed him, until adverse winds kept the ship penned in and provisions dwindled. Then hunger drove some of them to slaughter several cows. Their flesh bellowed aloud, even on the spits, and the hides crawled.

The gale dropped, the men embarked, but a black cloud immediately came overhead. Hyperion had appealed to Zeus, and now the god came down to blast the ship with one thunderbolt. The only survivor was Odysseus, who rode out the sea and came ashore on the island of the beautiful Calypso.

In her cavern by the sea, Calypso cared for Odysseus tenderly. For seven years this went on, as she tried to make him immortal like herself. But he would only sit gloomily on the shore, staring across the sea in the direction of Ithaca.

Tiresias had told Odysseus of the plight endured by Penelope. Continually she was troubled by suitors—Odysseus being thought dead—who demanded that she choose a new husband. Penelope promised to decide after she had finished her weaving, which she would unravel every night. But her suitors had discovered her trick, and now were more restless than ever.

At this time Athena took pity on Odysseus. He had been her favourite before the sacrilege, and now persuaded Zeus to let the poor fellow return homeward. Calypso was informed of the gods' will and gave him an axe with which he fashioned a sturdy boat.

So off he sailed and landed amid heavy seas on the island of Phaeacia.

Odysseus, stripped naked by the violent surf, was discovered on the beach by Nausicaa, the king's young daughter. Her friends scampered away at the sight of his salt-caked body, but she stayed to hear his plea. "Twenty days have I struggled on the wine-dark sea," he said, "and I ask only that you provide some humble garment and lead me to your town."

"Your words show you to be neither villain nor fool," Nausicaa replied. "I will fulfil your wishes."

Nausicaa had suitable clothing brought to Odysseus, and led him to the palace. After being warmly entertained, he told his story in a way that touched the hearts of all. That very night, Phaeacian sailors transported the wanderer to Ithaca. He was home at last.

But ahead lay the greatest test of all. What support could he hope to find against the unruly mob of suitors besieging Penelope?

Just before Odysseus had returned, his son, Telemachus, came back after searching throughout Greece for his father. The suitors, resenting the young prince's opposition to them, now plotted his death.

When Telemachus appeared, Athena briefly transformed the aging hero to his former self. "Surely you are a god!" cried the youth in astonishment. "Be gracious, that I may sacrifice to you!"

"You see no god," replied Odysseus. "I am truly your father."

He kissed his son. Slowly the truth dawned on Telemachus. Then, throwing himself on Odysseus's neck, he cried tears of relief.

Odysseus now executed his plan. He stepped into the great hall of his palace, where the mob of suitors was lounging, and begged for scraps of food.

Then Penelope descended the staircase, and Odysseus was stunned to see that she was lovelier than ever.

"You have pressed me to select a new lord," said the queen, "and to prove your worthiness I give you the great bow of Odysseus. The winner shall be the man who can string it with ease and shoot an arrow through the rings of twelve axes set in a row."

The great bow was given to the first suitor. He stood and struggled to bend it, but his hands soon grew weary. He passed it on, but the next man met with no greater success.

Odysseus knew that his moment had arrived. "Hear me, suitors to our honoured queen!" he said. "Let me once try the strength of my aging limbs at this task."

The men were infuriated. "You shabby wretch," sneered one of them, Antinous. "Is it not enough that we let you dine in our midst? Know your place!"

Penelope intervened by saying, "If this stranger has the power to string this bow, let him try."

But Telemachus had joined in the plot with Odysseus and knew that bloodshed was imminent. "Mother, you know that the bow is a man's matter," he said. "Go now to your room and allow me to make the decision." And Penelope, surprised to see her son display so much authority, went to her bedroom, where she cried herself to sleep out of yearning for her true husband.

Odysseus took the weapon, inspecting it for any flaws it might have gotten in his long absence. And as effortlessly as a minstrel fitting a string to his harp, he strung the bow.

The suitors gasped in amazement. Then Odysseus, without rising from his seat, aimed at the axe-rings and missed not a one.

"Telemachus, I have not disgraced you," said Odysseus. He leaped up, took his stand at the threshold, and sent an arrow straight through the throat of Antinous. The others scanned the walls for their spears and shields, but all had been removed by Telemachus. Odysseus's bow hummed arrow after arrow, his son flung a barrage of spears, and soon the dead lay in heaps.

Odysseus called for the serving-maids. He ordered them to remove the bodies, sponge the hall clean, and fumigate it with fire and sulphur. Then he commanded that Penelope be told of her husband's return.

Athena restored the hero to his former magnificence,

and added even greater height and strength. When the queen reappeared, however, she gave no sign of recognition, and Odysseus became troubled. "After twenty years, no other wife could have kept out of her husband's arms!" he said.

"I remember too well the man who sailed from Ithaca," Penelope replied. "I will order the servants to make up the bed outside his chamber."

"Now who has moved my bed?" Odysseus demanded. "That would be some feat, because the bedroom was built around the trunk of an olive-tree, which serves as the bed-post!"

Penelope began to tremble. She had heard the proof she had been looking for. Then she threw herself into Odysseus's arms, and kissed him.

"I've always feared that some man would win me through deceit," she sobbed. "But only my husband would know the secret of the olive-tree." She clung to his neck, unable to let him go.

Odysseus wept as he held Penelope in his embrace. This was the happiness of swimmers, struggling against the rushing surf to stand on earth once again.

Meeting at Night

The grey sea and the long black land;
And the yellow half-moon large and low;
And the startled little waves that leap
In fiery ringlets from their sleep,
As I gain the cove with pushing prow,
And quench its speed in the slushy sand.
Then a mile of warm sea-scented beach;
Three fields to cross till a farm appears;
A tap at the pane, the quick sharp scratch
And blue spurt of a lighted match,
And a voice less loud, through its joys and fears,
Than the two hearts beating each to each!

Robert Browning

The Rightful Kingdom

A great mythic moment comes when Odysseus, after many wanderings, strings the royal bow. He has returned to claim the rightful kingdom.

Odysseus at first is lost in a world of marvels and must rely on his own resources. But energy flows, as always, from such experiences. He outwits the Trojans with his trick of the wooden horse,* outwits the Cyclops with his ruse, outwits Circe with the charmed herb.

But a new side of Odysseus is tapped when he meets Circe. A fearsome woman she is and yet, it turns out, gracious and compassionate as well. It is with her aid that Odysseus ventures upon the Land of the Dead—a trip demanding powers greater than mere cleverness.

What makes Odysseus's journeys so meaningful, states M.L. Finlay, is that "he returns with something like full knowledge of what life affords." The gods intervene, of course, and this aspect of Greek myth is hard for modern researchers to fathom. Yet the god's presence lends to Odysseus's adventure a moral dimension not found in other early myths. Chaotic as the events may appear, we see that Athena represents a principle of divine order.

Homer's Odyssey stands as the first quest romance—the great story of the hero's homeward return. His tale projects heroism, but also a longing for the harmonies of ordinary society: family and friends. It inspired James Joyce to imagine, in 20th century Dublin, an adventure tale based on the same journey.

Her eyes had called him and his soul had leaped at the call. To live, to err, to fall, to triumph, to recreate life out of life! A wild angel had appeared to him, the angel of mortal youth and beauty, an envoy from the fair courts of life.

JAMES JOYCE, *PORTRAIT OF THE ARTIST AS A YOUNG MAN*

---

*See pages 172-173.

Jim and Nora *Irish*

Every June 16, Dublin is crisscrossed by admirers of a novel, *Ulysses*. Written by James Joyce, it describes events of that single day in the year 1904—fictitious events, set in real places. Many wear period costumes as they relive these events on the "Bloomsday Stroll," so called after a major character named Leopold Bloom. He is the Odysseus in Joyce's great novel, which vividly updates the *Odyssey* of Homer.

Joyce, born in 1882, gained much of his early education from the *Odyssey*. But its pagan view of life contrasted with that of the Catholic Church, which commanded the allegiance of 95 percent of the Irish people.

For a while, Joyce aspired to become a priest, as spiritual matters held so much interest that earthly pleasures appeared puny by comparison. But then came an awakening to the things of this world, described vividly in his early novel, *A Portrait of the Artist as a Young Man*.

Fictionalized as "Stephen Dedalus," Joyce walks to a beach facing the sea and "Europe of strange tongues." Stephen hears his friends call his last name, that of the "fabulous artificer" Daedalus.* Suddenly, he has a vision of the Greek hero. "A hawklike man flying sunward above the sea."

Stephen takes off his shoes to enter the sea's waters—his baptism into the life of an artist. Then there comes an extraordinary vision.

"A girl stood before him in midstream; alone and still, gazing out to sea." The hawklike man is a Classical symbol, but the girl is a Christian one—the bird of the Holy Spirit.

It is the goddess. Stephen cries out to meet this "envoy from the fair courts of life" and to leap at her call. Stephen resolves to become a priest of art, fashioning worlds of the imagination.

Joyce's now-famous vision fictionalizes his first glimpse of Nora Barnacle. Raised on Ireland's west coast, the

*See pages 90-91.

daughter of an alcoholic baker, she was beaten by an uncle one night for staying out against orders. Within a week she had fled to Dublin and was working at a hotel when Joyce met her.

Although piously Catholic, Nora belonged very much to the world of the here-and-now. This red-haired beauty with a proud walk excited Joyce and he asked her out, on a day known to every lover of Joyce's books: June 16, 1904.

For Joyce, Nora became the perfect companion. And on the evening of October 8, just four months after they had first met, the two left Dublin on the night-boat to England, never to return. Yet during their many years in Europe, Nora served as Joyce's "portable Ireland." The native wit, humour, and remarkable wisdom of this unflappable woman fed his genius. She was his Maeve, his Mother Earth. *

Joyce was fascinated by the ritual of Mass, whereby priests transformed ordinary bread and wine into the body and blood of Christ. As a writer he did something similar. Always he looked for an epiphany** by which real-life events take on a spiritual glow.

The epiphany technique appears both in *A Portrait* and an earlier work, a short-story collection entitled *Dubliners*. But Joyce's masterpiece, presenting a vision of life found only in the greatest literature, is the novel whose title is the Latin form of Odysseus's name: *Ulysses*.

The mind's rich flow of images and thoughts is captured in a "stream-of-consciousness" technique. Where did Joyce pick it up? Apparently from letters written by Nora to him in 1909, when he briefly revisited Ireland. Scant punctuation, loose sentence structure, everything running together—these features of Nora's style were to be hailed as spectacular innovations when used by Joyce.

An enchantment with everyday reality, with the delicious quirks of mankind, make *Ulysses* a very funny book. "I go to bed and then that man sits in his room and continues laughing about his own writing," Nora complained. "And then I knock on the door and say, 'Now Jim, stop writing or stop laughing.'"

---

*See pages 58-66.
**See page 54.

Leopold Bloom, a Jewish advertising salesman, is depicted as a modern Odysseus journeying through Dublin before returning to his wife, Molly. The city represents the entire Mediterranean world, and the 20-year time span is reduced to an action-packed 24 hours.

There are many ingenious parallels. The Sirens are a pair of singing barmaids, luring passersby to drink. Aeolia and the bag of winds become a newspaper office and the "hot air" of journalism. The Underworld is a cemetery, where Bloom attends a funeral. Circe is transformed into a brothel-owner named Bella Cohen.

Stephen Dedalus reappears in the novel as a kind of Telemachus. His hope of finding a true father is realized when he meets Bloom. And Bloom visualizes Stephen as his own son, who had died at 11. Thus the dead are, in effect, brought back to life.

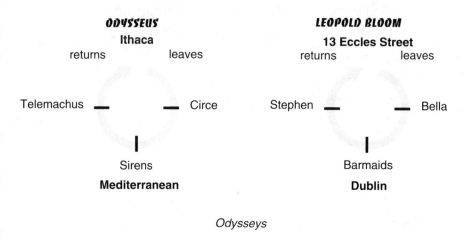

Odysseys

The book's publication was a feat in itself. In 1918, when one sexually-explicit section of Ulysses was printed in a U.S. magazine, the Post Office confiscated every copy on the charge of obscenity, and its editors were fined and fingerprinted. Finally in 1922, Sylvia Beach, an American operating a Paris bookshop, published the manuscript—a huge task, because it comprised much-corrected notes on little scraps of paper.

Joyce was firmly upheld by Nora in his dire struggle with poverty, blindness, customs officials, and censors. "If only I had married a ragpicker or a farmer," she once reflected, "or anything but a writer." Yet she loved Joyce—not for his genius, but for what was down-to-earth about him. And without Nora, he probably would not have been able to bring his towering works to the world.

Despite failing eyesight, Joyce completed his last book, *Finnegan's Wake*, not long before his death in 1941—a decade before Nora's passing. It was composed as an elaborate dream.

from *A Portrait of the Artist as a Young Man*

He turned to the flyleaf of his geography and read what he had written there: himself, his name and where he was:

Stephen Dedalus
Class of Elements
Clongowes Wood College
Sallins
County Kildare
Ireland
Europe
The World
The Universe

The Prize

The rock singer, after years of obscurity, steps forward to accept her award for female vocalist of the year. The substitute tackle, after three seasons as a benchwarmer, runs onto the field as his team receives the trophy.

The quest's goal is a prize, a reward for labours. And the Odysseus myth—both in itself and as lived by James Joyce—dramatically tells of crossing the return threshold to claim the prize of esteem.

Today, backpackers taking the regular Italy-to-Greece ferry will pass near the steep and wooded island of Ithaca. But few will know or care that this mythic isle is right there, off the starboard bow. They will be thinking about their own islands, shaping their own myths of adventure and quest.

Later comes the return, back to the normal world. There will be photos and souvenirs to show, of course, but a greater prize is that of experience.

To give others the benefit of that experience, to tell them about the dearly-won Grail, is often the hope. Yet people may not be eager to applaud the hero's deed. And perhaps, as Gord states, it might not even be known.

So Much Inside

I can well understand the futile efforts of the hero in myths, trying to explain his experiences to people on his return. For me, it's like coming back to school at the end of the summer holidays.

One has so much built up inside, so much personally-important experience. But it would be almost impossible to pass that eyewitness experience on to someone else.

No one will exactly know what great tasks you've accomplished, what you had to endure, how much you have grown inside. You return from your journey, and nobody at home assumes anything. Nobody knows what bubbles and quakes inside you, apart from what little overflows in the form of modest words.

But I suppose the hero must often accept such a return. Those who are unaware can hardly be expected to welcome you back with open arms and tears in their eyes.

The hero of romance is analogous to the mythical Messiah or deliverer who comes from an upper world, and his enemy is analogous to the demonic powers of a lower world. The conflict however takes place in, or at any rate primarily concerns, *our world*, which is in the middle....

NORTHROP FRYE, *ANATOMY OF CRITICISM*

17. Harmony

Hozho: Navaho word expressing life's basic goal: happiness, beauty, goodness, harmony

Gemütlichkeit: German word denoting a wished-for atmosphere: happiness, cosiness, well-being, harmony

Marduk and Tiamat *Babylonian*

In the beginning the whole world was water. Nothing could be found in the water, not a reed nor a grain of sand, and there was no sky. Apsu ruled over the fresh waters, and the salt waters belonged to Tiamat, mother of all.

For countless ages, the world was changeless. Then the waters were streaked with silt, fathered by Apsu and given birth by Tiamat. And over the silt ruled the first god and the first goddess.

Strands of silt wandered about and then thickened until they split the sea. The horizons appeared, each with its own god. Then the dome of heaven was filled with air and ruled by Anu.

Ea, lord of the earth, was fathered by Anu. Many other gods would follow, but none with the wisdom of Ea, who forever searched for the truth. No secret could be kept from him, and there was no magic feat he could not perform.

Gods in great numbers were born. They clustered, surged restlessly back and forth, and danced wildly.

Tiamat and Apsu, who had never known motion, were very much upset.

"No sleep at night, no rest by day!" Apsu cried. "These gods must be destroyed!"

"But these are our grandchildren," said Tiamat. "We should treat them gently."

But Apsu vowed to destroy the gods. Ea, knowing his intention at once, informed the other gods, and they were plunged into despair. But Ea, chanting a magic spell over a pitcher of water, poured its contents over Apsu and put him into deep slumber. Then Ea put him to death.

Tiamat, enraged, plotted revenge. She created eleven flaming monsters and placed at their head a new husband, Kingu. When they advanced, even Ea and Anu fled in terror. "Who can save us now?" they cried.

Ea built a secret chamber at the very heart of Apsu. Here, his wife gave birth to Marduk, who was greater than any god before him. Fire shot from his lips, lightning from his eyes. Born fully grown, he came before the gods' assembly and declared, "I will conquer Tiamat, but you must proclaim me as your leader!"

"Reveal your powers," the gods urged. They placed a garment on the earth, and Marduk with only one word made it vanish. With another word, it reappeared. "Marduk is King!" exclaimed the gods, and they placed a crown upon his head.

Marduk now armed himself for combat, first hanging a wondrous bow and arrows at his side. For protection against Tiamat's enchantments, he rubbed red powders on his face and hid a sacred herb in his tunic. He made a giant net to ensnare her, then mounted the chariot of the winds, and set the lightning before it. With the mace of the thunder in his grip and a fearful radiance flashing from his face, the king of the gods rode forth.

Kingu and his army of monsters fled in panic at once. But Tiamat stood firm, shouting, "Meet me in single combat and die!" Shrieking spells and shaking terribly, she lunged at Marduk with open jaws.

But Marduk was ready for Tiamat. Into her mouth he drove the storm winds, all the way down into her belly. The god flung his net, completely trapping Tiamat in its coils. Then he sent an arrow into her cavernous mouth, and when it pierced the heart, she slumped dead at his feet.

Marduk brought the thunder-mace down hard on Tiamat's skull. Her spurting blood was carried by the North Wind to far places. Then the god split her enormous body into two halves. From the bottom part he made the earth, and from the other he formed the sky.

In the sky Marduk placed lights. He made the moon a creature of the night, and every month gave her a new crown. But it would always dim at the approach of the sun, which was made to be her superior. Finally Marduk placed the stars in their constellations and sent a god into every part of the universe to be its ruler.

"Who will serve to us?" the gods asked Marduk. "We must have servants to support us while we do our tasks."

"I will make a puppet from bones and arteries," he replied, "and its name will be Humankind." And so it was Kingu's flesh being used for this purpose.

The gods built a great city for Marduk, Babylon, and placed in its centre a sacred temple, the ziggurat. When his kingship was reaffirmed, he proclaimed the rules and destinies of the universe. Each New Year this would be done in a ritual renewing the people.

In a chamber atop the ziggurat, the royal bed was prepared. Here Marduk and the goddess Ishtar were united in Sacred Marriage. This achieved, everyone knew that crops would grow abundantly and that all would be well.

The force that through the green fuse drives the flower

The force that through the green fuse drives the flower
Drives my green age; that blasts the roots of trees
Is my destroyer.
And I am dumb to tell the crooked rose
My youth is bent by the same wintry fever.

The force that drives the water through the rocks
Drives my red blood; that dries the mouthing streams
Turns mine to wax.
And I am dumb to mouth unto my veins
How at the mountain spring the same mouth sucks.

The hand that whirls the water in the pool
Stirs the quicksand; that ropes the blowing wind
Hauls my shroud sail.
And I am dumb to tell the hanging man
How of my clay is made the hangman's lime.

The lips of time leech to the fountain head;
Love drips and gathers, but the fallen blood
Shall calm her sores.
And I am dumb to tell a weather's wind
How time has ticked a heaven round the stars.

And I am dumb to tell the lover's tomb
How at my sheet goes the same crooked worm.

DYLAN THOMAS

Establishing Peace

After the triumph, it is time for that thing called existence. Drinking deep from the cup of life, we experience harmony.

It's like playing baseball and reaching the playoffs. We have had our bruises, and maybe there was bad blood with another team. But now the hurt is transformed into something higher. There is an exultation.

The Marduk myth, given in the epic known as the *Enuma Elish*, was the creation story of ancient Babylon. The people enacted it in an elaborate rite, known from old clay documents luckily preserved. It took the form of an elaborate pageant held every New Year.

In the pageant's first days, Marduk—played by the real king—was said to have disappeared into the Underworld, to fight an epic battle with the monster Tiamat. The people mourned Marduk's absence and ran about "searching" for their leader. Finally, the king re-emerged in triumph. On the tenth day, he was united with the Chief Priestess in Sacred Marriage.

Here, as in other ancient communities, the rite expressed a universal harmony. Earth had returned to its point of origin, wound up like a clock for the coming year.

Next, the king would ride a chariot in a fine marriage procession, his consort joining him in a boat on wheels. On the eleventh day, the king set down laws just as Marduk had done. And on the twelfth, farmers began the year's ploughing, confident that all would be well.

The ancient Babylonian temple, the ziggurat, had seven terraced storeys, representing the planets' seven spheres—the source of our very ancient expression "in seventh heaven." Its tip, where the Sacred Marriage occurred, was the lightning-rod, the fuse, through which the energies of heaven poured into the earth.

A Babylonian ziggurat

It was in Babylon, it seems, that gods were first assigned to the major heavenly bodies.* Apparently this scheme coincided with its week of seven days, which was adopted around 400 A.D. in Rome and still governs our lives.

---

*See pages 260-261.

With righteousness in the heart, beauty will be in the character.
With beauty in the character, harmony will be in the home.
With harmony in the home, order will be in the nation.
With order in the nation, peace will be in the world.

CONFUCIUS

The Sons of Heaven *Chinese/Japanese*

Doom eventually came to the world's first civilizations, those of Babylon and Egypt. But that of China, formed not quite as early, exists to the present day. Thus it is the oldest culture in the world.

China's mythology centred upon heaven—not in the sense of an afterlife, but of universal harmony. The Chinese felt awe at the cosmic progression of the stars and the orderly passage of the seasons. And people fit into the universe, they believed, exactly where the forces of heaven and earth connected.

Yu-Ti, the Emperor of Heaven, had counterparts on earth who ruled by a "mandate from heaven." These earthly emperors performed a priestly role, conducting the sacrifices by which earth addressed heaven. During the Chou dynasty (1122–249 B.C.), emperors began to call themselves the Sons of Heaven.

In the 6th century B.C., Confucius, the great Chinese philosopher, stressed that emperors must follow the way of Heaven. He also taught respect for one's ancestors, still important to the Chinese today. Indeed, the idea that royal ancestors rule from heaven was basic to emperor worship from the start. This provided a link between the spirit world and the living.

The same era produced a religion of the Tao, meaning "way" or "path." To follow the natural way, as animals do, would bring all things into harmony. For Yin (passivity, darkness, winter, etc.) must be attuned with Yang (activity, light, summer, etc.). The Taoist symbol shows such harmony between Yin and Yang that each invades the other's hemisphere.

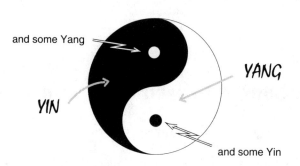

Yin and Yang

Harmony is symbolized by the layout of the Chinese capital city, Beijing. It is perfectly aligned to the four cardinal points of the compass. At its heart is the Forbidden City and at its centre—at the centre of China and the ancient Chinese world itself—is the Hall of Supreme Harmony. Built in 1609, it still holds the throne once occupied by the emperor.

In the Hall of Supreme Harmony, says a classic text, "earth and sky meet, the four seasons merge, wind and rain are gathered in, and Yin and Yang are in harmony."

At the winter solstice (around December 21) the Yin of winter was said to hold all things in its embrace. So that the Yang of summer might release itself and allow the growing season to begin, the emperor would have to approach heaven.

Throughout the year, the emperor faced south from the Forbidden City so as to receive his subjects' worship. But at the winter solstice, he would be carried southward to the Altar of Heaven, then northward to mount it, for it was the emperor, now, who did the worshipping.

The vast courtyard was built as a square to symbolize the earth. The marble altar is round to represent heaven, with shrines for the sun, moon, and five planets. So when the emperor mounted the altar's three terraces, he symbolically passed from earth to heaven. And from heaven, through his person, all power and goodness descended.

Century after century, the monarch rose at dawn each winter solstice to pray and then preside over the sacrifice. Even after the railway came to China (in the mid 1800s), all trains would be stopped on the day of the solstice, for fear that the sound might disturb the sacred moment. This unfathomably ancient rite, perhaps four thousand years old, did not come to an end until 1911.

Meanwhile in Japan, emperors ruled as well. Also called Sons of Heaven, they first gained the throne some 25 centuries ago. But not until 608 A.D., when an embassy returned from the Chinese court with new administrative ideas, did Japan's system become truly imperial.

Later the emperors were established in the city of Kyoto, laid out in a checkerboard pattern modelled after that of the Chinese capital. And chronicles were written to tell the unusual myths of these ancient emperors.

Amaterasu, the sun-goddess, says the myth, was the ruling deity. She was given a five-strand necklace as a symbol of her supremacy. Her brother, Susanoo, received a sword which showed his status as god of the ocean, but many arguments developed between the two.

Once, when Susanoo approached heaven, he made such a noise that Amaterasu asked for proof of his goodwill. He proposed that they should create children by the exchange of pledges. So Amaterasu, taking his sword, chewed it up and blew three goddesses from her mouth. Susanoo crunched her jewels in his teeth, then breathed out five gods—from the oldest of whom descended the first emperor.

Even up until 1946, the emperor of Japan was declared to be a god. Children would lose their sight, it was said, if they looked directly at the Son of Heaven. So if he went out in his carriage, the Japanese had to shutter all windows above street level so that no one could look down.

Emperor Hirohito came to the throne in 1926 as the 124th Living God. Then two decades later, after Japan's defeat in World War II, he renounced "the false conception that the emperor is divine."

The prince, Akihito, ascended to the world's oldest monarchy four hours after Hirohito's death. In the brief and silent ritual he was given replicas of ancient imperial treasures—the sword and jewels first received by the gods.

Chinese Emperor's Sacrificial Ode

Let me give praise, give praise—
The way of Heaven is shown.
It is not easy to preserve it,
But say not that Heaven is remote.
For it rises and descends above us,
Daily heeding what we do.

I remain only a child,
Inexperienced at giving honour.
But daily I grow in learning,
As I aspire to the glow of wisdom.
Help to raise me up
And show a virtuous life.

As Above, So Below

There will always be wrangling. People are forever exploding in anger, giving vent to their hatred in murder and destruction. But we may also expect the return of harmony, a time when things have somehow worked out.

To learn whether an undertaking is likely to succeed on a certain day, many have turned (and still turn) to astrology. This works on an ancient principle: "as above, so below." Earthly events are said to be influenced by movements in the sky—notably the zodiac, a dozen star constellations in a narrow corridor running a complete arc around the sky.

As the earth revolves around the sun, a different zodiacal constellation comes into view each month. In the evening as the sky darkens, this constellation will swing above the eastern horizon as if on a seesaw with the sun. Our zodiacal "sign"—the one in the sky at our birth—is said to produce personality traits, positive or negative.

Scientific studies of astrology have revealed no factual basis for its claims. Still, to contemplate the stars' harmonious sweep through the heavens is also to reflect on whatever harmonies operate within ourselves.

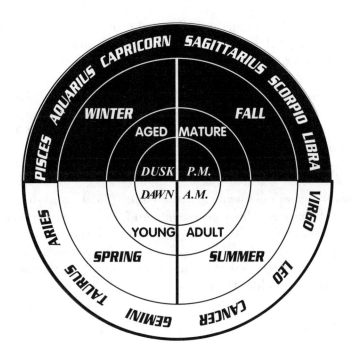

The Zodiac

This chart aligns each of the seasons with the zodiacal constellations ascendant at the time, and also with the four "seasons" of human life.

Astrology was born in ancient Babylon, spreading into Europe as well as eastward to China. The zodiac and its various powers were decreed by Marduk after his triumph, as the myth states. And here is Paul as Marduk, plunging into the midst of disorder and establishing peace.

The Foiled Revolution

Being a camp counsellor, of course, puts you in an authoritative position. But controlling the lives of the campers—that's the ultimate power.

Last summer I was awakened at about 3 a.m. by yelling and laughter. I figured someone else would handle it but finally felt obligated to investigate.

When I tried to open my door, I found it tied shut, and as I attempted to budge it, the oozy slime of Vaseline spread over my hands. These kids had thought of everything. It was a well-planned revolution.

Furious by this time, I managed to kick the door open. The grounds looked as if they had been decorated by a madman. Rolls of toilet paper were strewn everywhere, obscenities were spelled out in toothpaste on cabin walls, campers ran about half naked.

Apparently no other counsellor had heard any of this revolt. It was up to me to restore order.

When the campers saw me, silence came quickly, and they all took refuge in their beds. This was not enough for me. I made every one of these beasts, every last It-wasn't-me-Pauls, pick up each fragment of toilet paper, wash each wall, and then make their beds. I did not have to use force, yet they were suddenly at my command, though I was only a year or two older than them.

When peace was restored, I cleared my throat and returned to my one-roomed castle.

A man who has a vision is not able to use the power of it until after he has performed the vision on earth for the people to see.

BLACK ELK, OGLALA SIOUX SHAMAN

18. Revolt

✳

So long as there is life in the world, each generation will react against its predecessor, correct it, go beyond it. The house that accommodates the father never quite suits the children.

RICHARD LIVINGSTONE

The Olympians *Greek*

Chaos, formless and flowing space, came into being. And out of Chaos arose Gaia, wide-bosomed Earth, a firm standing-place for all.

While Gaia was asleep, she gave birth to the starry sky, Uranus. Equal to herself and covering her on all sides, he provided a home for the blessed gods. When Uranus sprinkled fertile rain upon Gaia, the waters gathered as streams, making the world a green habitat for countless species that crawled and walked, swam and flew.

Gaia's first children with Uranus were the Hundred-handed Giants, with fifty heads and a hundred arms. The Cyclopes appeared next, each with one wheel-like eye in the middle of its forehead. Then Gaia produced a superior race, the Titans—twelve majestic and beautiful forces of nature.

But Gaia was horrified to find Uranus thrusting all of these creatures into the earth's innermost regions. The sky-god lay so closely on her that they had no room, so she appealed to the Titans to rebel.

Cronus was the youngest and craftiest of the Titans, and he volunteered. Gaia presented him with a huge sickle made of hardest flint. Then at night, when Uranus slumped on Gaia, Cronus slashed at his genitals with the sickle. By castrating his father, he instantly separated sky from earth.

Uranus recoiled in pain and rose to his own lofty regions, never again to approach Gaia. Yet a terrible dread now troubled Cronus—that he too would be overthrown by his children.

So when Cronus mated with his sister Rhea and she gave birth, he resolved to destroy the child. Snatching the infant from Rhea's embrace, he opened his mouth and swallowed it.

Rhea had a second child, and it met the same fate. Five times Rhea conceived, five times Cronus gobbled down the newborn baby. But with her sixth child, she deceived her husband by handing him a large stone wrapped in cloth. Cronus duly devoured it without knowing that the real infant, Zeus, was safe and sound.

When Zeus came of age, Rhea urged him to seek vengeance on his father. She made him Cronus's cup-bearer. One day Zeus added a drug to the food, and Cronus became so ill that he vomited. Then all five of the swallowed children—along with the stone—came spewing out.

And now, under Zeus's leadership, the children of Cronus declared war against their father and the other Titans.

Zeus turned the tide of battle in his favour by drafting Uranus's monstrous sons. The Cyclopes forged deadly weapons—best of all the thunderbolts Zeus loved to hurl. The Hundred-handed Giants were like so many machine guns, shooting thick volleys of stones. Against all this fire-power, the Titans had no chance, and they suffered defeat.

The Titans fled westward to the distant Isle of the Blest. Here Cronus ruled over them in an everlasting Golden Age. But Atlas, the Titans' commander, was punished by Zeus and forced to hold up the sky on his back.*

The victors made a home on the high peak of Mount Olympus and were called the Olympian gods. Zeus, their chief, ruled the heavens as the All-Father. His brother,

---

*See pages 258-259.

Poseidon, commanded the seas from his golden palace beneath the waves, but was still considered as one of the Olympians. This was not true of Zeus' third brother, Hades, who lived in the Underworld as its king.

Three sisters survived the bitter conflict to gain Olympian glory. Demeter became the vegetation goddess; her spirit from that time on resided in all crops. Hestia was worshipped as goddess of the hearth. Hera, through marriage with Zeus, ruled as Queen of Heaven.

Zeus had children by many women. Hera bore two of them: the war-god Ares and Hephaestus, god of the forge. The latter had the enviable fortune of marrying the love-goddess, Aphrodite. Zeus's passion for the Titaness, Leto, led to the birth of Artemis and her twin brother Apollo,* and still another produced Hermes, the wing-footed messenger god.

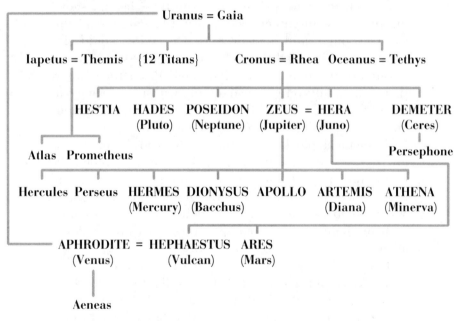

Greek gods and heroes

---

*See pages 68-69.

In the war that brought the Olympians to power, one of the Titans went over to the other side. This was Prometheus, whose name meant "forethought." He foresaw the Olympians' victory, and took their side.

Until that time there had been no mortal creatures. Now the gods fashioned them from a mixture of fire and earth, and Prometheus was asked to give them living characteristics. But his brother Epimetheus ("afterthought") objected. "Let me fashion these new beings, and you can inspect my work," he said, and Prometheus agreed.

Epimetheus began with the animals. He gave speed to some, nimbleness to others, and strength to a favoured few. Some he encased in armour, others he wrapped in a thick hide or coat of fur. Soon he used up this supply of features, leaving none for the creature known as humankind.

Prometheus took special interest in these beings, showing them how to gather food and use language. Still this wasn't enough, and he reflected. "One thing would give them warmth and light as well—a little bit of fire."

But fire belonged to the gods, and Prometheus knew that Zeus would refuse to share any with these new creatures. So the Titan decided to climb up Mount Olympus and secretly steal a spark of the divine fire.

Prometheus plucked a fennel plant, whose spongy hollow would conceal a burning coal. Then he climbed the mountain's jagged flank, entered the gods' palace, and approached the hearth where the goddess Hestia worked. When her back was turned, he deftly scooped an ember with his fennel-stalk, then sped down Olympus's slopes again.

The divine element uplifted the life and soul of humankind. But when tiny flickers of light punctured the darkness, Zeus saw them. He summoned Prometheus to answer for his crime and decreed that he be nailed to the rocks.

Prometheus was led away, but not before he had worried the king of gods with a prophecy: "Your fate will be like that of your father, Cronus, and his father, Uranus, before him. No god is aware of his fate, for I alone have this knowledge."

In the Caucasus mountains, Prometheus was fixed to a crag by a stake driven through his body. Every day an eagle came to gnaw away his liver, which grew whole in the night only to be torn again—and again and again, every day and every night.

Every hero becomes a bore at last.

RALPH WALDO EMERSON, "REPRESENTATIVE MEN"

Stealing the Fire

Heroes in myth, gaining triumph, become monarchs of all they survey. Then inevitably, they are faced with revolt.

In this Greek myth based on the 8th-century B.C. poet Hesiod's account, rebellion happens when a youth castrates his own father. But the culprit, Cronus, in turn becomes the evil father. He is sent packing by Zeus—who dreads a similar fate at the hands of Prometheus.

Fire-theft often appeared in world mythology, the deed usually done by tricksters such as Prometheus. However, he was different from the others in being more serious about his goal. Defying the gods in the hope for something better, he represented the idea of youthful energy hurled against aged authority.

Napoleon after being exiled to St. Helena* saw himself as Prometheus. "I have stolen the fire of heaven and made a gift of it to France," he declared. "I am nailed to the rock to be gnawed by a vulture." At the same time, Shelley took the British Museum's massive statue of Rameses II as the subject for his sonnet Ozymandias, a powerful condemnation of tyranny.**

John Milton's *Paradise Lost* tells of Lucifer (Greek: "Light-carrier"), once the brightest of God's angels. When God creates an earthly creature and gives it an immortal soul, Lucifer grows so jealous that he leads a rebellion in heaven. Though defeated by Christ and thrown with his followers into hell, he comes to Eden and corrupts humankind so as to win power on earth.

---

*See page 179.
**See page 169.

Rebels are admired in some eras, hated in others. Interest in this Greek origin myth has recently shifted from the aggressive male gods to the earth-goddess Gaia. Concern for the environment has turned our attention toward what brings harmony, rather than disruption.

This new respect for Mother Nature is clothed in scientific theory. How was the earth able to support life? All factors became regulated, the physicist James Lovelock suggests, by life itself. Life adjusts rainfall, the atmosphere's temperature, and the saltiness of the oceans. All the earth's creatures work together as a master control team, to keep its surface alive and fertile. Lovelock, learning that the Greeks' most ancient earth goddess was said to act similarly, named his theory the *Gaia Hypothesis*.

Always, however, the king must die. Nature decrees it, for a new generation must arise. Leaves wither, but as Robert Frost writes, they "go down past things coming up."

In Hardwood Groves

The same leaves over and over again!
They fall from giving shade above
To make one texture of faded brown
And fit the earth like a leather glove.

Before the leaves can mount again
To fill the trees with another shade,
They must go down past things coming up,
They must go down into the dark decayed.

They *must* be pierced by flowers and put
Beneath the feet of dancing flowers.
However it is in some other world
I know that this is the way in ours.

ROBERT FROST

The Birth of Frankenstein *British*

To believe that rules are made to be broken, that all things are possible, that everything might be changed! That's how it was during the Romantic revolt, two centuries ago. The world, it seemed, would have a new beginning.

In that era, as in the 1920s and 1960s, many dreamed of discarding outmoded notions about human relationships. One philosopher, William Godwin, declared the world's misery is rooted in its fixed laws. He argued that humanity could be radically improved by sweeping those tyrannical laws away, along with the priests and kings who made them.

Mary Wollstonecraft, the first great champion of women's rights, equalled Godwin in fame. In *A Vindication of the Rights of Women* she wrote, "Strengthen the female mind by enlarging it, and there will be an end to blind obedience." Women are fit to be the intellectual companions of men, she argued. They must avoid becoming the prey of "tyrants and sensualists," as "the former only want slaves and the latter a plaything."

When Wollstonecraft was abandoned by her first husband after the birth of their daughter, she nearly drowned herself in despair. Then she met Godwin, and an ideal union came about.

Godwin disapproved of marriage. "Nothing can be so ridiculous," he argued, "as to require the overflowing of the soul to wait upon a ceremony." But because Wollstonecraft respected it, he agreed, and they were married. Sadly, in 1797 she died from an infection caused by the birth of her second daughter, also called Mary.

Young Mary had an extraordinary education, as her home was a meeting-place for many gifted souls. The famous poet, Samuel Taylor Coleridge, came over for tea one day to recite the whole of his haunting *Rime of the Ancient Mariner*.

Mary Wollstonecraft Shelley

Mary spent many hours by her mother's grave, reading her works, and here in 1814, she was courted by the young poet, Percy Bysshe Shelley. He had met her through Godwin, whose ideas he admired—and tried to carry out. "Love," Shelley argued, "should be free: to promise for ever to love the same woman, is not less absurd than to promise to believe the same creed."

That same year he had married Harriet Westbrook, who had given birth to one child by him, and would soon have another. Three months later Mary, 16 and very beautiful, decided to live out her parents' principles by running away with Shelley.

In 1816, the lovers came to Geneva, Switzerland. Here for the first time they met Lord Byron, by far the most famous of all the Romantic poets. Their friendship was a creative stimulus of rare power, but the most memorable work to emerge from the months the three spent together was written not by these two poets but by Mary, then only 19. It was called *Frankenstein; or The Modern Prometheus.*

"Incessant rain often confined us for days to the house," Mary wrote in her diary. To pass the time in their villa, they told horror tales to one another. Every night they plunged deeper and deeper into the torments of the dead.

On the night of June 16, Byron read from Coleridge's *Christabel,* which tells of a girl destroyed by her mother's ghost. The reading was so hard on Shelley's nerves that he ran screaming through the villa, until they drugged him with ether. But Byron was nonplussed. "We will each write a ghost story," he said .

"When I placed my head on my pillow, I did not sleep," Mary wrote about that night. There had been much talk among the three of them about the prospect of imitating Prometheus, who created humanity from clay and stole fire on its behalf.

"My imagination, unbidden, possessed and guided me," said Mary. "I saw the hideous phantasm of a man stretched out, and then, on the working of some powerful machine, show signs of life." She imagined a doctor, Frankenstein, vowing to save humankind by shaping a new form of life—but his creation turns into a monster.

Frankenstein's monster, pathetic as it is, has power of speech. So it is able to argue that the real monster is not himself, but the doctor. "You, my creator, detest and spurn me," it cries. "How dare you sport thus with life?"

It was just a century before that science had first defined the laws of nature. To violate these laws, it was felt, was to risk unleashing all it potential horrors. Horace Walpole's novel, *The Castle of Otranto,* written in 1765, had dramatized just that.

The castle's wicked prince, Manfred, pursues Isabella into its gloomy vaults, and various supernatural events happen until he repents and becomes a monk. This was the first *Gothic* novel, and in its day made the reader's hair stand on end. Horrible, incomprehensible things happen in mysterious moonlit castles, on murky stairways, within ghost-haunted dungeons.

What Mary Shelley did was to turn Walpole's villainous prince into a scientist. Dr. Frankenstein's creation, patched together from corpse fragments, is a rational being who craves knowledge and love, but is denied them by his creator. Then loneliness drives it to violence; so the doctor is shown as the Mad Scientist, governed by the head rather than the heart. And Mary, by inventing him, gave birth to what is now called science fiction.

Frankenstein also experiences guilt, as did many creative people in the Romantic era. Revolting against established power made them feel outcast and alone.

Later Mary raised an obvious question: "How I, then a young girl, came to think of, and to dilate on, so very hideous an idea." Should we compare Frankenstein with Godwin—who, hypocritically, disowned Mary until she had a conventional marriage? Or with Shelley, who upset her by putting his free-love ideas into practice? Or with herself, as someone who had wronged Shelley's wife, Harriet?

Harriet, humiliated and distraught by Shelley's desertion, wrote, "At nineteen I could descend a willing victim to the tomb." In December of 1816, she did just that, apparently by drowning herself. Mary, full of remorse, saw "many of my own sorrows as the atonement claimed by fate for her death."

The couple returned to England and married, in order to gain rights to his and Harriet's children. But the request was denied by the courts, and they took this as a sentence of exile. Living in Italy, they saw three of their own four children perish. Then in 1822, Shelley himself lost his life in a mysterious boating accident.

Mary, at this time only 25, returned to England. She continued to write novels which dealt, like *Frankenstein*, with guilt and the longing for affection. Once she was advised to send her one surviving child to a school where he would learn to think for himself. "Teach him to think for himself?" she replied. "Oh, my God, teach him rather to think like other people!"

Rebellion to tyrants is obedience to God.

MOTTO ON THOMAS JEFFERSON'S SEAL

Control Over Nature

"Children shudder at the smell of newness," writes Isaac Babel, "as a dog does when it scents a hare." In modern times the thirst for newness—the "new and improved" as emblazoned on a product's label—seems almost unquenchable. For we are gripped by the myth of progress.

Stories of human triumph over nature hold a special appeal. These tell of heroes such as Isaac Newton (defining natural laws), Henry Ford (mass-producing cars, to put the countryside within easy range), Madame Curie (harnessing the atom), and so on. People like the idea of going to the outer limits of scientific progress.

Faith in progress is said to be the central belief in modern mythology. History was once described as cyclical—the same thing over and over—but our myth gives it a direction. This idea comes mainly from the ancient Hebrews, who believed that God prepared a spiritual destiny for humanity. From this faith has sprung the myth of progress: paradise regained by our own efforts.

Progress means control over nature. We enjoy clearing land at a cottage, or mowing down dandelions on a lawn. Our race has risen to dominance over all forms of life, and the Frankenstein myth presents this as a kind of revolt against nature. But Greenpeace activists fight as rebels on nature's behalf*—as does John in his protest against "senseless killing."

The Pheasants

At a camp I know, thousands of pheasants are raised every year to be hunted by high-salaried businessmen. My father, being the president of a growing company, was invited for a trial membership, and he brought me along.

I talked with a female guide, Cathy, while the hunters went ahead. She informed me how dogs chase the birds into the air and then the men shoot them. One of the guides retrieves their corpses, so these men never even see blood.

I am against the senseless killing of any creature. Cathy told me that on the average day, 250 pheasants are slaughtered. Now there is no way that 20 men will eat or use that many birds. She didn't tell me what they do with the leftover birds, but I can tell you that it's not justified.

Now I had enough of this. I had to do something. So I went against authority.

The pheasants are kept in a large pen until required, about a thousand in a very small space. I opened the door and started to let them all out.

Well, my dad caught me. So unfortunately, only about twenty got away, but it was a good try. My father yelled at me with disgust.

What I did, I do not consider wrong. What's wrong is what goes on at that camp. It may seem like just a place for hunting, but to change such a peaceful woods into a war zone is wrong.

---

*See pages 28-31.

Step on a crack,
You'll break your mother's back;
Step on a line,
You'll break your father's spine.

Step in a ditch,
Your mother's nose will itch;
Step in the dirt,
You'll tear your father's shirt.

TRADITIONAL AMERICAN RHYME

✳ 6 Lovers Meeting

Primavera

O Mistress Mine

O Mistress mine, where are you roaming?
O, stay and hear; your true love's coming,
    That can sing both high and low:
Trip no further, pretty sweeting;
Journeys end in lovers meeting,
    Every wise man's son doth know.

What is love? 'Tis not hereafter;
Present mirth hath present laughter;
    What's to come is still unsure:
In delay there lies no plenty;
Then, come kiss me, sweet and twenty,
    Youth's a stuff will not endure.

WILLIAM SHAKESPEARE, *TWELFTH NIGHT*

Shakespeare's verse strikes an ancient theme. Lovers keenly anticipate reuniting, but how long their joy will last is anyone's guess.

Something of the same idea appears in Sandro Botticelli's *Primavera*, or "Allegory of Spring." It presents Venus as the mother-goddess—we note her pregnancy—who brings divine love and beauty to the earth. A subtle halo around her head, formed by the trunks of trees, suggests that she is also Mary, who inherited many virtues of the pagan goddesses.

The love-goddess, arousing desire, brings forth all the bounty of the earth. Yet the sadness of love's brevity runs through the triad of Graces at left, where Chastity is solemnly initiated into the mysteries of love. Her sisters Voluptuousness and Beauty lead her, and Cupid helps out by taking aim at her head.

19. Love-Goddess

✳

I'm tired of Love: I'm still more tired of Rhyme.
But Money gives me pleasure all the time.

HILAIRE BELLOC

Aphrodite and Her Lovers *Greek*

How did the goddess of love come into our world? Her origins are strange. In that long-ago hour when Cronus wounded the sky-god Uranus,* his genitals fell into the sea. Foam gathered from the blood, grew into a bright cloud, and congealed into the ravishing form of Aphrodite.

Aphrodite emerged on a great sea-shell, and floated to the island of Cyprus. Wherever she stepped, flowers and lush grass sprang forth from the soil. Animals along her path, stung with desire, mated in the shadows.

Maidens rushed out to clothe Aphrodite, for human eyes would be dazzled by so much beauty. On she went to Mount Olympus, home of the gods, and there became the bride of Hephaestus, the crippled blacksmith god. But fidelity was not to be something this goddess would know. Ares, the god of war, fell instantly in love with her, and she returned his passion.

Hephaestus was naturally upset by their affair, and so he hung a gossamer-thin bronze net in Aphrodite's chamber. This net fell on the lovers, trapping them in mid-embrace. Hephaestus then hobbled into the chamber, scolding the couple, and the other gods came running as well.

Apollo was fascinated by the sight. "Now if you were Ares in this situation," he remarked to Hermes, "you still wouldn't mind too much, would you?"

---

*See pages 205-206.

Hermes readily agreed. "Let everyone be looking on, the goddesses as well," he said, "and it would still be a delight."

Ares had a rival in Adonis, a very handsome youth, who had been born from a myrrh-tree. Aphrodite doted on him from the time he was an infant.

Adonis's great love was hunting. He would roam the hills in search of game and was often accompanied by Aphrodite. "Watch out for the fierce boar," she would warn him, "for its tusks are sharp and as swift as lightning!"

However, one day, after the love-goddess had left him, Adonis did happen to rouse a mighty boar. He hurled his spear, but only grazed the beast's side. The enraged boar pursued him and buried its tusks deep into his groin.

Aphrodite, hearing the youth's moans, instantly flew to his side. As he lay dying, she cried aloud her grief, reproaching Fate for taking away her lover.

"Woe for Adonis!" the goddess cried. "And everlastingly, his fate will be lamented as I lament it now. But from his blood, a flower will grow, red of hue and fragile like himself."

That flower is the blood-red anemone, with petals so weakly attached that they quickly fall to the ground.

The Racer's Widow

The elements have merged into solicitude.
Spasms of violets rise above the mud
And weed and soon the birds and ancients
Will be starting to arrive, bereaving points
South. But never mind. It is not painful to discuss
His death. I have been primed for this,
For separation, for so long. But still his face assaults
Me, I can hear that car careen again, the crowd
    coagulate on asphalt
In my sleep. And watching him, I feel my legs like snow
That let him finally let him go
As he lies draining there. And see
How even he did not get to keep that lovely body.

LOUISE GLÜCK

Mysteries of Birth and Death

Growing up, we hear distant rumours of a happiness unsurpassed. She who makes it all happen is the love-goddess. Century after century it is love that yields life's richest meaning.

Aphrodite promises entry into untold realms of infinite delight— and also of the sharpest pain. The heroic journey might seem hard enough, without the torments of love. Yet love, when it is right, brings final release from infancy into full maturity.

Although we now tend to look upon Aphrodite as only a sex-goddess, she was once closely linked with the mysteries of birth and death. In a play by Aeschylus, here is what she has to say:

The holy Sky longs to penetrate Earth
who likewise yearns for her marriage.
Earth, made fertile by raindrops from Sky,
brings forth her brood for mankind.

In Rome an obscure goddess of pot-vegetables, Venus, took on the attributes of Aphrodite and rose to national importance. Mars, a vegetation god, also won popularity after taking over the myth of the Greek war-god Ares. Today, Venus and Mars are well-known as the greatest lovers in all of mythology.

Early Christianity condemned certain temples "dedicated to the filthy devil answering to the name of Venus—a school of wickedness for all worshippers of indecency." This refers to the practice of sacred prostitution, performed in her name at Corinth.

Looming far in the background is Ishtar, the Babylonian love goddess.* Aphrodite is clearly a Greek version of her and a very ancient one indeed, as shown by her origin from the primeval sky-god's blood. In myth, Aphrodite first appeared among humankind at the island of Cyprus, part way between Asia and Greece.

Her shrines appeared here around 1200 B.C. The Greek poet Homer wrote that the goddess was bathed ritually here to renew her powers, being clothed afterwards by those elegant beauty-givers known as the Graces.

Aphrodite's cult had much to do with death. Adonis's fate, repeating that of Tammuz and Osiris, kept alive the myth of the Dying God. Every year in Athens, women joined in a ritual lament over his effigy—much as Tammuz was mourned in the Ishtar cult. For, like her 1950s personification Marilyn Monroe, Aphrodite appeared both aggressive and vulnerable.

---

*See page 24.

Had I been toothed like him, I must confess,
With kissing him I should have killed him first.

WILLIAM SHAKESPEARE, *VENUS AND ADONIS*

Most Shatteringly in Love with Marilyn
American

Hollywood in the 1920s created a myth of the celluloid goddess. Movie-star mythology was believed even by those within the industry, film cutter Gladys Baker being one of them. She tried to make her little girl, Norma Jean, look and smile like the famous actresses.

The stars' footprints in front of Hollywood's Chinese Theatre fascinated Norma Jean. She found that hers matched those of the silent screen idol Rudolph Valentino, who had tragically died young.

In 1934, at the age of eight, Norma was placed in an orphanage after her mother was declared schizophrenic. Later, she lived in nine foster homes and was often abused. But Christian Science, presenting God as love and the world as innocent, gave her hope. "Divine love," she would say, "always will meet every human need."

She was married off at 16, and her teenage husband soon went to war. While he was gone, she looked for theatrical work in Hollywood. And a strong will drove her to seek fame.

Her little-girl voice endeared her to older men—stand-ins for the father she never knew—and her big chance came in 1950, with a featured role in *The Asphalt Jungle*. From the moment she appeared, walking as only she could walk, people asked, "Who is that blonde?"

So she became a star—with a new name, Marilyn Monroe. And her voluptuous body, combined with that fetching voice, produced the image of a love-goddess who seemed strangely vulnerable. "She has an innocence which is so extraordinary," said Dame Sybil Thorndike, the British actress. "Whatever she plays, however brazen a hussy, it always comes out as an innocent girl."

So when *Gentlemen Prefer Blondes* had its premiere at the Chinese Theatre, the cement now received Marilyn's signature. The star had arrived at the temple. Yet soon she would be driven to describe Hollywood as "a place where they pay you ten thousand dollars for a kiss and fifty cents for your soul."

Marilyn's face, after minor plastic surgery, was perfect. The fluff of ash-blonde hair, the dreamy blue eyes, the moist red lips of her open mouth—all this, and her incandescent, earthy, flamboyant vitality, contributed to this goddess's cult. It is still very much alive today.

Marilyn had powerful men for lovers. In 1954 she married baseball hero Joe DiMaggio, at the time America's most celebrated athlete. Always protective, he was angered by publicity over her famous hot-air-vent scene in *The Seven Year Itch*. "I'd have been upset, you know," said the director of the film, Billy Wilder, "if there were 20 000 people watching my wife's skirt blow over her head." This image became a major icon in Marilyn's cult—but the marriage broke up within a year.

Marilyn, desperate to discover herself, now broke with Hollywood and went to New York to study acting with the noted drama coach Lee Strasberg. The effort paid off in the movie Bus Stop, for which she invented her character's accent, clothes, and personality. "She had always been treated very badly by producers, cameramen, actors," said her director, Joshua Logan. "Treated like a dumb blonde, which she wasn't. She was a brilliant blonde."

When Sir Laurence Olivier made *The Prince and the Showgirl* with Marilyn, he succumbed at once. "By the end of the first day, one thing was clear to me. I was going to fall most shatteringly in love with Marilyn," he recalled. "She was so adorable, so witty, such incredible fun, and more physically attractive than anyone I could have imagined."

Marilyn and Venus

In 1956, Marilyn married the country's leading playwright, Arthur Miller. Appearing to him as "a poet on a
street corner trying to recite to a crowd pulling at her
clothes," she was later fictionalized as the heroine in his
play, *After the Fall*.

At the time she keenly desired a child. But the marriage, which ended four years later, produced only miscarriages. And Marilyn's career had begun to falter.

Increasingly she had trouble showing up on the set and remembering her lines. While making *Some Like it Hot,* she stumbled so often over the line, "It's me, Sugar," that the scene required 47 takes.

Always eager to be loved, Marilyn was plagued by self-doubt. "I can't have children, I can't sustain loving relationships, I suffer from depression," she confessed to one of her lovers near the end. "I often wish to die even though I'm sickly afraid of death."

John Kennedy, both before and after becoming President, had an affair with Marilyn. (His father had openly flaunted Gloria Swanson as his mistress, once taking her along with his wife on an ocean liner to Europe.)*

On May 29, 1962, a birthday celebration for Kennedy was held at Madison Square Garden, and Marilyn attended to offer a tribute. Late as usual, she finally took the spotlight, fortified by too many glasses of champagne, and was jokingly introduced by the actor and Kennedy brother-in-law, Peter Lawford, as "the *late* Marilyn Monroe."

Cooingly, Marilyn sang Kennedy a sultry "Happy Birthday, Mr. President." Then the man she called Jack said, "I can now retire from politics, after having 'Happy Birthday' sung to me by such a sweet, wholesome girl as Marilyn Monroe."

On August 4, Marilyn phoned Lawford and murmured in a slurred voice, "Say goodbye to Jack and say goodbye to yourself." The next day she was found dead, having taken a fatal overdose of barbiturates. "A probable suicide" was the judgment on Coroner's Case No. 81128.

"She had a luminous quality," Lee Strasberg said in his eulogy to Marilyn, "a combination of wistfulness, radiance, yearning—that set her apart and yet made everyone wish to be part of it."

---

*See page 94.

The Pretty Maid

Where are you going to, my pretty maid?
I'm going a-milking, she said.

May I go with you, my pretty maid?
You're kindly welcome, sir, she said.

Say, will you marry me, my pretty maid?
Yes, if you please, kind sir, she said.

What is your father, my pretty maid?
My father's a farmer, sir, she said.

What is your fortune, my pretty maid?
My face is my fortune, sir, she said.

Then I can't marry you, my pretty maid.
Nobody asked you, sir, she said.

CHILDREN'S RHYME

Red Roses and Chocolates

Love is confusing because it has enough force to knock us senseless, yet we must go through a formality to make it acceptable. Our society still honours many refinements from the days of courtly love when lords wooed ladies in their castles.*

Giving red roses and chocolates on a certain day sacred to lovers is among these ritual courtesies. Spare a thought for the fearsome god whose rituals gave rise to Valentine's Day.

Pan, the Greek god of forests and pastures, had the feet and horns of a goat. He invented reed pipes, on which he played music expressing the wild impulses of nature. *Pan* means all (as in *pan*orama: view of all the land) and the god lived everywhere in the wilderness—where sounds made by him are apt to produce unreasoning terror, or "panic."

Pan's name among the Romans was Faunus. At his rite held annually on February 15, Lupercalia, goats would be sacrificed, and their skins sliced to serve as whips. Naked youths ran through the street,

*See page 248.

using the whips on any women who held out their hands, thus ensuring their fertility.

In Asia Minor, around 270 A.D., a Roman soldier named Valentinus fell in love with a young Christian girl. He also embraced Christianity and chose to become a priest, so he renounced marriage. Yet he was said to be exceptionally kind toward young lovers. Valentinus died a martyr's death—one sad February 14—and the Lupercalia was christianized in memory of his name. Thus he became the patron saint of all lovers.

Valentine's Day comes but once a year, however, while those medieval courtesies are everyday duties—and not necessarily well-appreciated, as Joanne shows.

A Bit Far

I remember once my girlfriend and I went out on a date with these two guys. Talk about courtly love! It was incredible!

First they asked us to please not wear jeans but to get dressed up. OK, fair enough. They came to the door (my friend stayed at my house) and when introduced to my parents, shook their hands. Not unusual.

They then escorted us to their car, opened our sides first, let us get in and shut the door before going to their side. Impressed?

In the restaurant they took our plates and served us. This was after holding the door of the car open for us, letting us go into the restaurant while they parked, escorting us to our table, holding our chairs out, making sure we were comfortable, and ordering for us.

I was in fits of laughter. I mean it was nice but come on, they went a bit far. I felt like a useless, blithering invalid.

Science writes of the world as if with the cold finger of a starfish; it is all true; but what is it when compared to the reality of which it discourses? where hearts beat high in April, and death strikes, and hills totter in the earthquake . . .? So we come back to the old myth, and hear the goat-footed piper making the music which is itself the charm and terror of things . . .

ROBERT LOUIS STEVENSON, "PAN'S PIPES"

20. Romance

Do you love me,
Or do you not?
You told me once,
But I forgot.

ANONYMOUS

Jason and Medea *Greek*

Jason and the Golden Fleece

Beware of the man with one foot bare!" old King Pelias was warned. The prophecy filled him with dread. Having seized the throne of Iolcus from his brother Aeson, he feared being overthrown.

Pelias's response was to have Aeson's children murdered. So when Aeson's wife gave birth to a son, the family announced that he had died during the delivery. Then the infant was smuggled away and raised in secrecy.

Many years later, Pelias learned that a stranger had appeared in the marketplace. Curious, he went there and saw a broad-shouldered youth wearing only one sandal. Pelias shuddered with fear. "Who are you?" he asked.

"I am Jason, son of Aeson," said the youth, who had lost a sandal while crossing a river. "I have come to regain the throne which is my father's."

"That may well be," Pelias replied. "But before I ever yield up the throne, you must bring back the Golden Fleece."

What was the Golden Fleece? It belonged to a winged ram, which had once swooped down to rescue a child prince and his sister about to be sacrificed on a mountaintop. The ram flew with the boy to Colchis on the Black Sea's eastern shore. Here the beast was offered in sacrifice and its fleece hung in a sacred grove, guarded by a serpent that never slept.

Jason, who knew the story well, agreed to go. He was joined by the noblest heroes in the land, fifty in all. They were known as the Argonauts, after the name of their ship, the *Argo*.

When launching-time came, the *Argo* refused to budge. But Orpheus, the greatest of singers, made music so charming that it happily slid into the waves.

The Argonauts first came ashore at Lemnos, where the women had killed all the men for infidelity with slave girls. They welcomed these worthies most warmly—so much so that it was some time before the *Argo* sailed again.

Guarding the entrance to the Black Sea were the Clashing Rocks, which would come together whenever a living creature passed between, crushing it. Jason cleverly released a dove, which made the rocks sweep forward, clipping a few of its tail feathers. At the instant when the great boulders separated again, the Argonauts frantically rowed their ship into the opening. With a deafening roar the rocks ground together, but were only able to tear off the *Argo*'s stern ornament. And from that time, the Clashing Rocks have remained immobile.

The gods favoured Jason, whom they loved. They knew that the King of Colchis, Aeetes, would not easily allow him to take the Golden Fleece. So the king's daughter, Medea, had to be persuaded to help the young hero, and this task fell to Aphrodite, goddess of love. She enlisted the help of her winged son, Eros (Cupid).

The Argonauts sailed across the Black Sea, landed at Colchis, and were welcomed by Aeetes at the palace. It was here that the beautiful Medea saw Jason for the first time. Cupid chose this moment to let fly an arrow, and it entered deeply into her heart. At once, she felt the agonies of love.

After a banquet was given to the Argonauts, Jason revealed his aim to Aeetes. The king exploded with rage. "Get out of my kingdom before I have your hands chopped off!" he roared. "You seek no fleece, but the throne of Colchis!"

"We're here at the bidding of Fate," Jason calmly replied, "and only for as long as it takes to receive this prize."

"Well then, let's see if you're worthy of it," said Aeetes. "I have two fire-breathing bulls with hooves of bronze. In the span of one day I yoked them, ploughed the field of Ares the war-god, and sowed the furrows with dragons's teeth. From these, armed warriors sprang up, and I killed them all. You must do the same to earn the Golden Fleece!"

Jason, gathering his courage, accepted the challenge.

When Medea witnessed this exchange, she was torn between loyalty to her father and love for Jason. That night she dreamed of Jason, who came to carry her off as his bride. Awakening, Medea determined to offer her help, for she had the power to work magic.

She brought him a container of special ointment. At first she was powerless to speak, as she gazed at him in a spell of love. Then she tenderly placed the magic ointment in his hands.

"For one day, this will make you invincible," said Medea. "The bulls will give you no harm. And when you go away from here, remember how I saved your life."

"I won't leave without you," he said. "Come with me to Iolcus, and live there as my wife." And Medea, aching with Cupid's wound, agreed.

The next day Jason rubbed the ointment on his body and faced the bulls. Breathing streams of fire they flew at him, but Medea's charm did its work and quickly he brought them to their knees. He then harnessed them to the yoke, and their bronze hooves dug into the earth as he ploughed the fields.

Instantly, helmets shot up and an army of warriors rose into view. But Jason, acting on Medea's instructions, threw a stone into their midst. Each soldier thought that the man next to him had thrown it, and they set upon one another like savage hounds.

Jason strode in among the soldiers, reaping the crop with his sword until all had been killed. Then he asked the king to honour his promise. "Tomorrow," Aeetes muttered.

That night, Medea warned Jason of treachery. "Row at once to the grove of the Golden Fleece," she said, and the Argonauts stealthily brought their vessel to the spot.

Medea led Jason into the woods, and soon they saw a shimmering cloud. It was the Golden Fleece, hanging on the branches of an oak tree.

Alongside the treasure was the serpent with a thousand coils. It reared up, hissing, but Medea began to sing softly. The monster's fierce head drooped, and finally sank to the ground in slumber. Immediately, Jason seized the Golden Fleece.

The two lovers quickly returned to the *Argo*, but not before Aeetes ordered every able-bodied man to join in pursuit. The massive Colchian fleet, commanded by Medea's half-brother Apsyrtus, swept over the sea like a flock of birds, as the Argonaut rowers pulled with all their might.

Medea now plotted against Apsyrtus. That night when the pursuers and the pursued made camp, she sent a message saying that she had been carried off against her will. She called on Apsyrtus to rescue her at a designated meeting-place.

Jason waited there in ambush and killed Apsyrtus with his sword. The rest of the Argonauts raged through the Colchian camp, sparing no one. When the *Argo* sailed at dawn, there was no pursuit.

One evening, the *Argo* came ashore at Iolcus. Jason triumphantly went to Pelias and presented him with the Golden Fleece. But it soon became clear to him that the king was reluctant to fulfil his promise.

Again Medea employed her magic. To Pelias's daughters she said, "I know how to make your old father young again." And to convince them, she demonstrated her powers on an aged ram.

In a large cauldron Medea mixed a brew of magic herbs and many other ingredients—the entrails of a wolf, a crow's head, a stag's liver—before carving the ram into thirteen pieces and flinging them inside. She sang her charms and out leapt a lamb.

The daughters were convinced. While Pelias slept, they killed him and cut his body into pieces, which they plunged into Medea's cauldron. But now, she had vanished. Without her magic, Pelias never would emerge from the potion, either old or young.

Jason and Medea now took the throne, as king and queen of Iolcus. Later, they became the parents of two sons. It would be pleasant if our tale ended with their happiness, but that was not to be.

Pelias's son meant to avenge his father's death. He raised an army and Jason and Medea fled to Corinth, where the royal family offered shelter. And here Jason, caring more for ambition than family joys, became engaged to the princess, Glauce.

Medea nearly went mad with anguish. How could Jason

betray his wife, after she had done so much for him? And unable to return to her homeland, she would have no honourable way of supporting her children.

Once more, Medea returned to her magic arts. Anointing a wondrous robe and coronet with her drugs, she sent them to Glauce as a wedding present. As soon as the girl put them on, flames burst forth and consumed her entire body.

Then Medea, certain that her children were doomed to die by someone else's hands, made an appalling decision. "I who gave them life will take it from them," she said. "Come, in one brief moment forget that you are their mother." And Medea killed both of her sons, and fled.

Grief overwhelmed Jason, and he began a life of wandering throughout Greece. One day he came upon the *Argo*, now a rotten hulk. He reflected on the vanished hours of glory, when he and fifty warriors went forth in quest of the Golden Fleece.

The moment he stepped on board, the rotting vessel broke in two and crushed him to death.

Erasure

Falling out of love
is a rusty chain going quickly through a winch.
It hurts more than you will remember.
It costs a pint of blood turned grey
and burning out a few high paths
among the glittering synapses of the brain,
a few stars fading out at once in the galaxy,
a configuration gone
imagination called a lion or a dragon or a sunburst
that would photograph more like a blurry mouse.
When falling out of love is correcting vision
light grates on the eyes
light files the optic nerve hot and raw.
To find you have loved a coward and a fool
is to give up the lion, the dragon, the sunburst
and take away your hands covered with small festering bites
and let the mouse go in a grey blur
into the baseboard.

MARGE PIERCY

Falling In and Out of Love

Falling in love, many believe, is the highest adventure. We dream of going with our beloved to misty mountains, or down endless canals of bliss in a hired gondola. It is a plunge into our depths, astonishing and often scary as familiar things are left behind.

Falling out of love is equally shattering, as the Jason myth shows. And romantic love, promising eternal joy in a private world, often betrays us by giving acute pain. *Medea*, a play by Euripides, places the lovers' story in a tragic context.

Romance means both the experience and a kind of literature, made up of stories of love and adventure. Love will triumph in the end, it says. Barriers blocking fulfillment will inevitably fall, even perhaps at the cost of riches or status or fame.

Mining this inexhaustible vein is the traditional romance novel, or "love-pulp." It shows the heroine forever intent on one aim, honourable marriage. Women in the early U.S. pulps had to be innocent—"pretty, between 18 and 24, earning her own living, pure in thought and deed" as one editor put it. And always the tales ended happily. Greater equality between the sexes has generated a steamier kind of romance, although men are usually still dominant.

Pain and still more pain are what we may expect on daytime drama, or the "soaps." The nickname comes from the frequency of soap commercials, which fit in well because moral cleansing so often is the theme. Daytime drama's sustained anguish forges an intense emotional bond—so that someone playing a villain's role runs the danger of being assaulted by an aggrieved viewer.

Situation comedy, like daylight drama, deals with human relationships, but with less emotional power. Its cheeriness provides relief from the sorrows of soapland. The most discussed topic is health, which the soaps treat primarily in terms of its impact on relationships. Easy answers are hard to come by, yet a traditional morality dictates that decency will triumph.

Great art, of course, takes us much deeper into the love relationship. In novels such as Leo Tolstoy's *Anna Karenina* and Gustave Flaubert's *Madame Bovary*, characters are destroyed by passion when love and death, the two greatest adventures, come together.

I want to paint men and women with that something of the eternal which the halo used to symbolize...to express the love of two lovers by a wedding of two complementary colours, their mingling and opposition, the mysterious vibration of kindred tones.

Vincent Van Gogh

Reason Over Passion *Canadian*

At the wedding of Margaret and Pierre Trudeau

Pierre Trudeau, coming to Ottawa as a member of parliament in 1965, seemed to bring a new era of youth and progress. He had charm and wit, a red rose on his lapel every day, a buckskin jacket, a way of joining his fingertips meditatively, and a Mercedes 300SL.

In 1968, the chance came for him to run for prime minister. Pierre flew to the paradise island of Tahiti to give it some thought. Here, on a raft in the middle of a lagoon, the 49-year-old bachelor first met Margaret Sinclair.

"I found her eyes extraordinarily beautiful," Trudeau later said of Margaret, 29 years his junior. "She is a very earthy woman. A sensual woman with both feet on the ground."

Margaret, the daughter of a former cabinet minister, was a rebellious but idealistic girl of uncommon loveliness. "I dreamed of being a rich, celebrated, beautiful, totally happy woman," she recalled, "with an extremely famous husband and many beautiful children."

The next time Margaret saw Pierre, he was campaigning to be prime minister. "Trudeau! Trudeau!" shouted the mob as it surged forward into a stadium. He noticed Margaret, broke through and kissed her on both cheeks before being swept on. Not for another two years would they meet again, on their first date—for dinner, atop a mountain overlooking Vancouver.

When Trudeau was elected, Canadians were proud to have one of the world's most brilliant leaders. And one day on Parliament Hill, Pierre obliged a pretty girl by kissing her, behind an upraised briefcase. "Why not?" he said, "It's spring." This and other antics aroused in the Canadian public, uncharacteristically, what was known as "Trudeaumania."

Then, in 1970, a very different Trudeau emerged during the Québec separatist crisis, which he ended by invoking the War Measures Act to suspend civil rights. Later he worked toward a rights charter that would have subjected his own action to approval by the courts.

Pierre took "reason over passion" as his motto; Margaret, by her own account, was a "flower child." Yet for the sake of Pierre, North America's most eligible bachelor, she gave up marijuana and put aside thoughts of "a romantic fling with another lover."

On March 4, 1971, the two were secretly married, Margaret having sewn her own wedding dress and baked a simple cake. This story of Cinderella and her prince fascinated the world, and would do so for the next six years.

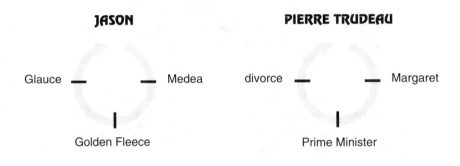

The Romantic's journey—Jason, and Trudeau

"I spent much of the first two years either pregnant or nursing a new baby," said Margaret. In 1971 a boy, the first child born to a serving Canadian prime minister in 102 years, appeared on Christmas Day—the day's significance not lost on their adoring public. To underline the mythic aura even more, two years later Margaret's second son also was born on Christmas Day!

The child-bride remained within the walls of her castle at 24 Sussex Drive. "Oh, I'm just Old Mother Earth," she said when asked for comment. "I wanted to be a wife and mother, and I've committed myself totally to that." But during the 1974 election, Margaret did emerge to campaign with her husband. "A man who's quite a beautiful guy," she would say, introducing him to adoring crowds as Trudeaumania raged again. "He has taught me all about loving."

Perhaps the peak of this romantic story came on the night of Trudeau's smashing victory when, before the cameras at the Chateau Laurier, in Ottawa, Margaret kissed the prince she had blessed with her help. Rarely had a Canadian couple looked more loving than at that moment. Yet only a few months later, the castle walls began to crack.

Pierre's routine, Margaret wrote, was numbingly unvaried. Arriving home at 7:45 p.m., he swam "44 laps, never more, never less, every evening. Seventeen minutes later the little boys would begin their fifteen-minute swimming lessons with him." Then came dinner and for precisely three-quarters of an hour, its digestion. "The forty-five minutes up, Pierre would start working again. Time with Wifey was over. That's when the loneliness really hit me."

In September 1974, Margaret was admitted to a Montreal hospital. Her stay was for "a rest and some tests," said the Prime Minister's office, but Margaret in a press conference openly stated that she was suffering from "severe depression." Later a third son was born to her.

In 1976, on a state visit to South America, Margaret made a series of protocol gaffes that aroused widespread indignation. Pierre, interviewed on French TV, defended her. "The woman always remains a bit subjugated by marriage," he remarked. "Women are now beginning to leave this confinement, but it takes a great deal of maturity on their part—and on that of the man."

Later that year, Margaret became so angry in a dispute with Pierre that she attacked a quilt embroidered with his famed motto, Reason Before Passion. "I grabbed at the quilt," said Margaret, "wrenched off the letters and hurled them down the stairs at him one by one, in an insane desire to reverse the process, to put passion before reason just this once."

Meanwhile Pierre faced another political crisis, the election of the independence-seeking Parti Québecois. "Now you're never going to be able to get out of politics," Margaret told him. Early in 1977, without informing the public, the couple agreed to a 90-day trial separation.

On the day of her sixth wedding anniversary, Margaret undertook what she later described as her "ultimate freedom trip." She went to Toronto for a concert by the Rolling Stones and, when members of the group went on to New York, she followed them there as well. On her return to Ottawa, a columnist reported a violent argument between Pierre and her, climaxed by "a punch in the eye, husband to wife." Then came an official statement: "Pierre and Margaret Trudeau announce that, because of Margaret's wishes, they shall begin living separate and apart."

The public condemned what it saw as her wickedness. "Overnight Pierre became the most famous single father in the world," she observed, "and his popularity rating rose 17 percent in the polls."

Margaret went to live in New York City and became the centre of media attention. She had made a decision—a courageous one, in the view of many Canadians—and now she had to struggle with its consequences. In the election of May 22, 1979, Trudeau was ousted from office. "I felt stricken by his defeat," she said, "and the shame, hurt, and humiliation were mine just as much as his."

But impulsively, Margaret went that night to a Manhattan night club, where a cameraman caught her dancing. "They portrayed me to the world the next day," she recalled, "dancing, as it were, with my 'naked midriff' and my 'dishevelled hair', over my husband's political pyre."

Margaret remarried, and found herself only three blocks from 24 Sussex Drive, raising another family. Pierre made the decision to resign as prime minister on February 29, 1984, while pitting himself against the elements on the night of one of the worst blizzards in recent years.

 ✳

To love and to remember; that is good:
To love and to forget; that is not well:
To lapse from love to hatred; that is hell
And death and torment, rightly understood.

CHRISTINA ROSSETTI

Dangers and Delights

A teenaged girl meets a handsome computer consultant at a rock concert. She defies her parents by going to Spain with him and helping to establish a business. After having several children by this man, she is dropped for another woman.

A young machinist goes off with friends to fish at a spot belonging to a private resort. Its owner intervenes, until a female employee gets him drunk and they are able to catch the limit. She becomes the machinist's wife, but they can't get along and things end badly.

Hidden today within such tales is the old myth of Jason and Medea. And mythology is full of stories showing love as a dangerous thing.

Consider the Sirens,* who inspire males to swim madly ashore and be turned into skeletons. Here is the well known myth of the "fatal woman," *femme fatale.* It would be easy to apply this category to Medea, a witch, yet we see that she is a woman of extraordinary qualities.

There is also the "fatal man," putting a notch on his belt after each conquest. And a painful encounter with one of these, or his female counterpart, might induce people to swear off love forever. But usually the delights of love, such as Glenn describes, outweigh its dangers.

---

*See page 183.

The Next Slow One

I made my way a little closer, just so I wouldn't miss the opportunity to ask her during the next slow one. I waited what seemed like hours before the next slow song came on, and without thinking I rushed up to her and said, "Hi Carolyn, wou-wou-would you like to dance?"

She said, "Sure."

My God, I asked her in front of her friends. She must think I'm used to doing this. We walked toward a bunch of people on the dance floor, my heart in overtime.

I stopped to face her. She put her arms around my neck, and I was left with no choice except to put mine around her.

I started wondering if her eyes were closed, because some of the people around us had their eyes closed. So I closed mine. How nice it was to be close to a girl, moving with the music and feeling the dulled vision of coloured lights on my eyelids.

Lovers and madmen have such seething brains
Such shaping fantasies, that apprehend
More than cool reason ever comprehends.

WILLIAM SHAKESPEARE, *A MIDSUMMER NIGHT'S DREAM*

21. Marriage

Rest in Peace
Until We Meet Again

EPITAPH, WIFE IN MEMORY OF HER HUSBAND,
HINDHEAD CHURCHYARD, ENGLAND

Arthur and Guinevere *British*

The Britons had fallen on troubled times. Bloody conflict raged over the succession to the throne, and many feared that the Saxons might easily overrun a leaderless land.

Then Merlin the magician emerged from his home in the Welsh forests and came to London. He persuaded the archbishop to summon all of the knights. On arriving they saw, next to the cathedral, a large stone pierced by a sword.

The knights read a golden inscription: *"Whosoever Pulls This Sword From The Stone Is Rightly King Of All England."* Many put their strength to the test, but the sword could not be budged. So it was left there while the knights went off to compete in a tournament.

Sixteen years earlier, a baby had been conceived on a night of sorcery. Merlin had worked his magic so that the then king, Uther, could satisfy his passion for the beautiful Saxon Lady, Igraine. But when the baby was born, it had been stolen away from her and placed in the hands of Merlin, who named it Arthur.

Young Arthur was at the tournament that day, serving as a squire to Sir Kay. That knight, breaking his sword, said, "Arthur, be a good fellow and bring me a new sword from home." But when the youth went off, he saw a fine sword in the churchyard, unclaimed. This would save him a trip, he thought.

Arthur went over to the stone, grasped the sword's handle, and easily drew it out.

Arthur handed the sword to Sir Kay, who recognized it at once. "You have withdrawn this sword," he exclaimed, "after the best knights of the land have failed!" Arthur was surprised as everyone crowded around him and cheered.

"Let him be king!" the people shouted. "God save King Arthur!" And so it was. Under Arthur the Britons became united, and won a decisive victory over the Saxons. The king then established his capital at Camelot.

"My nobles want me to marry," Arthur said to Merlin one day. "They want a queen."

"Is there someone you love more than all the others?"

"Yes, Guinevere, the most beautiful woman alive!"

"That she is," Merlin agreed. "And yet marriage with her would be wrong, for I see that one knight, Sir Lancelot, will have a deep love for her and Guinevere for him. But alas, this knowledge will not change your heart from its desire."

And indeed, Arthur did make Guinevere his wife and queen. Her father owned the Round Table, which had been built by Merlin, and he gave it to the couple as part of the dowry. Arthur was so pleased that he said to Merlin, "Grant me fifty knights of prowess and piety."

Forty-eight men were assembled for the splendid marriage ceremony, and these became known as the Knights of the Round Table.

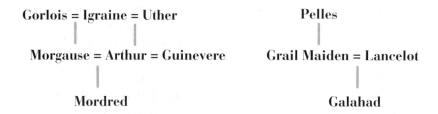

Arthurian family trees

Of all the knights of King Arthur, Lancelot was the most famous—handsome, generous, merry, courageous, full of grace and honour. But although he had the highest regard for Arthur, turmoil began the moment Guinevere buckled on Lancelot's sword for him. Exchanging a glance of complete adoration, Lancelot and the queen gave their hearts to each other. All would suffer just as Merlin had foretold.

To Lancelot, Guinevere was perfection, he could love no other woman. But he also worshipped Arthur, and several times rescued him from danger. This was the tragedy, that all three had extraordinary tenderness for each other, and Lancelot was torn between ecstatic passion and noble purpose.

Lancelot's adultery was the cause of his failure to attain the Holy Grail,* and on his quest he had confessed his sin to a hermit. The knight promised to dally with Guinevere no more. But as soon as the lovers saw each other again, this vow was forgotten and they were together whenever possible, day and night.

Arthur had once been seized with passion for Morgause, a daughter of Igraine by previous marriage. He was thus her half-brother but, unaware of this relationship, the two had had a son out of wedlock named Mordred. "You have lain with your sister," Merlin had informed the king, "and sired a child who shall one day destroy you and all of your knights."

Now this prophecy came true. It was this child, now a young man, who finally informed Arthur about the queen's adultery.

Arthur could not believe in this treachery. So he decided to test Guinevere, by going on a hunt without Lancelot. That night, Mordred came with thirteen other knights to the door of her chamber. "Traitor knight," he shouted, "come out of the queen's chamber!"

Lancelot was there, of course. "We are betrayed!" Guinevere cried. "I fear that our love has come to a mischievous end."

"You have always been my lady," he said, taking her in his arms and kissing her. "All I ask of you is to pray for my soul if I am slain."

---

*See pages 47-50.

Lancelot unbarred the door, and killed the first knight who tried to attack him. He struck with great speed, strode in among his assailants, and killed all but Mordred, who escaped. Then Lancelot swiftly rode to rally his kinsmen. "Arthur no doubt will be advised to punish the queen," he told them. "What course should we take?"

"Guinevere must be rescued," said Bors, who was Lancelot's nephew, and the others agreed.

According to the law, Guinevere was guilty of treason and should be burned. With great sadness, Arthur pronounced this verdict and secluded himself to avoid seeing her being led to the stake.

But rescued she would be. Lancelot rode with his knights straight to Camelot, killed many of Arthur's men, and made off with Guinevere to his own castle, Joyous Garde.

Arthur, learning what had happened, fainted from sorrow. Nothing more was left for him to do but lead his remaining knights to besiege Joyous Garde. In the fierce battle which followed, Bors knocked Arthur to the ground. With drawn sword, he stood above him and shouted to Lancelot, "Shall I end this war now?"

"Strike not, for I have never wished to see my lord either slain or shamed!" Lancelot cried. Then he pleaded with the king: "Arthur, for God's love remember all my service to you and make an end of this war!"

"Alas, that this war ever began!" said the king, tears springing from his eyes.

All withdrew from the battlefield. Later, the Pope issued a judgment—that Arthur should once again receive Guinevere.

"So madam, I leave you and this noble fellowship forever," Lancelot quietly told the queen. He would live on his lands in Brittany, leaving behind all that he loved most.

Lancelot kissed Guinevere and brought her to the king. When he turned to leave, a storm of weeping overcame them all. They were nearly out of their minds with sorrow.

Arthur's trials were not at an end, however. Mordred, had appeared to serve his father devotedly, but he knew that his bastardy would deprive him of the crown. He plotted against the king, and soon England was ravaged by civil war.

The warring knights finally gathered at Camlann. Arthur, who had held the Britons together for a generation, knew that the Saxons were massing to take advantage of Mordred's revolt. The knights' battle at Camlann, clearly, would be their last.

The fight lasted all day, as a hundred thousand lives were lost. Then at dusk beside a lake, Arthur saw Mordred. "There stands the traitor who brought on all this suffering," he said to himself. Thus came about a heart-rending struggle between father and son.

First one man had the advantage, then the other. Finally, Arthur sent his spear right through his son's body. Yet Mordred, even as he fell dead, managed to pierce the king's helmet with his sword.

Arthur was greviously wounded. But three queens approached, sailing on a small barge, to heal the fallen king.

On seeing Arthur, they wept and shrieked with dismay. The barge then sailed away until none could see it any longer, bearing Arthur to the Isle of Avalon. Some say that King Arthur is not dead and will come again at a time when England is in peril. Others say that he lies in a tomb, and on it is written: *Here Lies Arthur, The Once And Future King.*

Dearly beloved: We have come together in the presence of God to witness and bless the joining together of this man and this woman in Holy Matrimony. The bond and covenant of marriage was established by God in creation, and our Lord Jesus Christ adorned this manner of life by his presence and first miracle at a wedding in Cana of Galilee. It signifies to us the mystery of the union between Christ and his Church, and Holy Scripture commends it to be honoured among all people.

THE BOOK OF COMMON PRAYER
(ANGLICAN/EPISCOPALIAN)

We have taken the Seven Steps. You have become mine forever. Yes, we have become partners. I have become yours.
Hereafter, I cannot live without you. Do not live without me.
Let us share the joys. We are word and meaning, united. You
are thought and I am sound.

May the nights be honey-sweet for us; may the mornings be
honey-sweet for us; may the earth be honey-sweet for us;
may the heavens be honey-sweet for us.

THE "SEVEN STEPS" WEDDING RITE
(HINDU)

Till Death Us Do Part

The marriage bond is a central concern in the tale of Arthur.
Although it includes much Celtic hero legendary lore, Arthur was a
real man—a 6th-century leader of the "Britons," who had been citizens of the Roman Empire and staunchly opposed the invading
Saxons.

It was a 12th-century French writer, Chrétien de Troyes, who
turned Arthur into a king. He invented an adulterous "game of love"
between Guinevere and Lancelot, although nothing like this was
probably known to the roughhewn knights of Arthur's time.

This game of love came out of what we call chivalry. Such formal-
ities as opening the door for a woman originated from those at
medieval European courts. From these we get our modern idea of
"courtesy." Earlier it had been a man's world, where wives were regularly mistreated and beaten.

The emphasis on love, in this and other medieval tales, was new.
In ancient Rome, love had been expressed in verse as a kind of hunt
by the man. By the 11th and 12th centuries, however, it had become
a more serious matter, solemnized by the Christian marriage ritual.

Guinevere, in Welsh tradition, was regarded as a goddess in a vir-
tual religion of love. It may seem odd that she was sentenced to
death by burning, but because a queen was sacred, it was believed
that otherwise the earth would be contaminated by the magic in her
bones.

Goodbye to Greer County where blizzards arise,
Where the sun never sinks and a flea never dies,
And the wind never ceases but always remains
Till it starves us to death on our government claims.

Farewell Greer County, farewell to the West,
I'll travel back East to the girl I love best,
I'll travel back to Texas and marry me a wife,
And quit cornbread for the rest of my life.

TRADITIONAL AMERICAN

The King of Rock 'n' Roll *American*

At the wedding of Priscilla and Elvis Presley

Elvis Presley, driving his truck on deliveries in Memphis, would often pass Sam Phillips's Sun Recording Studio. He noticed that it advertised custom-recording services, and one day in 1953 he dropped in—"to make a record for my mother, just to surprise her."

Phillips had been looking out for something special. "If I could find a white man who had the Negro sound and the Negro feel," he often said, "I would make a billion dollars." When Elvis came in to make his recording, Phillips took interest, and later decided to "give the kid a try" at doing a blues number.

Several recording sessions followed, and then came an historic moment—on July 6, 1954, during a break. "Elvis picked up his guitar, started banging on it and singing 'That's All Right Mama'," guitar player Scotty Moore recalled. "The door of the control room was open, and Sam came running out and said, 'What the devil are you doing?' We said, 'We don't know.' He said, 'Well find out quick and don't lose it'."

Elvis Presley had become the first white performer to sing like a black man.

That night, the sound of popular music changed. When "That's All Right Mama" and its country flipside were played on WHBQ, so many requests flooded the station that the deejay spun only this record—one side and then the other—for the rest of the evening. He made a point of mentioning that he had attended Humes High School, which listeners well knew was for whites only.

Thus began the media exposure of the man who became known as the "King of Rock 'n' Roll." In American mythology Elvis still reigns, long after his death, over the world's most influential musical culture.

The young singer's fame grew quickly as he was vaulted into the leadership of America's restless teenagers. There was a growl of rebellion in his voice, a sneer in the corner of his upper lip. And in the throes of song, he would set his hips wildly gyrating. "I jump around because it's the way I feel," he said. "I can't even sing with a beat at all if I stand still."

Such anxiety grew over the image given by "Elvis the Pelvis" that on the Ed Sullivan Show in 1957, he was filmed "above the waist" as soon as it seemed that the notorious bump-and-hump was about to begin. "I want to say to Elvis Presley and the country," Sullivan was thus able to declare, "that this is a real decent fine boy."

Teenagers largely abandoned the slow fox-trot, to dance uninhibitedly like Elvis. In high schools across the continent, there was suddenly adult concern over dress codes, as formal wear became too restrictive for a new way of letting the body go wildly to the beat.

That year Elvis, now called the "king of rock 'n' roll," bought Graceland Mansion in Tennessee. White-pillared in the plantation style, it was a gift for his mother, Gladys. This became the home base for Elvis and the "good ol' boys" who surrounded him.

In 1958, Elvis was inducted into the army. Media attention focussed on the ritual of the G.I. haircut, to which his three-inch sideburns were sacrificed. There is truth in John Lennon's statement that "Elvis died when he joined the army"—especially because it was followed within weeks by the death of Gladys.

Elvis was devastated. After her casket was brought in, he would talk to her, saying how pretty she looked: "My Momma's all fixed up, it looks like she's going some place." On the day of the funeral he would collapse, be picked up, collapse—over and over again.

The loss of Gladys, who had meant security to Elvis, hung as a dark cloud over the rest of his life. "I could wake her up any hour of the night," he recalled, "and if I was worried or troubled about something she'd get up and try to help me."

While posted in Germany, Elvis met 14-year-old Priscilla Beaulieu. He ardently wooed this beautiful and untouched girl, intent on shaping her into a woman as perfect as his mother.

After Elvis returned to civilian life, Priscilla came to live in Graceland. Elvis had promised her stepfather that when she turned 21, marriage would occur. This happened in 1967 (at a Las Vegas casino). The relationship was finally consummated, and Priscilla immediately became pregnant.

But at Graceland, Elvis's "ideal" woman grew bored. He sent Priscilla out to learn karate. She fell in love with her instructor, Mike Stone, and divorced Elvis in 1973.

Her child by Elvis, Lisa Marie, is the sole heir to the fortune of the only musician ever to sell a billion records.

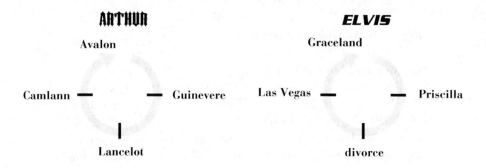

The hero-cycles of Arthur, and Elvis

Then came the heyday of groups like the Rolling Stones, whose music was based on the grittier forms of black music. The king lost touch with American youth, which began to see him as something of a joke.

But Elvis made a comeback, with sold-out shows in Las Vegas. Wearing a gem-encrusted white jump-suit, he would sing his famed *Trilogy*, fusing "Dixie," "All My Trials," and "The Battle Hymn of the Republic." Referring both to the black civil rights movement and the anguish of the Civil War, *Trilogy* encapsulated the myth of the South.

By the age of 40 Presley had earned $100 million, all of it spent. His craving for peanut-butter-and-banana sandwiches made him balloon to 116 kilograms, he had trouble remembering the words of songs that he now sung in a withered voice, and heavy drug use began to take its toll.

On August 16, 1977, the world was electrified by the news that Elvis had died. Some 100 000 fans converged on Memphis, hoping to file past the coffin of the man who had given his all—the king, dressed in a white suit.

Today as ever, this man ranks among the most beloved mortals in music history. Elvis is cherished for his generosity and politeness, his talent and success, his love of fun and simplicity of heart, his patriotism, his obedience to God, his tender devotion to his mother—and even for his self-deluding marriage to Priscilla.

Elvis will return, say the tabloids. He has become a god to his worshippers. And the shrine, Graceland, is now as famous as George Washington's Mount Vernon home.

A week after the funeral, Gladys Presley's body was transferred to a marble crypt alongside Elvis's in what became known as Meditation Gardens. Following an attempt to steal his body, it was placed in an immense vault with an inscription from Washington's home: *"God Saw That He Needed Some Rest And Called Him Home To Be With Him."*

Each August 15, starting at 11 p.m., some 10 000 admirers begin walking up the path from Graceland to the Meditation Gardens, bearing candles in a moving rite of remembrance.

Thus within the depths of human beings, as within the universe, lies the hidden cave where the Virgin who is infinitely receptive and infinitely fertile, and has been chained and hidden all our lives, awaits the coming of the divine hero, so that what is higher in us can be reborn.

MARTIN LEV, *THE TRAVELLER'S KEY TO JERUSALEM*

Summoned by the Maiden

A male hero is summoned by the maiden, ancient myth says, to rescue or release her. She is kept under her father's thumb, held in a cave, bound to a railway track, placed within a circle of flame. She holds powers of fertility and joy, wisdom and love—but these are held back until the hero wins her, and the two are reborn into a higher state of being.

Hard knocks have been delivered to this myth, by feminist concerns and the strains of modern life. Yet it is still upheld by the marriage rite, which affirms joy and harmony among all things. And with the birth of an heir, a blessing to parent and grandparent alike, the quest for a loving marriage begins again.

Panikos described the folk-oriented marriage customs observed on his native island of Cyprus—Aphrodite's island.* We note especially how fertility is affirmed, while God "looks down" on the earthly cycle of life. This link between heaven and earth signifies the ideal of Sacred Marriage.

A Wedding in Cyprus

Marriage is the union of a man and woman in holy matrimony. It is the beginning of a new life for the married couple, vowed by the rituals to love and togetherness for eternity. It is a sad and happy occasion for everyone, in rejoicing by traditional ways.

At the bridegroom's house all the friends of the groom have shown up waiting for him to get ready for the walk to the church. The musicians arrive and start to play while the barber shaves the spouse-to-be. Parents and relatives start to sing a song, about how he was born, how his parents struggled to raise him, and how it's his turn now to make a life of his own.

They begin the walk to the church while the musicians are still playing. Everyone follows behind. The father walks with the son, and the mother close by, and the same with the bride. The bride and groom meet at the church and walk in together. The old bearded priest wears the crown, and decorations of flowers in the church give it a beautiful fragrance.

After a while, the priest asks God to bless the couple and look down on them as man and wife. He places rings on their fingers, connected

---

*See page 220.

with a ribbon which symbolizes togetherness and life. Holy wine meaning the blood of Christ is given to both to drink, and also there's the bread which symbolizes Christ's body. Then they are led by the priest to walk in a circle a few times.

After church they all congratulate the couple and step outside while the bell is rung by little kids pulling on the rope. Pictures and movies are taken and they all leave to the big party where dancing will take place.

But first there is the dancing of the bed. A mattress is placed on the floor and when the music starts, the ladies come with their homemade sheets and pillows to dress the bed, and everybody forms a circle to watch. Crosses are stitched on all four corners and in the middle.

Then ladies with infants place them on the bed and roll them over. Usually it's a boy first and then a girl. This means that the couple will bear children and the first one will be a boy and then even a girl. Then the bed is raised in the air by both men and women and they dance in a circle for a few minutes. Money is also placed on the crosses, and the couple will use it for a home and to support each other.

The dancing and singing go on for hours into the night, sometimes until sunrise. Now comes what everyone has been waiting for, the dance of the bride and groom. First the bride starts to dance and then the groom behind. They dance in a circle and the people go up to them with money and pin it on them.

One of the most dramatic things is when the grandparents dance. They forget about their manly ways of being mean and the boss, and the affection that they kept inside of them is released as they dance with their canes in hand, smiling and having a lot of fun. Everyone looks at them and then join in, and even the shy ones who didn't dance say inside of them the hell with it and join in.

This is in Cyprus where tradition still exists. Life is portrayed many times in the singing of friends and the couple joining with God, and the rings and the dancing in circles you would say symbolize the cycle of life of mankind.

If you and your folks like me and my folks
Like me and my folks like you and your folks,
Then me and my folks like you and your folks
Like you and your folks like me and my folks.

ANONYMOUS

7 Till We Have Built Jerusalem

Jacob's Ladder

from Milton

And did those feet in ancient time
   Walk upon England's mountains green?
And was the holy Lamb of God
   On England's pleasant pastures seen?

And did the Countenance Divine
   Shine forth upon our clouded hills?
And was Jerusalem builded here
   Among these dark Satanic Mills?

Bring me my Bow of burning gold!
   Bring me my Arrows of desire!
Bring me my Spear: O clouds, unfold!
   Bring me my Chariot of fire!

I will not cease from Mental Fight,
   Nor shall my Sword sleep in my hand
Till we have built Jerusalem
   In England's green and pleasant land.

WILLIAM BLAKE

Myths tells of a land of peace and happiness called paradise. Blake's well-known poem, based on the legend that Christ once visited England, expresses the hope of creating there a perfect society—a new Jerusalem.

Blake himself is the artist of *Jacob's Ladder*, which shows a staircase spiralling to heaven from the dreaming Jacob (*Genesis* 29). Ascending angels represent the human soul, while divine wisdom is symbolized by those coming down through the stars to earth.

Blake was growing old when he expressed these two splendid visions. Such spiritual insights often come late in life, near the end of our earthly trials and triumphs. Existence, growing ever more strange and improbable, becomes an unfolding of mysteries.

22. Golden Age

Children today are tyrants. They contradict their parents, gobble their food, and tyrannize their teachers.

SOCRATES, 5TH CENTURY B.C.

The Four Ages of Mankind *Roman*

First there was the Golden Age, a time of perfect goodness. There were no crimes, no courts, no judges, no jails, not even laws. Because peace prevailed, no soldiers nor weapons were to be found anywhere. The people remained healthy and youthful, danced and laughed all day, and experienced death as a kind of peaceful sleep.

All year the hills remained clothed with green trees, and the metals slept undisturbed deep below. Animals lived at peace with one another and with humankind. The earth was untouched by the plough's blade, yet it yielded berries and acorns for all. The rivers flowed with milk, and the oaks dripped golden honey. In an everlasting springtime, soft breezes caressed the flowers.

When Saturn was dethroned by Jupiter,* he fled to the remote Isle of the Blest. Here the Golden Age continued to be enjoyed by him and the other Titans.

Elsewhere, Jupiter divided the year into seasons and thus began the Silver Age. With extremes of hot and cold, it became necessary to build houses. As the Earth stopped giving food freely, beasts had to be harnessed for ploughing, and grain had to be sown in the furrows. Although people lived a long life, they were subject to violent quarrels and tragic, untimely deaths.

The Bronze Age followed. People now devoured flesh as well as bread. Arming themselves with bronze weapons, they took pleasure in battle.

*See page 206.

In the Iron Age, our own, the earth was overwhelmed with crime. Truth gave way to deceit, loyalty to treason, modesty to greed. The land, once held in common, was divided up into possessions. Forests were stripped bare of their trees, and people laboured in the depths of the earth to gouge out its treasures.

War became an obsession, and men and women lived by plunder. Sons wished to see their fathers dead, so as to grasp their inheritance. Parents fought with their children. Even brothers and sisters loathed one another. And every god abandoned our blood-soaked earth, the maiden Justice leaving last.

It was a movie about American bombers in the Second World War and the gallant men who flew them. Seen backwards by Billy, the story went like this:

American planes, full of holes and wounded men and corpses took off backwards from an airfield in England. Over France, a few German fighter planes flew at them backwards, sucked bullets and shell fragments from some of the planes and crewmen. They did the same for wrecked American bombers on the ground, and those planes flew up backwards to join the formation.

The formation flew backwards over a German city that was in flames. The bombers opened their bomb doors, exerted a miraculous magnetism which shrunk the fires, gathered them into cylindrical steel containers, and lifted the containers into the bellies of the planes. The containers were stored neatly in racks. The Germans below had miraculous devices of their own, which were long steel tubes. They used them to suck more fragments from the crewmen and planes. But there were still a few wounded Americans, though, and some of the bombers were in bad repair. Over France, though, German fighters came up again, made everything and everybody as good as new.

When the bombers got back to their base, the steel cylinders were taken from the racks and shipped back to the United States of America, where factories were operating night and day, dismantling the cylinders, separating the dangerous contents into minerals. Touchingly, it was mainly women who did this work. The minerals were then shipped to specialists in remote areas. It was their business to put them into the ground, to hide them cleverly, so they would never hurt anybody ever again.

The American fliers turned in their uniforms, became high school kids. And Hitler turned into a baby, Billy Pilgrim supposed. That wasn't in the movie. Billy was extrapolating. Everybody turned into a baby, and all humanity, without exception, conspired biologically to produce two perfect people named Adam and Eve, he supposed.

Kurt Vonnegut, Jr., Slaughterhouse Five

Better in the Old Days

"Things were better in the old days," some say. "People used to care more about other people." And myths, throughout the world, tell of some better time long ago. In native North American tales, we often hear of a time when human beings lived with animals in perfect harmony.

The myth of the Golden Age, a long-ago era of peace and abundance, was described by the Roman poet Ovid (the basis for our retelling).

In Roman times, the Golden Age was recalled in a rite called the Saturnalia, which happened in late December. A temporary king was chosen by lot from among the people, and for a month he would do and have whatever he wanted. At the ritual's end, this mock king would cut his own throat on Saturn's altar.

Saturnalia goes back to the cave-dwellers' dread of the year's darkest time: would the dwindling sun entirely disappear? Would it ever fully return? To make its rebirth happen, people celebrated as the days grew longer. And we still can look to important celebrations at this time of year.

Even though the gods described here are no longer worshipped, their presence is still with us. Saturn, the Greek Cronus, is remembered in the week's last day, Saturday. As Father Time, he carries an hourglass and a death-sickle shaped like the waning moon—and New Year's Day cartoons often show him in this way, the fresh year being represented as a baby.

The week as a whole, in fact, has been steeped in mythology since

Babylonian times. It starts with the two main sky-travellers, the sun and moon, which are usually associated with the male and female powers, respectively. The fifth and sixth days are linked with the gods' chieftain and the love-goddess.

The Days of the Week							
	1	2	3	4	5	6	7
English	Sunday	Monday	Tuesday	Wednesday	Thursday	Friday	Saturday
French	Dimanche	Lundi	Mardi	Mercredi	Jeudi	Vendredi	Samedi
Babylonian	Shamash	Sin	Nergal	Nebo	Marduk	Ishtar	Ninib
Greek	Helios	Selene	Ares	Hermes	Zeus	Aphrodite	Cronus
Roman	Sol	Luna	Mars	Mercury	Jupiter	Venus	Saturn
Northern	Sun	Moon	Tyr	Odin/Woden	Thor	Freya	Saturn

Saturn rules over the remote island of a Golden Age. Here, says the Roman writer Hesiod, "bounteous Earth thrice yearly bears fruit as sweet as honey." Similar is the Valhalla of Scandinavian myth, a place of reward for great heroes chosen from among those slain in war.*

A modern parallel would be the "hall of fame" memorializing sports heroes. One stands at Cooperstown, New York, where the game is said to have been "invented" by Abner Doubleday in 1839. As in ancient Greece, where offerings were made at the tombs of heroes, baseball fans come to do homage before the bronze statues of great players.

Even on the level of a humble playground game, like hopscotch, the eternal dimension is found. A German term for it is Himmelhupfen, heaven-hopping.

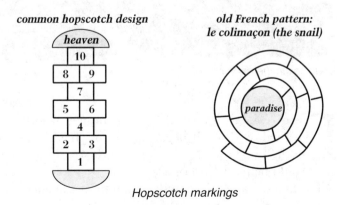

common hopscotch design

old French pattern:
le colimaçon (the snail)

Hopscotch markings

---

*See page 268.

People down to one sandwich would see the guy next to them with no sandwich and split it. Woodstock pulled the very best out of us.

Everybody was thrilled that there were so many of us. We thought, "Hey, we're going to change everything."

DAVID CROSBY, OF THE ROCK GROUP CROSBY, STILLS, NASH, AND YOUNG

Woodstock Nation *American*

Woodstock in the morning

There is a bad myth about the famed Woodstock Festival of 1969. It began an era of greed, says this myth, by showing the music industry how much money could be made from rock 'n' roll.

What follows is another myth, much nicer to believe.

A pilgrim's quest, traditionally, is for union with the divine. The goal of pilgrimage might be a holy city such as Jerusalem or Mecca or Benares. Or its destination could be a sacred river or mountaintop, or a Hall of Fame raised in memory of heroes. The quest could also lead to a festival.

In the 1960s, the term "festival" was applied to rock concerts, one-shot affairs often promoted as a kind of love-in. By far the most famous, the most mythical, was the one known simply as Woodstock.

The Woodstock Festival, promising "three days of love and music," came from an earlier plan to hold it at Woodstock, in upstate New York. This was an art colony inhabited by a visionary rock superstar, Bob Dylan. However, he never graced the event, which was ultimately held 100 kilometres away near Bethel, New York.

On August 15, 1969, some 400 000 people converged on Bethel, whose name in Hebrew means "holy spot." Festival-goers hitchhiked, rode motorcycles, drove old hearses and Day-Glo vans. Finally caught in a massive traffic jam, they received 30 000 sandwiches, made by Jewish ladies and distributed, free, by Catholic sisters.

Many pilgrims walked the last few kilometres from Bethel to the meadow where the concert was being held— a superb natural amphitheatre filled with a crowd that stunned the imagination. "Wow! Phhew!" exclaimed Richie Havens when he stepped to the mike as the festival's first performer. "I mean like wow! Phhhew!"

For three days and three nights the festival continued, with musical sets running so far behind schedule that many groups didn't perform until early in the morning. And among those performers there would be several who had only a few months left in their lives: the Who's drummer Keith Moon, Janis Joplin, and Jimi Hendrix.

Because no one had had any experience with anything of this scope, water and food supplies were far from enough. Yet in a family spirit there was much sharing, and the people who lived on communal farms nearby distributed free whole-wheat porridge with raisins.

These were the "flower children." They wore love beads, fringed buckskins, tie-dyed headbands, granny gowns, leather vests, beards, and shoulder-length hair. Of course, many wore nothing at all as they waded into a nearby pond, summoning up the ancient image of a Golden Age.

The previous generation had created undreamed-of prosperity for their children, and on that same month had even placed men on the moon. But this tribe sensed even greater possibilities—global peace, ecstatic harmony, an uncontaminated earth. Joni Mitchell summed it up in her song about the Festival, telling how we must get "back to the garden."

Four months later, thousands of people trekked to a speedway at Altamont, California, where a free Rolling Stones concert was promised. Here, a security force was made up of the outlaw motorcycle gang, Hell's Angels. And even as Mick Jagger impersonated His Satanic Majesty, the bikers savaged the audience, leaving four people murdered.

To those who had expected a reprise of Woodstock, the outcome seemed like the Fall from Eden. It was the loss of innocence, a descent from the divine to the demonic. Altamont revealed what realists knew all along: that the world still awaited the Golden Age's return.

In marble halls as white as milk,
Lined with a skin as soft as silk,
Within a fountain crystal-clear,
A golden apple doth appear.
No doors there are to his stronghold,
Yet thieves break in and steal the gold.

CHILDREN'S RHYME

Paradise Lost

The term "paradise," meaning a place of bliss, comes from an ancient Persian word. Originally it referred to a walled enclosure, and later, to an oasis where a person might drink pure water beneath shady palms.

Eden, meaning delight or luxury, is a paradise lost. Here Adam and Eve, of the Old Testament, walk with God "in the cool of the day." And sometimes feeling trapped, we long to regain a joyful innocence in such an ideal place—a cottage on a northern lake, a perfect ski run, glistening sands on remote tropical beaches.

In a similar way, childhood is often seen as a time of perfect happiness. Bathed in love and protected by our parents, we had fun all day—or so we remember it. And as Karl shows, we may find a nostalgic delight in a child's innocence.

Only the Very Young

We were sitting down on a rickety old dock with our feet in the water. Jessica was telling me about something. Her pretty little five-year-old face was filled with the type of wonder that only the very young can possess, unspoiled by bitterness.

Although we were a dozen years apart, we could easily get on the same wavelength. For a joke, I told Jessica that I had just seen a water snake. She didn't believe me, yet her witty mind saw an opportunity for fun.

She told me not to think of water snakes. "Think about something nice," she said. "Think about . . . riding a motorcycle."

A few seconds later, I heard a little voice exclaim, "There's a water snake!" Jessica was trying to scare me, and she laughed heartily at her little joke.

Then her dad came for her in a canoe. As it slowly moved away, time seemed to click back into place.

The only paradise is paradise lost.

MARCEL PROUST

23. World Tree

In the old days when we were a strong and happy people all our power came to us from the sacred hoop of the nation, and so long as the hoop was unbroken, the people flourished. The flowering tree was the living centre of the hoop and the circle of the four quarters nourished it.

BLACK ELK, OGLALA SIOUX SHAMAN

Odin the Dark Horseman *Scandinavian*

In the beginning there was only a vast, yawning deep. Then north became north, and a fountain began spouting there. It grew into a raging torrent and gave birth to twelve rivers which immediately froze. A crushing weight of ice filled this great deep.

South became south, brewing fiery winds that blew on the ice. From the melting ice emerged the giant Ymir and a cow to provide milk. As the beast licked the salt in the ice, her hot tongue revealed strands of yellow hair. When a torso and limbs emerged, the creature rose up and walked. This was the first god.

A second generation of gods appeared. Then came a third, among whom was Odin. A master of magic and poetry with powers surpassing those of any other being, Odin became the great god of the north.

One day Odin and his brothers fell into a bitter dispute with Ymir, and they killed him. From his body, they formed the world as we know it.

The heavens were shaped from Ymir's skull, the clouds from his brains, the earth from his flesh, the trees from his hair. Ymir's eyebrows became Midgard, soon to serve as the home of the human race.

Surrounding Midgard was an ocean, formed out of Ymir's blood. Its outer shore was the land of the giants, whose mountains were created from his bones. The World Serpent lay in the ocean, completely filling it so its jaws grasped its tail.

And from what remained of Ymir's body sprang the World Tree, Yggdrasil. This colossal ash tree supported the entire universe, binding all the worlds in wholeness.

One of Yggdrasil's roots lodged deep within Midgard. Another rose into Asgard, fortress of the gods. And a third extended down to Niflheim, where it was gnawed perpetually by a dragon.

At the World Tree's base were two wells. One belonged to the wisdom god, Mimir, *He Who Thinks*. He drank from it to learn the truth, and after his death his skull remained there for consultation.

The other well belonged to the three Norns, who sprinkled Yggdrasil's roots with water every day. Urd, incredibly old, knew the human race's past. Verdandi understood

The Norse universe

the present, and Skuld interpreted the future. Like the Fates of ancient Greece, the Norns held the threads of destiny and could pronounce the fate of both people and gods.

Odin craved wisdom above all. When he asked Mimir for permission to drink from his well, he was required to give one of his eyes as a pledge. And then to win knowledge from the magical writings known as runes, he hung himself on the World Tree.

For nine days and nights Odin suffered on Yggdrasil, a sacrifice to himself. Rocked by the wind, he waited in vain for anyone to come and relieve his agony. Finally, deep below his feet, he saw the runes.

Odin bent down to lift the magic writings. Falling from the World Tree, he at once began to grasp their meaning. Now like the Norns, he could prophesy human fate.

Odin's throne was in his palace, Valhalla. Each night two ravens were to be seen on the god's shoulders. They flew throughout the world during the day to bring report of all they had seen.

Putting on the vast cloak of the sky, with a broad hat concealing his face, Odin would ride his eight-legged horse across the heavens. He wandered the whole world, often intervening in the lives of his favourites. Sometimes the god would leave his body asleep on earth, becoming a bird or wild beast, but usually he appeared as a dark horseman.

Odin had many names. One was Lord of the Gallows, for often he would sit beneath the hanged, trying to learn the wisdom of the dead. He Who Makes Mad was another. For he could fill warriors with frenzy. Before battle, warriors would invoke his name, and anyone not favoured by Odin would be utterly paralysed with terror.

Those who died as heroes went to Valhalla, their hall of reward. Eight hundred warriors, shoulder to shoulder, could stride through each of its 540 doors, and daily they feasted on the meat of a boar. Each morning the beast was roasted, but by night it had became whole again. The men could fight and slash one another to pieces, for like the boar they would recover completely from any wound.

Odin's Ordeal

I hung heretofore
on the tempest-tost tree,
swung nights full nine.
Stung with a spear,
offered to Odin -
myself, to myself!
Tied to that tree
whose roots run deep;
how deep, no one knows.

Nourished by none
denied all drink
down into depths I peered.
Suddenly, saw the runes.
Groaned to grip them,
fell in a faint.
Set free by their force,
winning the wisdom
I rejoiced in rebirth.
Word by word
I was led to the light;
from vision, to vigour.

ICELANDIC POEM

Ygg's Horse

Trees give wood for shelter, as well as nuts and fruit. They have
wonderful strength and the power to achieve a kind of rebirth each
spring. Each season they are transformed, producing seeds which go
down to the earth from which the trees emerged in the first place.

Trees may be just trees for us, but in myths they are among the
most potent of symbols. On Yggdrasil, Odin suffers a kind of death
before regaining his vigour through self-sacrifice.

Odin's ordeal typifies that of the shaman.* Siberian shamans will sacrifice a horse, then ride its soul to the heavens on what they claim to be eight-legged steeds, just like Odin's. Yggdrasil means "Ygg's [Odin's] Horse" and the gallows in folklore are known as the "hanged man's horse."

So Odin was called the God of the Hanged Man. Most of Denmark's "bog people," whose well-preserved bodies are from his era, met death by strangulation. Although these people may have been offerings to Mother Earth, most scholars believe that they were sacrificed to Odin—who was absorbed in the wisdom of the dead.

Odin was a god who walked on earth among mortals. Yggdrasil's trunk connected the divine world, Asgard, with Midgard, where human beings live out their lives.

Yggdrasil was possibly an ancestor of the Christmas tree. First mentioned in a 14th-century chronicle as a "paradise tree" figuring in a play, it was subsequently set up in homes. In 1841, Prince Albert introduced the Christmas tree to Britain from his native Germany, so that many in the English-speaking world now "gather around the tree" as tender sentiments flow.

Also linked with the World Tree is the yule log. Christmas occurs at the year's darkest hour—a carry-over from ancient times when people wished to be sure that light would return in the spring. They held fire festivals, from which the yule log survives.

The Hebrews observed such rites, and today during Hannukah, candles burn in the Jewish household—one being added for each of eight nights. This is observed in mid-December. Several weeks earlier the Hindus enjoy a festival of lights honouring Divali, goddess of good fortune. Parallel to this response to midwinter darkness is the Chinese solstice ritual.**

---

*See pages 79-81.
**See page 200.

Old Roger

Old Roger is dead and laid in his grave,
LAID IN HIS GRAVE, LAID IN HIS GRAVE;
Old Roger is dead and laid in his grave,
H'M HA! LAID IN HIS GRAVE.

They planted an apple tree over his head,
OVER HIS HEAD, OVER HIS HEAD;
They planted an apple tree over his head,
H'M HA! OVER HIS HEAD.

The apples grew ripe and ready to fall,
READY TO FALL, READY TO FALL,
The apples grew ripe and ready to fall,
H'M HA! READY TO FALL.

There came an old woman a-picking them all,
A-PICKING THEM ALL, A-PICKING THEM ALL,
There came an old woman a-picking them all,
H'M HA! A-PICKING THEM ALL.

Old Roger jumps up and gives her a knock,
GIVES HER A KNOCK, GIVES HER A KNOCK,
Which makes the old woman go hipperty-hop,
H'M HA! HIPPERTY-HOP.

TRADITIONAL ENGLISH

Right Jolly Old Elf *International*

St. Nicholas was a bishop who long ago lived in what is now Turkey. An anonymous manuscript, now in Cairo's Coptic Museum, tells this story:

There once was a family which had lost all its wealth. Without dowries, the three daughters were now doomed to a life of misery. One night in secret, the saint slipped three bags of gold coins through the window of the family's home. But the father discovered the saint and tearfully asked, "Why have you hidden such wonderful deeds?"

"When you offer gifts," said St. Nicholas, quoting Jesus, "do it in secret, not letting the left hand know what your right hand is doing."

St. Nicholas was revered by merchants, who adopted his three bags of gold as the pawnbroker's symbol. Sailors long ago regarded him much as the Greeks had Poseidon, god of the sea. And, of course, English-speaking people know him as "Santa Claus," who still wears the red tunic of a bishop.

Today in Amsterdam, Holland, a white-bearded Sint Niklaas annually rides in a big parade. His white horse is said to take him over the rooftops, bringing gifts to be placed in the children's shoes beside the fire. On December 5, the Saint's feast is still held, with the traditional gift-giving.

But at one time, Sint Niklaas was widely denounced as a "heathen." He much resembled Odin, galloping across the skies on a horse, his identity concealed. Also, like Odin, he would offer gifts and punish bad deeds.

Although the Puritan colonists of New England frowned on pagan Christmas customs, many of these practices came to North America as other European immigrants flooded her shores. The Dutch invited Sint Niklaas to Nieuw Amsterdam, later taken over by the British and renamed New York. That, perhaps, was when English-speaking people adopted the figure they called "Santa Claus."

One December day in 1822 in New York, Clement Clark Moore was shovelling some snow with Jan, his pot-bellied and white-bearded oddjob man. After Jan drove off to the tune of sleighbells, Moore was inspired to write a poem: "A Visit from Saint Nicholas."

It much delighted Moore's children. Copied and recopied by friends, it was finally published in a New York newspaper and soon became known around the world.

Moore, clinging to his scholarly reputation as the compiler of a Hebrew dictionary, didn't acknowledge his authorship for fifteen years. But he created the modern Santa Claus, just as surely as Homer gave personalities to the Greek gods.

"A right jolly old elf," we read in Moore's poem. Elf? The modern Santa is certainly sizeable, and for this we can thank artist Haddon Sundblom, who in 1931 illustrated for Coca-Cola a large, grandfatherly man. It was this image which has since appealed to people's imagination. It also triggered a commercial exploitation that many dislike.

Still the myth of Santa Claus, for all its commercialism, continues to provide children with a way of experiencing life's magic. Even after learning who Santa really is, children will conspire with their parents to keep alive the myth of St. Nicholas. Jolly Saint Nick, riding a sleigh drawn by eight tiny reindeer, comes to their very rooftop, and like the St. Nicholas of old he leaves gifts in the best possible way—secretly.

To show a child what has once delighted you, to find the child's delight added to your own, so that there is now a double delight seen in the glow of trust and affection, this is happiness.

J. B. PRIESTLEY

Perfect Shapes

Paradise is about perfection, and here are two "perfect shapes."

The tree-shaped tetrakys fascinated followers of Pythagoras, well-known for his theorem. The dots, arranged in rows of one to four, add up to ten. A trinity of dots at the bottom is overarched by seven others, associated by the Pythagoreans with notes of the musical octave. And isolated at the centre is a number which they considered absolute, the one.

The other is the cross—humanity's most ancient symbol, dating from as long ago as 10 000 B.C. It may suggest a union of the divine and the earthly, and a reconciliation of tensions between the two. It can also mean the Four Directions and the four roads leading to and from the centre.

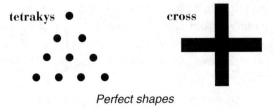

Perfect shapes

The Christian cross is often shown in medieval art as a tree, centre of the worshipper's life. For the Scandinavians, Yggdrasil served as the centre of the world—as ziggurats did for the Babylonians, and Serpent Mountain for the Aztecs.

Two other trees appear in the Bible, at its beginning and end. The first (*Genesis* 2:17) bears a Forbidden Fruit which brings suffering into the world. The second (*Revelation* 22:2) gives promise of paradise.

The more benevolent aspect appears in the Christmas tree, focal-point of family joy in many a home at winter's darkest time. This living-room-size World Tree kindles a vision of warmth and hope—a paradise of shared love, as Maria indicates.

Around the Table at Christmas

Christmas is wonderful at my house. Everyone knows their true role in the family. My mother graciously prepares dinner with great experience; my father prepares the fire-place and when he strikes the match I notice the pride in his eyes; my brothers usually talk with each other about work; and I prepare the table, setting the family candle in the middle of the table.

When everything is ready my mom calls to us, "Venite a mangiare," and we gather around the table. My father kisses my mother first, then the children kiss my father's hand and each cheek, in the order of birth. His eyes are filled with proud tears as he cries in front of us. Then we all kiss my mother and she also cries, and the children kiss one another.

The room glows with love as my father sits down at the head of the table, with my mother by his side and the result of their union before them. All is forgiven at Christmas, when respect for position within the family is strongest.

The Tree of Life

And he showed me a pure river of water of life, clear as crystal, proceeding out of the throne of God and of the Lamb. In the midst of the street of it, and on either side of the river, was there the tree of life, which bare twelve manner of fruits, and yielded her fruit every month: and the leaves of the tree were for the healing of nations.

THE REVELATION OF ST. JOHN THE DIVINE, CHAPTER 22

24. Renewal

They that wait upon the Lord shall renew their strength; they shall mount up with wings as eagles; they shall run, and not be weary, and they shall walk, and not faint.

ISAIAH 40:31

Balder's Return *Scandinavian*

Of the deities who lived in Asgard, the most handsome was Balder, the sun-god. He was also the happiest—until one day when gloom descended on him. Odin, Balder's father, asked what had brought on such despair.

"I dreamed that I would die," said Balder.

Odin shuddered but replied, "How could you be harmed? You have no enemies."

Balder said nothing. Odin went to his wife Frija, and they tried to decide how to lighten their son's mood.

"Let everyone and everything swear an oath never to injure him!" said Odin.

"Yes," Frija agreed. "I will tell them all."

And Frija went to all gods and people, all giants and dwarfs, all metals and stones, all diseases and poisons, even water and fire. All of them swore never to harm Balder—all but one. In her hurry, she had overlooked one small shrub growing on Asgard, called mistletoe.

This oath brought good sport to the gods. They flung spears at Balder, marvelling at how they veered off on approaching his body. Even heavy rocks, no matter how well-aimed, changed course in mid-flight. The gods shouted with laughter, and finally Balder forgot his gloom.

Only Loki remained unamused. A mere fire-demon, he was jealous of the sun-god and all this fun irritated him. Unable to control his jealousy any longer, he went to Frija, disguised as an old woman, and inquired about the oaths.

Have all things sworn to do Balder no harm?" Loki asked. "Every single thing?"

"All except for one tiny plant, surely too small to be harmful," Frija replied. "Its name is mistletoe."

Loki rushed off and soon returned to the scene of the gods' merriment. He noticed that Balder's brother, Hodur the blind god of winter, was not participating.

"You ought to be shooting as well!" Loki told him, placing a small dart in his hand. "Here, take this and I'll help you to aim it."

Hodur threw the dart at Balder, and this time it went straight to the mark. Down fell the sun-god, instantly dead.

It was the mistletoe, of course. Loki had found the plant, shaped it to a point, and guided it straight into Balder's heart.

The grief-stricken gods lifted Balder's body and carried it to his great dragon-ship. A funeral pyre was built, and the body was placed upon it. The sight overwhelmed Balder's wife, who cried out in remorse and sank lifeless to the ground. When the pyre was set ablaze, her body was beside his.

The evening wind filled the dragon-ship's sails, and sent it drifting out to sea. With the beginning of darkness, the flames rose higher and higher. Then the glare died to a flicker, and the spent ship sank into the ocean.

Balder was gone. But Frija, filled with hope that he might be brought back, cried out, "Who will ride to Niflheim, to restore Balder to us again?" Hermod the Swift, Odin's son, volunteered.

Mounting Sleipnir, the eight-footed horse that could outrun the wind, Hermod rode into the cave leading to Niflheim. Past Garm the blood-smeared hound he galloped, then downward for nine days and nine nights until, beneath the lowest of Yggdrasil's roots, he came to Helgate.

Hermod, digging his spurs into Sleipnir's sides, soared over Hel-gate into the vast hall of the Underworld. Here he saw Hel, Loki's ghastly offspring, thrown here by Odin to become queen of the Underworld. Half of her face was pink, the other half blue like a corpse's.

Here too, seated on a lofty throne, was Balder. Hermod went before the queen and pleaded for his return. "I must see how greatly this god is loved," she replied. "Deliver this message: if all things in the world mourn for Balder, he shall return."

Hermod remounted Sleipnir at once and started off on the gruelling journey back to Asgard. The gods, hearing his message, despatched messengers to all parts of the universe with that one request.

Earth, stones, trees, animals, people—all mourned the passing of Balder. Yet when the mission was almost complete, the messengers found an old witch who would not agree to weep for Balder. "I loved him not, living or dead," she croaked. "Let Hel keep her dead!"

The messengers used all their persuasive powers upon the witch, but she would not change her mind. When the gods learned the sorrowful news, they knew that this creature, indeed, must be Loki. No one else would be capable of so much evil. The gods were angry.

Loki fled to a distant mountain and hid in a small hut. The gods followed. They discovered a fish net in the cabin and dragged the nearest stream. When they caught a huge salmon, it struggled violently to escape. Thor grasped it by the tail, and instantly Loki appeared. The jealous demon had been caught.

Loki was bound in chains and fastened to a rock. A serpent was suspended above him so that the poison from its fangs dripped onto his face. Loki's faithful wife held out a goblet to catch the venom, but whenever she carried it away to empty it, the drops made the demon writhe in anguish, and earthquakes disturbed the world.

The death of Balder brings on Ragnarok, the Twilight of the Gods. Three harsh winters, unrelieved by a single summer, freeze the earth and bury it with blizzards. The sun grows weaker and weaker, turning blood-red, and then disappears. Disorder visits the land as the bonds of human loyalty snap. Brother turns against brother, father against son.

Loki breaks his chains and joins the evil children that he has sired: the firebreathing wolf Fenris, with an upper jaw that touches the heavens and a lower that scrapes the earth; and the World Serpent, flung at birth into the ocean, who has now grown to such a length that it encircles the world and bites on its own tail.

For Odin the time has come to fight. He calls on Heimdall, the watchman, who summons all the gods and heroes with a shrill blast on his horn. The World Tree, from its roots to the uppermost branches, begins to shake.

Odin leads this company of warriors, to the plain of the Last Battle. He himself is the first to fall, swallowed by the cavernous jaws of Fenris. But his son, Vidar, holds the wolf's lower jaw apart while he twists the other upwards, until with a resounding crack it breaks, killing the monster.

Then Loki marches forward to meet the valiant Heimdall, and in a desperate struggle they kill each other. Thor grapples with the World Serpent, a blow from his hammer crushing its skull. But it spews out so much poison into the air that Thor falls dead—even in the moment of victory.

Only one of the gods, Tyr, remains alive. Hearing the howling of Garm released from the infernal depths, he races to attack the beast. But when Tyr plunges his sword deep into its heart, Garm mauls him so terribly that he too dies.

The entire earth is now set on fire, feeding on all living things until none remain. The stars plunge from the sky. The ocean and all the rivers rise and overflow until everything is covered, until the field of the Last Battle can no longer be seen.

But slowly a new earth emerges. From the waves it arises, green and pure. Again the cataract falls, the eagle flies, fish swim beneath the cliffs. From fields unsown, plants grow abundantly.

And a new generation of gods appears. For the World Tree did not fall in the Last Battle, and in its branches the old gods' children have taken shelter. The flames cannot consume it, and the morning dew on its leaves gives nourishment.

Vidar and another of Odin's sons survive, as do two of Thor's descendants. And one day the world smiles as Balder, resurrected, returns.

The cricket sings in my heart. My heart sings in the cricket.

Zen Master

Good Fortune

Always, people yearn for better things in the future. Horoscopes and good-luck charms are part of life today, and anyone visiting the dead city of Pompeii will note how avidly its citizens, 2000 years ago, wooed the goddess Fortuna.

Doomsayers forever abound, of course. Many are beguiled by special numbers: lucky seven, or demonic 666, or the big round 1000. In 999 A.D., people were in a frenzy over the apocalypse that seemed certain to come, but the 2nd millennium A.D. arrived uneventfully.

Now its end approaches, and bookings have begun for a gala December 1999 cruise on the Queen Elizabeth II, from New York to the Great Pyramid, with Bruce Springsteen and Ronald Reagan among the optimists who have signed on.

We all want to peer into the future, fascinated by possibilities yet to come—a cure for cancer, perhaps, or peace on earth. When children unfold the little squares of the fortune game, eager for good tidings, they rehearse the hopes and fears of adults opening the day's newspaper.

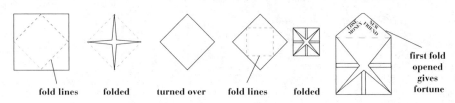

Children's fortune game

The world's ultimate renewal, many believe, will come only with its destruction. People often think of this as a specific and imminent event. A German preacher named Stoeffler announced in 1524 that the world's end would soon come as a horrendous flood. His alarmed parishioners built arks, but were so angry when the flood failed to materialize that they threw Stoeffler into a pond.

The bestselling non-fiction book of the 1970s, Hal Lindsey's *The Late Great Planet Earth*, told how the European Common Market would revive the Roman Empire and a Soviet invasion of Israel would trigger a nuclear war—the Battle of Armageddon told in *Revelation*.

Revelation, the last book of the Bible, has engendered many such frightening prophecies. It is possible, however, to see *Revelation* simply as the triumph of good over evil. The divine and human are joined in marriage, all of humankind's yearnings are fulfilled, and the world undergoes a final renewal.

Karma Repair Kit: Items 1-4

1. Get enough food to eat,
    and eat it.

2. Find a place to sleep where it is quiet,
    and sleep there.

3. Reduce intellectual and emotional noise
    until you arrive at the silence of yourself,
    and listen to it.

4.

RICHARD BRAUTIGAN

Somewhere the Hurting Must Stop *Canadian*

Terry Fox on the "Marathon of Hope"

O n November 12, 1976, 18-year-old Terry Fox had a slight car accident that gave soreness in his right knee. He played on the basketball team of his university near Vancouver, British Columbia, and the knee gave him trouble throughout the winter season.

Terry went to the doctor and received pain killers. Then one day, when he found it impossible to stand up, he saw a bone specialist. It was discovered that he had osteogenic sarcoma, a rare and malignant form of cancer.

Terry's family was around him, weeping, when the doctor gave word that the leg must be amputated. New drugs gave a 50 to 70 percent chance of survival, he said. Yet it was well known that sarcoma cells often drift elsewhere, usually into the lungs, and a few might have already spread within Terry's body.

Head Nurse Judith Ray cried too, but told Terry, "You can either mope or you can fight it." She explained how arrangements could be made for him to complete university and go on with his life. This made him see his trial as a challenge.

Then an article in *Runner's World* caught Terry's eye. It told of someone who had run on one leg in the New York Marathon. "I can do that too," he told Judith. And even before Terry's right leg was amputated, just above the knee, he had begun a fantastic dream—that he would be able to run across Canada.

Many people gave Terry help and encouragement during his hospital stay. He began to feel a debt to others, especially those in his ward. "I had to hear doctors tell people they had a 35 percent chance of living, and then to hear that person tell their family," he said. "My heart became larger during that time."

Terry began reading the Bible, and found in it a justification for hope. Also, he learned to run.

His left leg would make a double hop and the metal one a long stride. Blisters formed, however, and these bled copiously before turning to callouses. "It was just like running on coals," he said. "The blood would run all down my knee and my leg."

On August 30, 1979, Terry entered a marathon, intending to complete half of it. But after starting the race he was pestered by his boyhood friend, Doug Alward, into going the entire distance. This he did, in a time of three hours, nine minutes. For the first time, there appeared what would be a regular phenomenon whenever he ran—spectators weeping from the emotion of watching him.

One of Terry's dreams had been fulfilled. Then he focussed on the other, his cross-Canada run. Hoping that it might raise one million dollars for cancer research, he sent a letter to several companies seeking sponsorship.

"My quest would not be a selfish one," Terry wrote. He explained how he had been moved by the suffering in the cancer ward and felt a desire to somehow lighten it. "Somewhere," he said, "the hurting must stop."

Where did this 21-year-old youth find the inner resources to begin his odyssey? On April 12, 1980, in

St. John's, Newfoundland, Terry Fox dipped his artificial leg into the Atlantic and began the run that would be, as the Canadian motto states, *A MARI USQUE AD MARE,* from sea to sea.

"You sure got the nerve," Newfoundlanders said again and again to Terry as he battled gale-force winds and blizzards. With every step, his artificial leg gave him pain. In his diary for April 26 he wrote: "I cried because I knew I was going to make it or be in a hospital bed or dead. I want to set an example that will never be forgotten. It is courage and not foolishness. It isn't a waste."

Terry was a person with faults, like everybody else. Doug Alward, who accompanied him on the run, said, "Sometimes he didn't seem to give a damn about other people; at other times he gave an incredible damn. . . . It took me three months to figure out how tough it was. Tougher than any of us could ever know."

The "Marathon of Hope," Terry called it. But the media offered scant support. He ran all the way through the Maritimes and Quebec with little or no publicity. Then as he entered Ontario, people began to grasp the magnitude of his effort. Terry's image appeared almost daily on television. Suddenly his determination, his spirit, his shaman-like journey into the unknown entered the hearts of people all across Canada. Terry had become part of the nation's mythology.

His boyish handsomeness was part of the myth. Leslie Scrivener, in her compelling biography, tells of "a well-scrubbed, intelligent face, straight teeth, and an Adonis-like profile—which would make older women feel maternal and teenagers feverish." One onlooker, seeing Terry hobble into Toronto's Nathan Phillips Square to be greeted by 10 000 admirers, saw in his face "a tremendous look of peace."

Terry, once asked whether he was running to find himself, replied, "I'm not trying to find something. I've found what I want." There was a grimace on Terry's freckled face when he talked, and many experienced pity. "People thought I was going through hell," he remarked. "Maybe I was, partly, but I was still doing what I wanted and a dream was coming true."

Terry saw a vision of his arrival at the Pacific, of dancing in the waves, of exclaiming to himself, "I did it. I did it!" But on September 1, as he approached Thunder Bay, a cough racked his body, and he started to choke. "I was running with this pain in my chest and I began to think, you know, there's something wrong. This may be the last mile."

It was. Terry, on being examined in the hospital, was found to have cancer in his lungs. The right lung contained a tumour as big as a golf ball, and the other had one the size of a fist.

Now he travelled across the prairie and over the Rockies—not on foot but in a plane taking him home for treatment. He was already a symbol of courage across the land, but his utterances during the final crisis added even more to his lustre. "How many people," he asked, "have really put out an effort to fight for something they really believed in? I've lived a lifetime already."

A five-hour telethon, A Salute to Terry Fox, raised over $10 million for cancer research and provided a focus for the grief of Canadians across the land. Doctors tried Interferon in an effort to halt the disease, but it didn't work, and he was left gravely ill.

Then on June 28, 1981, Terry slipped into a deep coma from which he never awoke. His spirit, nevertheless, lived on: in the battle against cancer, in a fund-raising run conducted every year in his name, and in memories of a magnificent quest. "His attempt to run 4000 miles, from the Atlantic to the Pacific," said a statement issued by Prime Minister Pierre Trudeau, "elevated him into the exceedingly thin ranks of the truly heroic."

When Winter scourged the meadow and the hill
And in the withered leafage worked his will,
The water shrank, and shuddered, and stood still,
Then built himself a magic house of glass,
Irised with memories of flowers and grass,
Wherein to sit and watch the fury pass.

CHARLES G. D. ROBERTS

The Hope of the Future

"Every child," said the 19th century American writer, Henry David Thoreau, "begins the world again." Parents are invariably awe-struck to produce a brand new person, whom they will describe as their "hope of the future."

Life renews itself, over and over again. So many people being born, and falling in love, and giving birth, and then getting old! So many generations! But then far far back, there were no families called Smith or Kowalski or Chung, just the race of humankind. And beyond that?

Nothing renews hope more than the simple act of reproduction. Yet the outlines of this new lifespan will much resemble all those in the past—a truth that greatly impressed Val.

Mirror Image

Last weekend in the attic, I came across a box containing a part of my mother's life that I hardly knew existed. In this old faded box with broken corners were numerous snapshots and cards as well as other memorabilia representing an era I was no part of.

There were pictures of my mother when she was young, and I was stunned by the uncanny resemblance we share. It was like looking at a picture of myself.

This made me feel wonderful and at the same time frightened. Will I look exactly like my mother does now when I reach her age? It's almost like travelling ahead in time and seeing the future.

In this picture, the 17-year-old girl probably only has dreams of the future, the same as any girl that age. She has no idea that she will produce a baby who will grow into an exact physical replica of herself.

Will I in turn create children who will look exactly like this?

MOTHER: The Spring has come and you didn't know.

KID: And the grass is green. The branches are covered with leaves.

ALL: 1024   great great great great great great great great grandparents

512   great great great great great great great grandparents

256   great great great great great great grandparents

128   great great great great great grandparents

64   great great great great grandparents

32   great great great grandparents

16   great great grandparents

8   great grandparents

4   grandparents

2   parents

One   child

JAMES REANEY, *COLOURS IN THE DARK*

25. Endings

When the Earth becomes uninhabitable, Mars will gain a balmy and clement climate. Our remote descendants, if any, may wish to take advantage of this coincidence.

CARL SAGAN, *THE COSMIC CONNECTION*

Cuchulainn's Fame *Irish*

Cuchulainn

It all began one day when a lovely maiden named Dechtire was sipping a glass of wine. A mayfly landed in her drink and before she knew what happened, it slid down her throat.

That night in her sleep, Dechtire was visited by Lugh the sun-god. "I was the mayfly that entered your mouth," he said, "and a child has been planted in your womb."

So Dechtire had been made pregnant by a god, and no ordinary one at that. Lugh was the mightiest god of the People of Dana, who had come from Greece with their magic, never-emptying Cauldron of Plenty.

Dechtire delivered a son who was extremely strong-willed. His father, Lugh, often blazed in anger with a battle-flame, like the sun itself—and the boy would also show bursts of fiery rage.

Dechtire's brother was Conchobar, king of Ulster. Her son was determined to go to his court, some distance away. He made the journey at the age of seven, carrying a shinny ball for field hockey, and a tiny shield.

Arriving, the boy saw a troop of 150 boys playing shinny, and joined in at once. "Who is this little brat?" the boys asked.

They flung their spears at the intruder, but the boy easily caught all 150 of them with his shield. They hurled their shinny-balls at him, and he stopped every one with his chest. They threw their shinny-sticks, and he easily dodged them all. The boys, greatly impressed, made him their leader in a campaign of mischief.

Finally, the lad entered the palace. He was pursued, hid under a bed, and overturned it—along with thirty warriors on top—when discovered.

Conchobar was delighted to meet his nephew. "Come along to Cuchulainn's feast," he said, "after you've finished playing!" And the boy did, but found that the house of Cuchulainn, a blacksmith, was guarded by a fierce dog.

So strong was this hound that three men usually held it, using three chains. But even fiercer was the boy. He threw his shinny ball into the hound's mouth with such velocity that it came out the other end, causing instant death.

Cathbad the druid exclaimed, "You should be called 'Hound of Cuchulainn'—Cuchulainn!" And Cuchulainn (koo-KUH-lin) from that time on was the young boy's name.

Later Cathbad predicted, "Today, anyone taking up arms for the first time will have long fame, but a short life."

"If I become famous," said Cuchulainn, "a single day of life will be enough."

At once Cuchulainn went to Conchobar and demanded weapons. He tried a number of spears, but they shattered when he vigorously tried them out. So Conchobar provided his own arms.

Next, Cuchulainn demanded a chariot. And the same thing happened, with the king finally offering his own. Then off he went on his first exploit, fighting Nechta Scene's three murderous sons.

Suddenly the Warp-Spasm possessed Cuchulainn's body, which swelled terrifyingly. All fifty strands of hair on his head shot upright. His mouth twisted and spread to meet his ears. One eye shrank to a slit, and the other grew as big as his knee. His heart beat aloud like the repeated roars of a lion. His entire body swivelled within the skin until his heels faced forward. Then from Cuchulainn's forehead arose the hero-light, and from his scalp spouted a fierce jet of blood that streamed off to the four directions of the compass.

Cuchulainn made short work of the three brothers and attached their severed heads to his chariot. Then he captured a deer and a flock of swans and drove toward Emain Macha.

"Here comes my sister's son, quite berserk!" Conchobar said seeing the boy. "This means trouble unless we send out naked women!" So all the young women took off their clothes and ran out, causing Cuchulainn to hide his face in shame.

Cuchulainn was seized and plunged into a vat of cold water, which burst as the boy's heat instantly made the water boil. Thrust into another vat, he again made the water boil. Dunked a third time, he at last regained his normal appearance.

Now the men, fearing for the ruin of their wives and daughters, declared, "This lad must be married without delay." Cuchulainn went to the Gardens of Lugh and began wooing pretty Emer.

"May your road be blessed!" she said.

"A blessed country lies ahead, for sure!" he replied, admiring the beauty of her form.

"No man will visit that country," said Emer, "without taking a long journey." And so he did, all the way to the island of Scathach the warrior-woman. She taught him how to use the gae bulga, a horrendous belly-spear.

After learning many stratagems from Scathach, Cuchulainn returned to Emain Macha and finally to Emer, whom he married.

The earth-goddess Maeve ruled as queen of Connacht in the west of Ireland. Tall and stately, with hair that shone as golden as ripe wheat, Maeve had a good deal of vanity. And she wanted to own the Brown Bull, Ulster's pride.

The Brown Bull was the greatest of beasts, so broad that children could play on its back. Maeve's desire to possess it grew and grew, until she finally commanded an army of warriors to invade Ulster and bring it to her.

And so began the Cattle Raid. Ulster's defenders were helpless, for plague had weakened them, King Conchobar included. Only one man stood guard, and that was Cuchulainn.

Maeve's advance was stopped when Cuchulainn defeated her champions, one by one, at the ford of a river. Then she devised a trick. To Cuchulainn's oldest companion, Ferdia, she offered her daughter as a bribe to make him oppose his friend. Ferdia refused at first, but relented when she threatened to have poets compose verses against him.

Cuchulainn and Ferdia fought each other furiously. Yet at nightfall they embraced, tended each other's wounds, and slept on the same bed of rushes. After another day of combat, they retired in the same way. Then on the third

day, Cuchulainn accused Ferdia of fighting out of lust for
Maeve's daughter. They wounded each other more seriously that day.

Their duel was decided on the following day. Ferdia
severely wounded Cuchulainn, who in turn flung his gae
bulga with such accuracy that it pierced his friend's heart.

Cuchulainn made bitter lament. "Yesterday he was a
mountain," he cried, "today but a shade." No longer did
he have the will to fight against Maeve.

By this time Conchobar and his men had recovered
from the plague and entered the battle. But Maeve fought
magnificently, three times charging full tilt into the enemy.
Then at midday Cuchulainn joined in once more, terrifying her so much that she hid beneath her chariot. "It is
not my habit to slay women," he said, sparing her life.

Although Maeve's men were beaten, they did manage to
capture the Brown Bull, and triumphantly drove it to
Connacht. Ironically, though, it killed the White Bull and
escaped back to Ulster. Finally, the Brown Bull burst its
heart with frantic bellowing, and dropped dead.

Cuchulainn had saved Ulster's honour in its hour of
need, but Maeve now demanded his death, no matter how.

Before returning to the battlefield, Cuchulainn received
a drink from his mother, Dechtire, and it turned to blood.
Then he went out, bearing three spears, to face the foe at
the edge of the lake.

Maeve had assembled satirists, and one of them
demanded Cuchulainn's spear. Because in Ireland a poet
must be obeyed, the hero complied—but he threw his
weapon with so much force that it impaled this fellow and
nine men behind. Then the spear was hurled back, and it
killed Cuchulainn's charioteer.

Again a poet demanded one of Cuchulainn's spears, and
this time he flung it with little effect. When the missile
was returned, it killed his best horse and the other ran
away.

The third spear was demanded. Again Cuchulainn
threw it weakly. And on the return thrust, it struck the
hero with a fatal wound.

"I am thirsty," said Cuchulainn. Allowed to walk to the

lake, he drank for the last time. Then he staggered to a pillar stone, pulled himself upright, and tied himself to it with his belt.

Long did Cuchulainn stand there, defiant. Finally a crow was seen circling the hero, then landing on his shoulder. It was Morrigan, goddess of war.

Only then did the enemy dare to approach. They struck off Cuchulainn's head and took it to Maeve. The battle had lasted from Halloween to the beginning of spring.

Bess

Ours are the streets where Bess first met her
cancer. She went to work every day past the
secure houses. At her job in the library
she arranged better and better flowers, and when
students asked for books her hand went out
to help. In the last year of her life
she had to keep her friends from knowing
how happy they were. She listened while they
complained about food or work or the weather.
And the great national events danced
their grotesque, fake importance. Always

Pain moved where she moved. She walked
ahead; it came. She hid; it found her.
No one ever served another so truly;
no enemy ever meant so strong a hate.
It was almost as if there was no room
left for her on earth. But she remembered
where joy used to live. She straightened its flowers;
she did not weep when she passed its houses;
and when finally she pulled into a tiny corner
and slipped from pain, her hand opened
again, and the streets opened, and she wished all well.

WILLIAM STAFFORD

Cycle of the Human Life-Span

All of us add, in big ways or small, to the world's well-being. When death approaches, we might be forgiven for failing to contribute any more. Yet amazingly, people find the courage to hurl one more spear in the cause—or, as in Stafford's magnificent poem, to arrange "better and better flowers."

Cuchulainn's fate dramatizes the cycle of the human life-span. He embraces experience with gusto and dies a splendid death. The hero could also expect an afterlife, for the Irish imagine a more perfect paradise, the Otherworld, where sickness and age are unknown.

Maeve and Cuchulainn belonged to the Tuatha De Danann or "People of Dana," supreme in the land until defeated around 500 B.C. by the Celts. Then they became the People of the Mounds—turning into fairies and vanishing into an Otherworld within ancient burial mounds.

And what burial mounds! Newgrange, near Dublin, shows architectural subtlety comparable to that of the Egyptian pyramids, built at the same time (around 2500 B.C.). Beneath its 16-metre cone, dazzling with quartz stones, is the great round chamber symbolizing the womb of Mother Earth. Those buried here, it must have seemed, would surely be reborn.

Newgrange's stones are inscribed with many labyrinthine spirals*—symbols of continuity also found later in that Celtic masterpiece, the *Book of Kells*. A similar intricacy is found in James Joyce's *Ulysses*,** another great Celtic celebration of life.

The 2000-year-old story of Cuchulainn comes down to us by rare good luck. For the Irish, alone among all Celtic people, were able to preserve their myths. Other Celtic lands were conquered by the Romans, under whom local mythologies withered. (In our times U.S. culture, spread abroad largely through Hollywood films, has had a similar effect.)

In Ireland after Christianity came, the old myths were recorded by scribes who tolerated their earthiness. So the Cuchulainn story has come down to us in the *Tain Bo Cuailgne*, an epic comparable to Homer's *Iliad* in Greek legend. Here is the Celts' finest literary achievement, a tale that takes us right into a heroic age. And today the Irish rate Cuchulainn as the greatest of their mythic heroes.

---

*See page 141.
**See pages 189-192.

As the sun-god's offspring, Cuchulainn has a fiery rise and fall. Like the sun, he displays energies that increase until noon, then fade during a downward path toward dusk.

The sun also dwindles throughout the year, which the Irish considered to end on October 31. The Irish would equate a king with the sun and required that he have no blemish. So at this time, evidence suggests, an aging king might submit to a sacrificial death, perhaps at the hands of a younger man. He preserves the community by losing his life—a role played memorably by Cuchulainn.

February 1
spring begins

November 1
winter begins

May 1
summer begins

August 1
autumn begins

The Celtic year

So November 1 was a time of renewal. To do homage to the sun-god, the people would extinguish their hearth fires, then gather in a circle on a hill as a new blaze was ignited in his honour. Then from its flames, embers were carried into their homes to rekindle the hearth.

At this "crack in the year" the gates of life and death opened wide, and souls could walk abroad. This was the Night of Wandering Souls, when sacrifices of food were offered to discourage any from leaving the grave. Around 800 A.D. it was decreed that all saints must be honoured on this day, so that the preceding eve became hallowed—the hallowe'en.

I felt as if I were walking with Destiny, and that all my past life had been but a preparation for this hour and trial.

WINSTON CHURCHILL, REFERRING TO THE MOMENT IN 1940 WHEN HE BECAME BRITAIN'S WARTIME PRIME MINISTER

Their Finest Hour *British*

The British people in 1936 underwent a crisis. Their new king, Edward VIII, intended to marry a woman twice divorced, and they would never stand for this. So he abdicated without ever being crowned, explaining how he could not rule "without the help and support of the woman I love."

Edward's younger brother then came to the throne, as George VI, but a sense of foreboding still remained. Did this royal crisis foreshadow the fall of the British Empire? It was the biggest empire ever created, with a population four times that of the Roman Empire, taking in a quarter of the earth's surface and a quarter of its inhabitants.

Now Japan challenged Britain's holdings in the East. And in Europe, the threat of Germany grew as the Nazi party came into power under its Fuhrer, Adolf Hitler.*

In 1938, the British prime minister, Neville Chamberlain, returned from the notorious Munich Conference. He had "appeased" Adolf Hitler by granting him the German-speaking portion of Czechoslovakia. Bringing what he called "peace in our time," Chamberlain earned the public's praise.

But one man, Winston Churchill, expressed contempt for the pact. "The Government had to choose between war and shame," he said. "They chose shame, and they will get war too."

Churchill had once been a crusading leader in parliament. But during World War I, he took the blame for the failure of a military expedition and entered his "years in the wilderness." He was deprived of responsibility by his own party, led by Chamberlain—who thought him "a brilliant wayward child."

Hitler soon took all of Czechoslovakia, of course, and on September 1, 1939, his tanks rolled into Poland. So Britain declared war on Germany. Eight months later, the

---

*See pages 150-154.

Nazis made their long-awaited assault on France—coincidentally, on the very day that Chamberlain was replaced as Prime Minister by Churchill.

What a moment! Churchill had spent eleven years in political exile, a despised prophet of doom. And now, the people turned to him as their saviour.

On May 10, 1940, the Germans easily crossed into France, making her defeat a certainty. Three days later Churchill gave the first of his immortal wartime speeches, promising nothing but "blood, toil, tears and sweat." Some 200 000 British troops had landed in France, only to be overwhelmed by impossible odds. But a flotilla of 860 fishing boats and pleasure craft sailed from England to Dunkirk on the French coast and rescued the retreating British.

"We shall never surrender," Churchill boomed in the House of Commons soon after. And as the cheers burst forth, those nearby heard him mutter, "We'll beat the bastards over the head with broomsticks, it's all we've got."

Italy then opted to follow Hitler and the British were thus left all alone in Europe. Churchill gave still another speech, perhaps the most moving of all. "If the British Empire and the Commonwealth last for a thousand years," he declared, "men will still say this was their finest hour."

It was a heroic war against seemingly impossible odds. On August 1, 1940, Hitler gave the order: "Establish conditions favourable to the conquest of Britain." Two weeks later he unleashed his air fleet, and thus began the Battle of Britain. Fought in airplanes, it ranks as one of the most crucial struggles in history.

The Royal Navy had shown its vulnerability by losing a dozen ships in the sea battles near Norway; now Hitler saw the Royal Air Force as easy prey. Germany had 1100 fighter planes, and Britain 665. During the first two weeks, the R.A.F. shot down twice as many planes as the enemy, but nearly 600 of the 1400 pilots were lost.

Then a German plane erroneously dropped its bombs on London. At once the R.A.F. retaliated by bombing

Berlin, and Hitler, roused to fury, directed the attack away from R.A.F. air fields to London. The "Blitz" killed 30 000 Londoners—but at a heavy cost to the German air fleet.

In one massive assault on September 15, 1940, Germany lost sixty planes to Britain's twenty-six. Two days later, Hitler postponed his invasion plans until further notice. The Battle of Britain had been won by the defenders, whose island was thus preserved as a jumping-off point for the final invasion of Hitler's Europe.

Britain's greatest resource was Churchill himself, an overweight 65-year-old man whose energies were inexhaustible. Elevating ordeal into myth, he gave voice to the British spirit in his speeches. Churchill would visit the devastated streets of London, unceasingly bombed by German war planes, to flash the V-for-victory sign to Londoners. They returned it, crying, "Good old Winnie!"

Churchill's military leadership was extraordinary. "In his grasp of the broad sweep of strategy," said Lord Ismay, "he stood head and shoulders above his professional advisers." Not long after Dunkirk, Churchill was sending a tank brigade to the Middle East, which he recognized as a vital theatre of war.

On December 7, 1941, Churchill heard U.S. president, Franklin Roosevelt, say on the telephone, "It is quite true. They have attacked us in Pearl Harbor. We are in the same boat now." The U.S. entered the battle against Hitler; Britain joined the colossal war against Japan—and immediately lost her bastions at Singapore and Hong Kong. The role of world political leadership imagined by Churchill for Britain was now beyond her capacity.

On June 6, 1944, history's greatest invasion force crossed the English Channel to invade Hitler's France. But its commander was an American, Dwight Eisenhower, not a Britisher as Churchill had hoped. It was Eisenhower who accepted the German surrender on May 8, 1945. The Japanese defeat came three months later, ending a war which killed 25 million combatants and an equal number of civilians.

For the British people, Churchill seemed to represent the war, and they were sick of it. After its end, he was voted out of office, regaining the leadership only one more time. In 1953, during his last term in office, Elizabeth II conferred knighthood on Britain's great champion, and he became Sir Winston Churchill.

Meanwhile, the Suez Canal remained in British hands, the lifeline of its empire. But shortly after Churchill retired, it was seized by the Egyptians. Against them a British-French invading force was hurled, but these were no longer colonial times. The world was outraged, the troops withdrew, and the British Empire endured its death rattle.

Nine years later, Churchill himself died. For the first time in British history, the funeral of a commoner was attended by a monarch, Elizabeth II. As the coffin was borne down the Thames River, dock cranes were lowered in an awesome salute.

For the British, a special poignancy lay in the awareness that the Empire was no more. But in the Last Battle they had been led by a hero of towering stature, ever to be remembered.

When great causes are on the move in the world . . . we learn that we are spirits, not animals, and that something is going on in space and time and beyond space and time, which, whether we like it or not, spells duty.

WINSTON CHURCHILL, 1941

The Spiral May Go On Forever

Some endings are unutterably poetic. Josephine Baker, whose dancing amazed Paris in the 1920s, returned to stage a final gala at the
age of 68 and died of a heart attack soon afterwards. Lil Hardin
expired while playing the final chord of *The St. Louis Blues*, at a
memorial service for her ex husband, jazz great Louis Armstrong.

A teacher named Patrick Pearse dreamed of making Ireland independent of British rule. This aim was ultimately met, although he
was executed after the abortive 1916 Rising. Pearse had written mys-
tical poetry linking Cuchulainn with Christ—whose death brought
rebirth—and stood proudly before the firing squad as Cuchulainn
had done at the pillar stone.

Endings are also beginnings, for lives overlap as the human story
is replayed. The labyrinth symbolizes this, leading in and out in a
continuous spiral. Each crisis, each twist and turn in the way, will
release us into a new state of being.

And so it is with the universe itself. The spiral may go on forever,
and the hundred billion stars of our Milky Way form an unfathomably huge spiral. A spiral design informs most of the other galax-
ies—again, uncannily, some hundred billion in all.

But the thought of this vastness is hard to bear, especially when
death emphasizes our physical limits. Then we need the grandeur of
funeral rites to help us through the crisis. And within the family at
this time, scenes of great beauty often unfold—as in Jill's moving
description.

One Day at a Time

My father never seemed to play a big role in my life until he became sick. At this time we talked for endless hours on things, and I began to really admire and love him. Finally he admitted he was scared and did not want to die.

During his last few days we were all there for him. He would wake up, open his eyes, and see us in the room, one of us holding his hand. He was a beautiful man, and no one knows that, usually, until it is too late. We take so many things for granted.

The last day everyone had time with him alone, sort of the final conversation. It was so beautiful.

I will always remember what he said. Life goes on. Never be afraid to admit you're scared. Take one day at a time and enjoy everything as much as you can. You have always made me proud and I love you.

We both broke down and had a good cry just like I'm doing now. I'll always remember those few moments with Dad. It was like giving your whole self to something, your inner feelings. It was so beautiful, so hard to describe.

To this very day I cherish each moment and do not take as many things for granted.

I feel I have experienced something extremely special that no one else can experience. I have learned from this that death is not as scary as people think it is.

Your last moments with that person stay with people and help them to continue.

My love for my father has never been so strong, I think it is even stronger now that he is gone. I also find that I do not take my mother for granted. I don't rant and rave as I used to, and I can talk to her.

I find this strange, writing all these feelings down, because I just looked at the date. It's the 20th of September, which would have been Mom and Dad's 25th anniversary.

Make it so that time is a circle and not a line.

Simone Weil, *Notebooks*

Bibliography

Asterisks designate books that serve especially well as introductions to themes in mythology's vast field.

Sources for the Theseus myth include Ovid's *Metamorphoses**—well translated by Mary Innes (Penguin, 1955)—and Plutarch's *Lives*. This tale is delightfully retold in Nathaniel Hawthorne's *Tanglewood Tales* (reprinted Airmont, 1966) and in Edith Hamilton's superb *Mythology** (Mentor, 1953).

Superman at Fifty, edited by Dennis Dooley and Gary Engle (Octavia, 1987) gives many insights, as does E. N. Bridwell's introduction to *Superman from the Thirties to the Eighties* (Crown, 1983), a big collection of strips.

Joseph Campbell's *The Hero with a Thousand Faces** (Meridian, 1956) outlines a hero-cycle in terms of the quest for a prize, which must be painfully carried back to revitalize humankind. Maureen Murdock's *The Heroine's Journey** (Shambhala, 1990) maps the hero-cycle in feminine terms of personal transformation.

Ritual is exhaustively interpreted in J. G. Frazer's classic *The Golden Bough**, skilfully abridged by Theodore Gaster (Doubleday, 1961). Miriam Starhawk's *The Spiral Dance* (Harper and Row, 1979) plunges readers into the realm of goddess ritual.

Tom Chetwynd's *A Dictionary of Symbols** (Granada, 1982) gives a fascinating interpretation of major symbols, in terms of personal mythology and the unconscious mind. Useful as well is *The Dictionary of Graphic Images* by Philip Thompson and Peter Davenport (St. Martin's, 1980).

1 MY LONGEST JOURNEY

1. Beginnings

Huitzilipochli: A useful analysis is provided by Miguel Leon-Portilla in *Mythologies of the Ancient World**, edited by Samuel Noah Kramer (Doubleday, 1961). A full translation of the version by Bernardino de Sahagun, a 16th-century priest, appears in *The Great Temple of Tenochtitlan* (University of California, 1987), edited by Johanna Broda. David Carrasco's essay in this volume brilliantly analyses the temple's mythic background. Another well-illustrated archaeological account is Eduardo Matos Moctezuma's *The Great Temple of the Aztecs* (Thames and Hudson, 1988).

Two excellent creation-myth anthologies are *Sun Songs* by Raymond Van Over (Mentor, 1980) and Barbara Sproul's *Primal Myths* (Harper and Row, 1979).

Disney: Barbara Ford's *Walt Disney* (Walker and Company, 1989) is a readable biography. Shrewd comments on Disneyland appear in Randolph Delahanty's *California: a Guidebook* (Harcourt Brace Jovanovich, 1984).

2. Quest

Gilgamesh: N.K. Sandar lends a thorough introduction to his prose translation, *The Epic of Gilgamesh* (Penguin, 1960). Shirley Park Lowry's *Familiar Mysteries** (Oxford, 1982) concludes with a lovely account of the myth.

Greenpeace: Michael Brown's *The Greenpeace Story* (Prentice-Hall, 1989) provides a well-illustrated history of the movement.

3. Promised Land

Aeneas: A fine verse translation of Virgil's *Aeneid*, with full glossary, is that of Allen Mandelbaum (Bantam, 1961). Michael Grant's *Roman Myths* (Weidenfeld and Nicolson, 1971) also provides useful analysis, while Wendel Berry's *The Gift of Good Land* (North Point, 1981) sensitively deals with implications of promised-land mythology.

Martin Luther King: William Johnson's *King* (Warner, 1978) is an exciting dramatized biography, while Lerone Bennett's *What Manner of Man* (Johnson, 1976) provides an illustrated account.

4. Vision

Holy Grail: Thomas Malory's *Le Morte d'Arthur* is given complete in a Penguin two-volume set (edited by Janet Cowen, 1969), and shortened in a Faber edition edited by R. T. Davies. Updates include Tennyson's melodious verse retelling, *Idylls of the King* (not easy reading) and T. H. White's witty *The Once and Future King* (Fontana, 1962).

Chapters 7 and 8 of *The Power of Myth** by Joseph Campbell with Bill Moyers (Doubleday, 1988) offer insight into several aspects of epiphany and the Grail; Robert Segal's *Joseph Campbell: an Introduction* (Mentor, 1990) provides critical background. Thames and Hudson's outstanding *Art and Imagination* series* includes *The Grail: Quest for the Eternal* by John Matthews (1981).

Mother Teresa: Desmond Doig's *Mother Teresa* (Collins, 1976) offers an admirable account of her life; Malcolm Muggeridge's *Something Beautiful for God* (Collins, 1971) is also excellent.

2 I RECOGNIZED THE GODDESS

5. Mother

Isis: The only connected account of this myth is Plutarch's *On Isis and Osiris*. Additional details still come to light from newly-translated inscriptions, compiled in R. T. Rundle-Clark's *Myth and Symbol in Ancient Egypt* (Thames and Hudson, 1959). Eva Meyerowitz's *The Divine Kingship in Ghana and Ancient Egypt* (Faber and Faber, 1960) shows how old Egyptian rites may be discerned in modern African ones.

Yoko Ono: John Black's *All You Needed Was Love* (Perigee, 1988) tells about "the Beatles after the Beatles"; a negative approach is seen in Albert Goldman's *The Lives of John Lennon* (Morrow, 1988). Rogan Taylor's *The Death and Resurrection Show* (Blond, 1985) presents Lennon and other pop-music stars in terms of a magical journey.

6. Liberation

Artemis: Much of this retelling is based on Hesiod's *Theogony* (Penguin, 1973). Callimachus's lovely Third Hymn celebrates Artemis, and Homer's *Iliad*, Book I, gives the story of Hera's punishment. W. K. C. Guthrie's *The Greeks and Their Gods* (Beacon, 1950) offers scholarly background in a readable style.

The Language of the Goddess by Marija Gimbutas (Thames and Hudson, 1989) provides a wealth of background data on the Lady of the Wild Things. *The Goddess Within* by J. B. and R. J. Woolger (Fawcett Columbine, 1987), a guide to "goddess qualities that live within us all," gives illuminating interpretations of Artemis, Hera, and Athena, among others.

Joni Mitchell: Theodore Fleischer's *Joni Mitchell* (Flash, 1976) should be supplemented by Cameron Crowe's probing account in *The Rolling Stone Interviews*, edited by Peter Herbst (St. Martin's, 1981). "Blue" is well-analysed by Bob Sarlin in *Turn It Up!* (Coronet, 1973), and other songs are quoted in a stimulating folk-rock anthology edited by Bob Atkinson: *Songs of the Open Road* (Signet, 1974).

7. Sacrifice

Sedna: There are many versions of this great myth. A penetrating analysis is given in Alexander Spalding's article "Doctor Faust and the Woman in the Sea" (*Artscanada*, Dec. 1971/Jan.1972). Insights also appear in Alma Houston's *Inuit Art* (Watson and Dwyer, 1988) and the middle chapters of Edmund Carpenter's *Oh, What a Blow That Phantom Gave Me* (Holt, Rinehart and Winston, 1972).

Scholarly treatments of the shaman include Mircea Eliade's *Shamanism* (Bollingen, 1964), Holger Kalweit's *Dreamtime and Inner Space* (Shambhala, 1988), *Secrets of Shamanism* by Jose and Lena Stevens (Avon, 1988), Ward Rutherford's *Shamanism* (Aquarian, 1986) and Michael Harner's *The Way of the Shaman* (Harper and Row, 1990).

Joan of Arc: A readable illustrated account is *Joan of Arc* by Jay Williams (Harper and Row, 1963). Marina Warner's *Joan of Arc: The Image of Female Heroism* (Knopf, 1982) gives a well-documented modern approach to the famed martyr. *Witchcraft* by Pennethorpe Hughes (Penguin, 1965) briefly discusses Joan's trial in terms of medieval witchcraft prosecution.

3 THE POWER AND THE GLORY

8. Father

Daedalus: Norma Lorre Goodrich's *The Ancient Myths** (Mentor, 1960) gives the full sweep of mythic tales centred on the island of Crete. Leonard Cottrell's *The Bull of Minos* (Holt Rinehart, 1958) places them in an archaeological perspective. *Myths of the Greeks and Romans* by Robert Graves (Mentor, 1962) entertainingly retells this and other classical tales; *The Greek Myths** by the same author (Penguin, 1955) provides a wealth of speculative notes.

Kennedy: Theodore Sorensen's *Kennedy* (Bantam, 1965) is a detailed biography by the president's special counsel; *The Kennedy Imprisonment* by Gary Wills (Little, Brown, 1982) offers an unflattering portrayal of his father; the pre-presidential years are probed in *The Search for JFK* by Joan and Clay Blair. Lord Raglan in *The Hero** (Vintage, 1956) gives a 22-phase "hero pattern" which has been applied to Kennedy's career so as to award him a near-perfect score.

9. Tests

Hercules: His labours are described in Apollodorus's *Library*, his ultimate fate in Ovid's *Metamorphoses* and Sophocles's *The Women of Trachis*. An interesting chapter on Hercules appears in G. S. Kirk's *The Nature of Greek Myths** (Penguin, 1974)—an admirable scholarly approach to mythology in general.

Initiation ritual is discussed in Arnold van Gennep's classic *The Rites of Passage* (Phoenix, 1960). *The Wisdom of the Serpent** by Joseph Henderson and Maude Oakes (Macmillan, 1963) gathers together many initiation stories in the Western and Eastern traditions. Robert Bly's *Iron John* (Addison-Wesley, 1990) and Sam Keen's *Fire in the Belly* (Bantam, 1991) discuss, in present-day terms, the passage from boyhood to manhood.

Babe Ruth: Kal Wagenheim's *Babe Ruth* (Praeger, 1974) is a useful biography.

10. Trickster

Hare: The source for this tale is Paul Radin's retelling in *The Trickster** (Schocken Books, 1971) which also includes a probing commentary by Carl Jung. *Man and His Symbols*, edited by Jung (Dell, 1964) contains an illuminating chapter by Joseph Henderson. Marshall Fishwick's *Parameters of Popular Culture* (Bowling Green, 1974) deals interestingly with Br'er Rabbit.

Johan Huizinga's *Homo Ludens: a Study of the Play Element in Culture* (Beacon, 1955) places all of human achievement in the context of play. This theme is richly developed in Part Three, "Conscious Mythmaking," of Stephen Larsen's *The Mythic Imagination* (Bantam, 1990).

Bugs Bunny: Leonard Maltin's *Of Mice and Men* (McGraw-Hill, 1980) tells about his life and times, as does Steve Schneider's *That's All, Folks!* (Henry Holt, 1988).

4 AFTER GREAT PAIN

11. Monster

Windigo: The source is *Windigo: An Anthology of Fact and Fantastic Fiction* (Western Producer Prairie Books, Saskatoon, 1982) edited by John Robert Columbo. *The New Larousse Encyclopedia of Mythology** (Hamlyn, 1968) gives brief, well-illustrated accounts of this and all other important myths of the world.

Stalin: Michael Gibson's *Russia Under Stalin* (Weyland, 1972) gives an illuminating documentary account.

12. Underworld

Ishtar: Sylvia Brinton's *Descent to the Goddess: A Way of Initiation for Women* (Inner City, 1981) eloquently interprets this myth. See also Jean Bolen's *Goddesses in Everywoman* (Harper and Row, 1984) for an account of the parallel Greek myth of Demeter and Persephone.

Zelda: She is brought to life memorably in Nancy Mitford's *Zelda* (Avon, 1970). Phyllis Chesler's *Women and Madness* (Avon, 1972) provides a brief but insightful interpretation of her experience.

Labyrinth: Jill Purce's *The Mystic Spiral: Journey of the Soul* (Thames and Hudson, 1974), focussing on labyrinth symbolism, is another worthwhile volume in the *Art and Imagination* series.

13. Betrayal

Sigurd: *Legends of the World**, edited by Richard Cavendish (Van Nostrand Reinhold, 1982) retells and comments on this and many other tales from the five continents. Cavendish also edited *Man, Myth and Magic** (Purnell, 1970), a richly-illustrated survey of many mythic themes.

Hitler: The first chapter of Mircea Eliade's *Myths, Dreams and Mysteries* (Fontana, 1968) briefly analyses Nazi mythology in terms of Germanic folklore, as does the well-illustrated *Cult and Occult*, edited by Peter Brookesmith (Orbis, 1985). Joachim Fest's *Hitler* (Harcourt Brace Jovanovich, 1974) is a substantial study, while Gene Smith's *The Horns of the Moon* (Charterhouse, 1973) gives an interesting brief account. H. R. Kedward's *Fascism in Western Europe 1900-45* (Blackie, 1969) offers many insights into Nazi myth and ritual.

14. Destruction

Kali: Barbara Stanford's *Myths and Modern Man** (Washington Square, 1972) clarifies the story line of this and many other ancient tales. Her *Woman's Encyclopedia of Myths and Secrets** (Harper and Row, 1983) is another valuable reference work. Also pertinent is Chapter 11 of Erich Neumann's richly-detailed *The Great Mother* (Bollingen, 1955).

Huston Smith's *The Religions of Man* (Harper and Row, 1958) provides a clear introduction to Hinduism. Still another relevant *Art and Imagination* title is *Sacred Dance: Encounter with the Gods* by Maria-Gabriele Wosien (Thames and Hudson, 1974).

Isadora: Victor Seroff's *The Real Isadora* (Dial, 1971) is both detailed and dramatic.

5 KING OF KINGS

15. Justice

Agamemnon: Homer's *Iliad* and *Odyssey**, nearly three millenia old and still the greatest of all European literary masterpieces, have been given readable translations by W. H. D. Rouse (Mentor, 1949). Additional details derive from Ovid's *Metamorphoses*, *Iphigeneia Among the Taurians*, and *The Trojan Women* by Euripides, and *The Oresteia* by Aeschylus.

Both the epic and dramatic aspects of this tale are treated well by Michael Grant in his *Myths of the Greeks and Romans** (Mentor, 1962).

Napoleon: Two useful biographies are David Chandler's *Napoleon* (Weidenfeld and Nicolson, 1973) and J. Christopher Herold *The Age of Napoleon* (American Heritage, 1985).

16. Return

Odysseus: This account is based, of course, on Homer's *Odyssey*. M. I. Finley's *The World of Odysseus* (Viking, 1977) gives a superb picture of the epic's background, while *Pandora's Daughters* by Eva Cantarella (Johns Hopkins, 1987) analyses what it suggests about the status of women. A wealth of material is found in W. B. Stanford's *The Quest for Ulysses* (Phaidon, 1974).

Joyce: *The Essential James Joyce*, edited by Harry Levin (Penguin, 1963) contains *A Portrait of the Artist as a Young Man* and sections of *Ulysses*, with concise introductions to each. *James Joyce's Dublin* by Frank Delaney (Holt, Rinehart and Winston, 1981) is a lavishly illustrated guide to the novelist's world.

17. Harmony

Marduk: The Babylonian poem on which this account is based, *Enuma Elish*, is translated and annotated by Theodore Gaster in *The Oldest Stories in the World* (Viking, 1952). *Before Philosophy* by Henri Frankfort and others (Penguin, 1946) shows why Marduk's foe is the water, rather than hot winds as in the Horus tale.

John Perry's *Lord of the Four Quarters: Myths of the Royal Father* (Macmillan, 1966) places the Marduk tale in the context of the world's father-king myths. A feminist interpretation is given in Merlin Stone's *When God Was a Woman* (Harvest/HBJ, 1976).

Sons of Heaven: Two well-illustrated volumes describe Beijing's layout in terms of Chinese mythology: Lin Yutang's *Imperial Peking* (Elek, 1961) and *Peking: A Tale of Three Cities* by Nigel Cameron and Brian Blake (Harper and Row, 1965). Observations on the Chinese world-view are also given by Francis Huxley in Chapter 8 of *The Way of the Sacred* (Doubleday, 1974), a beautifully illustrated and penetrating study of mythic symbols. *The World's Mythology in Color** by Veronica Ions (Chartwell, 1987) gives scholarly interpretations of Japanese myth, and that of many other lands.

18. Revolt

Prometheus: This retelling is based largely on accounts in Plato's *Protagoras,* and in *Prometheus Bound* by Aeschylus. Edward Edinger's *Ego and Archetype* (Penguin, 1973) begins with a comparison between this tale and that of Adam.

James Lovelock presents his "Gaia Hypothesis" in *Gaia: a New Look at Life on Earth* (Oxford, 1975). Related "ecofeminist" concerns are given in *Reweaving the World*, edited by Irene Diamond and Gloria Orenstein (Sierra Club, 1990).

Frankenstein: A useful edition of Mary Shelley's *Frankenstein* is one with an afterword by Harold Bloom (Mentor, 1965). Radu Florescu's *In Search of Frankenstein* (Warner, 1975) traces the origins of this great modern myth.

6 LOVERS MEETING

19. Love-Goddess

Aphrodite: The famed Aphrodite-and-Ares scene is from Homer's *Odyssey*, Book VIII. Christine Downing's *Goddess: Mythological Images of the Feminine** (Crossroad, 1981) presents a very personal response to Aphrodite. Alexander Eliot's *The Universal Myths** (Meridian, 1976) entertainingly treats myths of love, and cites current Cypriot love-goddess rites.

W. H. D. Rouse's *Gods, Heroes and Men of Ancient Greece** (Mentor, 1957), a lively survey of Greek Mythology, concludes with a chapter entitled "Great Pan is Dead."

Marilyn Monroe: *Norma Jean* by Fred Lawrence Guiles is an absorbing, thoroughly researched biography. Her story is considered mythologically in Richard Dyer's *Stars* (British Film Institute, 1979) and Marjorie Rosen's *Popcorn Venus* (Avon, 1973).

20. Romance

Jason and Medea: The main source for this retelling is the *Argonautica* by Apollonius of Rhodes, while Ovid's *Metamorphoses* includes the Pelias incident. A beautiful treatment of mythic feminine images, including that of Medea (Chapter 3), is Manuela Dunn Mascetti's *The Song of Eve** (Simon and Schuster, 1990).

The mythology of romance is discussed interestingly in Chapter 2 of Kate Millet's *Sexual Politics* (Avon, 1969) and Part V of Antony Easthope's *What a Man's Gotta Do* (Grafton, 1986).

The Trudeaus: Margaret Trudeau's account of the marriage, given in *Beyond Reason* (Paddington, 1979) reads like a novel and tells the romantic myth that lures every woman in every age.

21. Marriage

Arthur: Arthurian books other than those listed for Chapter 4 include Bullfinch's *Mythology: The Age of Chivalry** (Mentor, 1962) and Geoffrey Ashe's *King Arthur: the Dream of a Golden Age* (Thames and Hudson, 1990), another *Art and Imagination* gem. Archaeological background is given in numerous other books by Ashe.

Elvis: W. A. Harbinson's *The Illustrated Elvis* (Grosset & Dunlap, 1976) gives a useful introduction. The unusual aspects of Presley's marriage are discussed by Priscilla herself in *Elvis and Me* (General, 1985). In the *Rolling Stone Illustrated History of Rock and Roll*, edited by Jim Miller (Random House, 1976), Peter Guralnick analyses his musical roots effectively.

7 TILL WE HAVE BUILT JERUSALEM

22. Golden Age

Four Ages: The source is Book I of Ovid's *Metamorphoses: The Western Way** by Caitlin and John Matthews (Arkana, 1985) interprets golden-age mythology in terms of the inward journey of self-discovery, along a path hallowed by ancient tradition. Northrop Frye's *The Educated Imagination** (Canadian Broadcasting Corporation, 1963) treats good-old-days notions in terms of "social mythology"—which becomes clear to those who educate their imagination.

Woodstock: Joel Makower's *Woodstock: the Oral History* (Doubleday, 1989) is a delight. The account by Geoffrey Stokes in Chapter 25 of *Rock of Ages** (Rolling Stone Press, 1986) puts both Woodstock and Altamont into clear perspective.

23. World Tree

Odin: Most of the material for his tale, and that of Balder, comes from the *Prose Edda* by Snorri Sturleson. R. L. Green's *The Saga of Asgard** (Penguin, 1960) is among the better retellings of these stories. Illuminating analyses are found in H. R. Ellis-Davidson's *Gods and Myths of Northern Europe** (Penguin, 1964) and Brian Branston's *Gods of the North* (Thames and Hudson, 1955). Part 6 of Rudolf Poertner's *The Vikings* (St. Martin's, 1975) presents Odin as a "Genghis Khan of the Clouds."

Roger Cook's *The Tree of Life: Symbol of the Centre* in the *Art and Imagination* series (Thames and Hudson, 1974) gives an engrossing study of the World Tree. Chapter X of Mircea Eliade's *Patterns in Comparative Religion** (Meridian, 1958) presents World Tree mythology in terms of a "nostalgia for paradise."

Santa Claus: Adriaan de Groot's *Saint Nicholas* (Basic, 1965) gives a thorough interpretation of the legends. The Christmas Tree's story is told in Sheryl Karas's *The Solstice Evergreen* (Aslan, 1991).

24. Renewal

Balder: Johannes Brondsted's *The Vikings* and Peter Brent's *The Viking Saga* (Weidenfeld and Nicolson, 1975) tell about the sacrificial rite behind this myth. Anne Bancroft's *Origins of the Sacred** (Arkana, 1987) connects the northern and southern branches of European mythology in terms of "the spiritual journey in Western tradition."

Terry Fox: Leslie Scrivener's *The Terry Fox Story* (McClelland and Stewart, 1981) provided much material for this retelling. *Terry Fox* by Jeremy Brown and Gail Harvey (General, 1980) offers a fine selection of photos.

25. Endings

Cuchulainn: The myth's background is well explained by Proinsias MacCann in *Celtic Mythology* (Hamlyn, 1970). Hugh Malet's *In the Wake of the Gods* (Chatto and Windus, 1970) explains how Irish kings were thought to incarnate the sun-god. Frank Delaney's *The Celts* (Harcourt Brace Jovanovich, 1987) is a companion to the British Broadcasting Corporation's exciting television series of that name.

Halloween is given detailed treatment in J. G. Frazer's *Golden Bough*—Part IV, "Dying and Reviving Gods," telling of food set out for hungry souls and lamps placed to guide them on their way; while Part VIII, "The Golden Bough," describes the firelightings and fortune-tellings of this time, when all was renewed.

Churchill: In Elizabeth Langford's *Winston Churchill* (Rand McNally, 1974) text and photos complement each other admirably.

Index

Major mythological themes indicated by boldface.

312

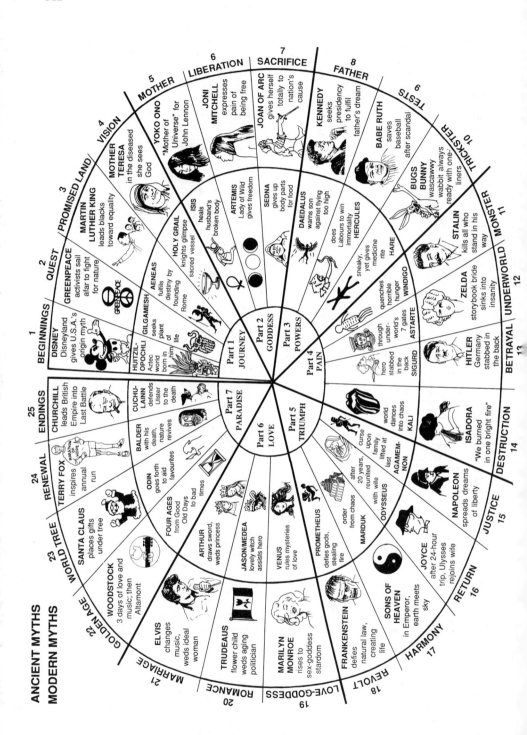

313

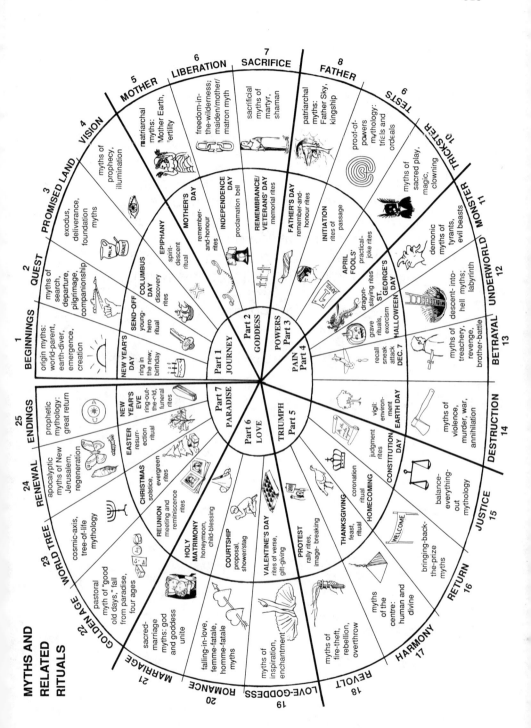

MYTHS AND RELATED RITUALS

May the wind be always at your back.
May the road rise up to meet you.
May the sun shine warm on your face,
The rains fall soft on your fields.
Until we meet again, may the Lord
Hold you in the hollow of his hand.

IRISH BLESSING